Buddhism

Dominique Side

Philip Allan Updates
Market Place
Deddington
Oxfordshire
OX15 0SE
Tel: 01869 338652
Fax: 01869 337590
e-mail: sales@philipallan.co.uk
www.philipallan.co.uk

© Philip Allan Updates 2005

ISBN-13: 978-1-84489-219-8
ISBN-10: 1-84489-219-0

In all cases we have attempted to trace and credit copyright owners of material used.

Cover photograph reproduced by permission of Graham Price.

Printed by Scotprint, Haddington.

Environmental information
The paper on which this title is printed is sourced from mills using wood from managed, sustainable forests.

Contents

Introduction

Why study Buddhism?

The purpose of studying Buddhism is not to study Buddhism but to study ourselves.

Suzuki Roshi, *Zen Mind, Beginner's Mind*

Buddhism opens the mind to a completely different understanding of the universe. In the Buddhist view, the universe seems to be far beyond the grasp of ordinary human beings. It is infinitely vast, encompassing unimaginably long periods of cosmic time through which it evolves, and including countless different worlds throughout the whole of space. These worlds contain many different types of beings, of which human beings are but one.

The Buddhist world is also one where suffering is a fact of life for most, but where it can be completely eliminated and true happiness is really possible. For Buddhists, this is not just a fantasy of how things could be or how we would like them to be: it is how they actually are. And to back up its vision, Buddhism offers plenty of practical methods aimed at broadening minds so that people can realise this for themselves, including meditation, ethical values, devotional practices and wisdom teachings.

The main message of Buddhism is that human beings have the power to change their lives and change themselves. In fact, the main thing that makes a Buddhist is a personal conviction in one's capacity to change for the better. Without this, Buddhism is pointless, because the goal of Buddhism is personal transformation. This transformation goes through many stages until one reaches enlightenment, which is the ultimate goal. Enlightenment means fully realising the limitless love and wisdom that are inherent in everyone. We could call it the ultimate in personal fulfilment, the true happiness we all seek. Buddhists believe it is part of our human potential, and that the Buddhist path is a way to develop this potential so that it flourishes for the benefit of all.

In the process of understanding and managing personal change, Buddhism has developed a detailed theory of psychology, sometimes called a 'science of the mind', on the basis of insights gained through meditation. It has also developed a system of ethics for guiding behaviour so that people make

their lives more rather than less happy. All this experience and knowledge translates into the Buddhist way of life as it is practised by people around the world. Put simply, Buddhism aims to help people to become better human beings.

The most radical aspect of Buddhism is that the journey to enlightenment goes beyond the limitations of being human. Many Western philosophers acknowledge that human sense perceptions and human language are limited, so we should not imagine that what we perceive is all that exists. Buddhism seeks to offer a practical way of breaking out of our human mould so that we can learn to see things as they are and not just as we think they are.

The teachings given by the Buddha on subjects such as karma, rebirth, nirvana, the existence of non-human beings and so on, all stem from the transcendental insights he gained through meditation, which are not commonly accessible to the ordinary human mind. That can make them difficult to grasp and believe in. To understand them fully, we would need to attain enlightenment ourselves. But this is the challenge that Buddhism offers: anyone who does what is necessary, it says, can attain enlightenment like the Buddha.

All religions address the questions of suffering, the nature of death, morality and so on, but Buddhism always explains its views through reasoning, so it is easier to understand why it comes to the conclusions it does. There is an element of faith in Buddhism, but there are no dogmatic beliefs in which people are expected to trust 'blindly'. That is why Buddhism is so accessible to people who are new to it, and to those people who distrust religious mysteries. It is a bridge between religion and philosophy, and between religion and science.

Facts
● There are 500 million Buddhists in the world today.
● There are 150,000 Buddhists in the UK (according to the 2001 census).
● There are 5 million Buddhists in the USA.
● Buddhism is the fastest growing religion in France, which now has 600,000 Buddhists.

> Buddhism has the characteristics of what would be expected in the cosmic religion for the future: it transcends a personal God, avoids dogma and theology; it covers both the natural and the spiritual, and it is based on a religious sense aspiring from the experience of all things, natural and spiritual, as a meaningful unity.
>
> Albert Einstein, *The Human Side*

About this book

On the World Faiths paper at AS and A2, Buddhism is consistently a popular option, yet there has been little material available for teachers or students. This book aims to fill the gap.

Buddhism

All the topics contained in the AQA, Edexcel and OCR specifications are included. The subject is presented in a relevant and interesting way, and debates within the tradition are explained to help students develop their critical appreciation of the issues. Each topic is supported by quotations, diagrams or tables where appropriate, and by sample essay questions based on past examination papers. A glossary of key terms and a list of further reading plus other resources (such as films) are also provided. This book should therefore serve as a comprehensive manual for both teachers and students.

Students at the school where I teach have said that studying Buddhism has opened their minds to a new and different way of thinking, and given them the tools to question their beliefs and assumptions. It is impossible for one person to do justice to such an ancient, rich and diverse subject as Buddhism, but at least I hope this book proves to be a useful classroom tool in stimulating a new generation of minds.

Acknowledgements

I wish to acknowledge in particular the help of Professor Peter Harvey, of the University of Sunderland, who kindly and helpfully commented on the draft, as well as that of Patrick Gaffney and Adam Pearcey. I am also indebted to the Tibet Foundation, London, for generously sponsoring the writing of this book. And finally, I am grateful to Graham Price for offering many photographs and to Pete Fry, of Zam Archives, for providing the line drawings.

Dominique Side

Chapter 1

Gautama the Buddha

The Ten Acts of the Buddha

The Buddha lived in northern India about 2,500 years ago. Scholars disagree about the exact dates of his life, but it is generally acknowledged that he lived some time between the sixth and fourth centuries BCE, and the dates most commonly accepted for the Buddha are 563–483 BCE.

He lived between the foothills of the Himalayan mountains to the north and the Ganges River basin to the south. He was born in Lumbini, in present-day Nepal, spent his childhood in Kapilavastu and attained enlightenment in present-day Bodh Gaya, India. He gave his first teaching in the Deer Park in Sarnath, where he spoke of the Four Noble Truths, and devoted the last 45 years of his life to teaching people as he wandered through the villages and towns of the Ganges basin. He passed away in Kusinara at the age of 80. The geographical area related to the Buddha's life is therefore relatively small and it is thought that his influence during his lifetime would have been quite localised (see Figure 1.1).

Figure 1.1 The Ganges River basin where the Buddha lived

1

Box 1.1

The Ten Acts of the Buddha

> **Box 1.1**
>
> **The Ten Acts of the Buddha**
>
> 1 Conception
> 2 Physical birth
> 3 Accomplishment in worldly skills
> 4 His youth: a life of pleasure and indulgence
> 5 Leaving the palace
> 6 Life as an ascetic
> 7 Victory over Mara
> 8 Enlightenment
> 9 Spreading the teaching
> 10 Death or passing away

Biographies of the Buddha first appeared many centuries after his death. By this time, the story had become an elaborate one, dramatised for the purpose of public storytelling. The oldest sources of information about his life are found in the Buddhist scriptures called the Pali Canon, but there his life is not recounted chronologically and has to be pieced together. As a result, Buddhists have developed a narrative framework for the Buddha's life story which is commonly recounted in terms of Ten Acts (see Box 1.1). A framework like this is useful for remembering the main points of his life. The value of the Buddha's life story for Buddhists stems from the fact that he was a human being, and therefore set an example they can follow. From the academic point of view, however, his life story is a blend of historical events and legend, and it is difficult to tell the one from the other.

1 Conception

According to Buddhist tradition, the Buddha's mother was Queen Mahamaya, wife of King Suddhodana who was leader of the clan of the Shakyas. Before he was born as a human being, he resided in the Tushita heaven, or Heaven of the Contented, a pure non-physical dimension that is one of the many heavens included in the Buddhist view of the universe.

The Buddha's conception and birth are said to have been marked by miraculous events, not unlike those of Jesus. As soon as his mind descended from the heavenly existence into his mother's womb, it is said that a tremendous light appeared in the world, and the event was marked by earthquakes. The queen dreamed that a splendid white elephant came down from the sky and entered her body. Symbolically, the colour white represents purity, and the elephant represents supreme power and majesty. Her dream was later interpreted to mean that her son would be either a great king or a great religious teacher. There is no indication that this was a virgin birth. During her pregnancy, the queen was naturally virtuous and felt no physical pain. Her pregnancy lasted 10 lunar months, which is said to be the norm for enlightened beings.

2 Physical birth

According to the custom at that time, women returned to their parents' home to give birth, so it was arranged for Queen Mahamaya to travel to the neighbouring kingdom of Koliya where her father was the king. On the way, she and her party passed by a garden called Lumbini Park where the queen ordered a halt. It was intended to be only a rest, but as she lay in the shade of a tree she gave birth to her son.

The story of the Buddha's birth is a striking one. It is said that Queen Mahamaya gave birth standing up, leaning gracefully against a sala tree. The baby emerged not from her womb but from her right side, with no blood or birth waters of any kind. Miraculously, two jets of water appeared from the sky, one cool and one warm, for bathing the baby and his mother. And the earth trembled to mark the event.

As soon as he was born, the Buddha was able to stand up and took several steps in each of the four directions of the compass. This is seen as symbolising the fact that his teachings would spread in all directions. At the same time, he declared that this would be his last birth and he was free from rebirth as a human being.

The child was named Siddhartha, meaning 'fulfilment of wishes'. One of the first visitors to the palace after his birth was a sage called Asita who was reputed for his wisdom and powers of clairvoyance. Asita predicted that the child would be out of the ordinary, and could become either a great king or a spiritual leader. But since King Suddhodana hoped his son would be heir to the throne, he deliberately shielded the child from anything that might trigger spiritual yearnings.

> **Box 1.2**
>
> **Names of the Buddha**
>
> The Buddha has various names:
>
> **Siddhartha** is the name given to him at birth, meaning 'fulfilment of wishes'.
>
> **Gautama** (or **Gotama**) is his family name.
>
> **Shakyamuni** means 'sage of the Shakyas'. He is called Buddha Shakyamuni to distinguish him from other buddhas.
>
> **The Buddha** is a title meaning 'the enlightened one' and in some traditions is used only when referring to him after his enlightenment.

 ## Accomplishment in worldly skills

The culture of India at this time was advanced and sophisticated. The Buddha was educated along with children of other noble families. He excelled at everything he did, including sports such as wrestling and archery, and was schooled in mathematics, languages, music and so on. He was tall, strong and handsome, and his good manners and kindness endeared him to everyone.

When he was young, his father took him to the annual ploughing festival and, as he was only a child, he was allowed to watch and rest under a rose-apple tree. As he was seated there his mind naturally fell into meditation, and he attained an advanced mental state quite effortlessly. This was the first mystical experience of his life. Time stood still for him and, as if to illustrate this, it is said that the shadow of the rose-apple tree had not moved from the time the attendants left him there to the time they came to collect him.

4   His youth: a life of pleasure and indulgence

All possible luxuries and comforts were provided for Siddhartha to ensure that he would be satisfied with his life as a prince. Three palaces were built for him, one for each season of the year (the hot season, the cool season and the rainy season). He was surrounded with beautiful parks and gardens, music and attractive attendants. He married the beautiful Yasodhara with much ceremony and rejoicing, and she gave birth to a baby boy named Rahula. The king thought that everything would turn out as he wished.

5   Leaving the palace

But Siddhartha grew bored and restless. One day he summoned his charioteer, Channa, to take him for a drive. He came across a tired old man by the roadside with no teeth, white hair, bleary eyes and legs so weak he needed a stick. The sight astonished him and he asked Channa what it could be. Channa explained that old age comes to us all. Siddhartha was so upset he turned round and returned to the palace.

He made three other trips out of the palace. On the second trip, he saw a sick person writhing with pain, his eyes bloodshot. Siddhartha was filled with compassion. On the third trip, he came across a funeral procession with mourners carrying a corpse to the river for its last rites. Siddhartha was stunned to realise that youth is not indefinite, and every one of us must die. Finally, on his fourth trip, he met a man with a shaven head, barefoot and wearing a simple robe, sitting quietly in meditation. He was an ascetic. There is a tradition in India whereby some men choose to leave their life in society and take up a lifestyle of hardship and simplicity, living in forests and surviving on alms food, as a way of seeking freedom from suffering. They are called *shramanas* or ascetics.

These four experiences marked a turning point in the Buddha's life. They are known as the Four Signs or Four Sights (see Box 1.3). They led him to decide to leave the palace and look for a solution to human suffering, and this quest is what motivated the rest of his life.

Box 1.3	
The Four Signs or Four Sights	
Old age	Death
Illness	The religious life

It is unlikely that the Buddha actually witnessed the Four Signs in this literal way, and hard to believe that he would have been as naive as the story portrays him. It may be more useful to read this part of the story as his growing disenchantment with pleasure and luxury, and his realisation that complacency cuts people off from the nature and meaning of life. Some people in our own societies can lead very sheltered childhoods, with their parents shielding them from the harsh realities of life. And even though we can be surrounded by

images of poverty, old age, illness, death and other forms of suffering, these do not always touch our hearts or arouse our sympathy. At other times, human suffering suddenly becomes very real and can change people's whole attitude to life, as when someone close to them is seriously ill or dies. The Four Signs or Four Sights can be understood as the process by which Siddhartha gained a personal realisation of the immensity of human suffering.

6 Life as an ascetic

Siddhartha renounced family life and left his palace at the age of 29. Tradition has it that he left at night in secret, to avoid his family's pleas for him to stay. He spent the following 6 years as an ascetic (see Box 1.4). He followed a number of teachers in the forest, and learned yoga and meditation from them. In addition, he practised mortification of the body: he fasted, held his breath for long periods until his head seemed to burst, stayed out in the burning sun in summer and bathed in icy water in winter. He would stand on one leg for long periods or would squat for days without sitting down.

> **Box 1.4**
>
> **Asceticism**
>
> There have been ascetic traditions in most world religions. Ascetics voluntarily choose pain and hardship for religious reasons, as a way to purify themselves of their sins. Fasting, for example, is a form of asceticism.

Long afterwards, the Buddha told his disciples that he learned a great deal from this experience. In particular it developed his discipline and willpower. However, in the end, he did not find the answers he was looking for, and his mind grew weak from lack of food.

One day a girl named Sujata found him in the forest and took pity on him. She offered him a bowl of milk rice, which immediately restored his strength. After this Siddhartha abandoned asceticism and, remembering his childhood experience under the rose-apple tree, realised that only meditation could lead him to enlightenment.

This episode of the Buddha's life is taken to mean that extreme attitudes are unhelpful. Even if the goal is freedom, truth and happiness, trying too hard to achieve it can be counter-productive. Extremes of puritanism or austerity do not bring the goal closer — and neither do the other extremes of indulgence and hedonism. At this point in his life, Siddhartha discovered that a balanced approach is best.

7 Victory over Mara

Siddhartha then chose to sit under a large peepul tree to meditate. At first he was confronted by worldly temptations in the form of demons — a religious experience similar to the temptations of Jesus in the wilderness.

The demon Mara symbolises the forces of desire and death. Mara is a deity who became powerful through previous good works, but uses his power to entrap people in sensual desire and attachment so that they stay within his realm of influence.

Mara wanted to prevent Siddhartha's enlightenment because it would make him free from death's clutches. According to the Mahayana account, Mara began by sending his own sons to arouse anger in Siddhartha. The sons, dressed as warriors, approached menacingly and released their arrows to kill him, but Siddhartha remained unmoved and as the arrows came near they turned into flowers. Next, Mara sent his daughters to try to seduce Siddhartha. Some were fat, some were thin, some were young and others were old, so Mara was confident that there was at least one the Buddha would find attractive. But the Buddha again remained unmoved, and the daughters eventually slunk away. Mara then tempted the Buddha's pride by offering him the whole of his kingdom provided he abandoned his quest for enlightenment, but the Buddha refused.

**Figure 1.2
The Buddha's
enlightenment**

Graham Price

Finally, Mara taunted the Buddha with the warning that nobody would ever believe him when he announced to the world that he had attained enlightenment. In response, the Buddha touched the earth with his right hand and called the earth goddess as his witness, whereupon the earth quaked in reply. Mara fled.

This story is a dramatisation of one of the Buddha's main religious experiences. It taught him that, before one can attain one's religious goal, it is necessary to overcome all desire, aggression, pride and other harmful emotions. The event is commemorated by many images and paintings, and particularly by statues of Gautama cross-legged in meditation with his right hand touching the earth (Figure 1.2). This episode can be seen as victory over evil, but evil in Buddhism is not primarily an external force; rather it is the power of our own negative emotions.

8 Enlightenment

Siddhartha then experienced various stages of joy and ecstasy known as the four *jhanas* (or *dhyanas*) of meditation. Gradually deepening his state of concentrated calm, he reached the fourth *jhana*, a state of great even-mindedness, mental brightness and purity. In this state, at each of the three watches of the night he

had three distinct insights in his meditation, known together as the 'threefold knowledge'. These insights are crucial, because they are the foundation of all his teachings.

- First, he saw countless numbers of his own previous lives, who he had been, his name, where he had lived and so on.
- Second, he understood the birth and death of beings in the universe, and what causes us to be reborn into different situations.
- Third, he attained omniscience, the all-knowing quality of enlightenment. This means that he understood the true nature of all things.

With the third insight, at dawn, the Buddha attained enlightenment. Upon his enlightenment he exclaimed, according to the Theravada tradition:

> Through many a birth I wandered in samsara, seeking, but not finding, the builder of the house (of the body). Sorrowful is birth again and again. O house-builder! (craving) You are seen. You shall build no house again. All your rafters (defilements such as greed and hatred) are broken, your ridge-pole (ignorance) is shattered. My mind has attained the unconditioned, it has achieved the end of craving.
>
> *Dhammapada* 153–54

And according to the Mahayana tradition of Buddhism, the Buddha spoke these words upon his enlightenment:

> No mind in mind;
> The nature of mind is luminosity.

The Sanskrit word for enlightenment is *bodhi*, which means 'awakening'. When we become enlightened, we wake up from the sleep of ignorance, from all the misconceptions we have about ourselves and the world. Enlightenment is a state of awakening that means we understand things as they really are. It takes us beyond human limitations into a dimension that transcends such things as space and time. The unique feature of the Buddha's message is that such a transcendental state is achievable for human beings during their lifetimes and not only after death.

9 Spreading the teaching

The Buddha spent his last 45 years wandering throughout northeast India explaining how everyone can attain enlightenment just as he did. He taught kings and poor people, men and women, old and young. Some of his disciples became monks and nuns, and others remained householders. On some occasions, he drew audiences of several thousand people. Even so, the Buddha's followers were a minority in the region, and lived alongside practitioners of India's other religions.

Westerners often judge the Buddha harshly for the way he abandoned his wife and son in pursuit of his religious goal. They think this is selfish and surely not an example for all to follow. The scriptures say, however, that during the period when the Buddha was teaching, he went back to the region where he had lived as a child and gave public teachings there. As a result, both his aunt and his son became monastics. Even the Buddha's father became reconciled to his son's way of life and respected him as a religious teacher.

All the Buddha's teachings were given during this period, and the scriptures were compiled on the basis of these teachings. During his lifetime, however, none of the Buddha's teachings were written down because writing was not common at that time.

10 Death or passing away

The Buddha was unwell for several months before he died, but he continued to wander on foot and teach. On his deathbed, he asked his monks whether they had any final questions for him. They remained silent. He then encouraged them not to hold back out of respect for him, but to ask any questions on their minds. Still they remained silent. He then spoke his last words: 'All conditioned things are subject to decay. Attain perfection through diligence.' His death was a final teaching on impermanence: all things come to an end, and one can never be complacent.

Figure 1.3 Stupa in Kathmandu, Nepal

Graham Price

The Buddha died at the age of 80 as a result of eating tainted food. Recent research has indicated that the Buddha probably suffered from a stomach complaint for several years before he died, and finally succumbed after eating a dish of either pork or mushrooms. According to Theravada Buddhism, he passed into each of the *jhanas* of meditation one by one, then into the four

Box 1.5
Stupas

Stupas are sacred monuments housing the relics of the Buddha or a Buddhist saint, or copies of the scriptures. These are placed in the centre of the stupa and become inaccessible because there is no door. Pilgrims walk round and round a stupa, reciting prayers. Each country in Asia developed its own particular style for building stupas. The stupa is an example of sacred architecture and symbolises the enlightened mind.

'formless' mystical states, and then into 'cessation of cognition and feeling'. He then gradually descended back into the first *jhana*, then back to the fourth, and attained *parinirvana* from there. For Buddhists he did not die in the ordinary sense, rather he attained the supreme nirvana, which is deathless.

He passed away lying on his right side, with his right hand under his head. In Sri Lanka there are many statues of the Buddha in this pose; they are used as reminders of the inevitability of impermanence and death.

His body was cremated. Some of his bones and teeth did not burn, and these were kept as sacred relics and placed inside eight stupas specially built to house them. These stupas became places of pilgrimage.

The Buddha did not appoint a successor. He told his followers that his legacy to them was his teachings, the Dharma, and this was the guide they should follow.

The stories of Angulimala, Sunita and Devadatta

There are several things we can learn from the stories about the Buddha's life as a teacher. First, they show how the Buddha related to other people, how he got his message across, and how he was seen by others. Second, they contain elements of his teachings and illustrate his values and his understanding of life. Third, they tell us about the social context in which the Buddha lived, about the beliefs and prejudices of his day, and the way the community of his followers developed. The following stories offer examples of conversion, the workings of karma and non-violence, and the Buddha's rejection of certain social values of his time.

Angulimala

One day the Buddha found the village of Savatthi deserted. People were terrified because Angulimala, a mass murderer, was in those parts. He had cut off a finger from each of his victims and wore 99 fingers around his neck — hence his name, which means 'necklace of fingers' (some accounts claim that he wore 999 fingers in his necklace). Despite this the Buddha walked along the road as usual. He suddenly heard the sound of footsteps behind him.

Angulimala shouted out to him, 'Stop, monk, stop!' The Buddha continued walking. When Angulimala had caught up with him he said, 'I told you to stop, monk. Why don't you stop?'

'I stopped a long time ago. It is you who have not stopped,' replied the Buddha.

Angulimala was startled by the Buddha's reply. He blocked his path and forced him to stop. The Buddha looked him straight in the eye like a friend or a

brother. Angulimala had never met anyone who radiated such serenity and ease, and who did not run away from him in terror. His curiosity was aroused: why did this monk feel no fear? And what did he mean about stopping and not stopping?

The two men entered into conversation. The Buddha explained that what he had learned to do was to stop harming and causing suffering to others. Everyone is afraid of dying; the duty of a monk is to protect life, not to destroy it. But Angulimala was cynical. 'Human beings don't love each other. They are cruel and deceptive. Why should I love other people?'

'There may be cruel people in this world, but there are also many kind people. My path can transform cruelty into kindness,' said the Buddha. 'Right now you are on the path of hatred, but it is up to you: you can choose the path of love and forgiveness instead.' Angulimala was thrown into confusion, but he could sense that the Buddha spoke from love and was worthy of respect. 'It is a great pity I did not meet you sooner,' he said. 'I have gone too far, I can't turn back.'

'No,' urged the Buddha, 'it is never too late.'

Their discussion continued for some time, and in the end Angulimala knelt before the Buddha and vowed to change his evil ways and to follow him. He was ordained as a monk and tried hard to practise meditation correctly and lead a disciplined life. Even the Buddha was amazed at the speed of his transformation. Just 2 weeks after becoming a monk, he radiated serenity and stability, and the other monks nicknamed him 'Ahimsaka', which means 'non-violent one'.

Sunita

Sunita was a homeless 'untouchable' who survived by sweeping the streets. It was the custom for low-caste people like him to stand at a distance from anyone of high caste who might approach.

One day, as he was busy sweeping the road, he saw the Buddha approaching with a group of monks. He looked in vain for a place to stand aside from them, but the best he could do was to flatten himself against a wall and fold his hands in a gesture of respect. To his dismay the Buddha came straight up to him, but far from being angry, as he had expected, the Buddha spoke in a

Box 1.6
Untouchables
The Indian social order was based on a hierarchy of four classes: priests, warriors/ kings, farmers, and servants. 'Untouchables' were the lowest class of servant. This system is associated with Hinduism and continues in India today as the caste system. In recent years, the untouchable leader Dr Ambedkar has inspired many untouchables in India to reject Hinduism and become Buddhists. There are now several million of these 'neo-Buddhists' in India, especially in Dr Ambedkar's home state of Maharashtra.

friendly way. He asked Sunita whether he would like to give up his job as a sweeper and follow him instead.

Sunita was astonished and delighted. He was used to being ordered about; nobody had ever spoken to him in a kind and respectful way before. He jumped at the chance and the Buddha ordained him there and then. In time, he became a respected and educated monk.

Devadatta

Devadatta was the Buddha's jealous cousin. They grew up together as children, and as an adult Devadatta became a monk and follower of the Buddha. But Devadatta was the archetypal troublemaker: he orchestrated three assassination attempts against the Buddha, and also tried to create a split within the Buddhist community. In the long term, he failed. The stories about his adventures show that, for all the Buddha's greatness, he did not succeed in converting everyone around him. They also illustrate the Buddha's non-violent approach to solving problems.

Devadatta tried to kill the Buddha on three separate occasions. First, he hired assassins to kill him, but they were moved by the Buddha's persuasiveness and became converts instead. Second, Devadatta climbed to the top of a mountain called Vulture Peak, and hurled a rock down on the Buddha as he was passing below. The rock narrowly missed him and wounded him slightly. Finally, Devadatta sent a wild elephant to attack him. The elephant charged down the road towards the Buddha, but as it neared him it unexpectedly slowed down and became quite tame. The Buddha used the power of love to subdue it.

Towards the end of his life, after his failure at creating a rival break-away group and after a long illness, Devadatta finally repented his behaviour and had himself carried on a litter into the Buddha's presence. He cried out, 'I seek refuge in the Buddha,' and was received back into the community. The Buddha prophesied that he would eventually attain enlightenment.

Critical evaluation

Modern academic scholarship looks critically at these traditional accounts of the Buddha's life. As we have already seen, not all episodes need to be accepted literally, but they can still be seen as meaningful. The difficulty is knowing where to draw the line between legend and historical fact, and it will probably never be known exactly what is fact and what is embellishment.

Among the points which scholars dispute is the question of whether Siddhartha was brought up in a kingdom or in a republic. There is no evidence to show that Shakya was a kingdom and many scholars now believe that it was

a democratic republic relatively uninfluenced by the hierarchical values of the Brahmin priesthood (see Chapter 2). Buddhist writers may have felt it brought more prestige to say that the Buddha was a prince.

> Everything in the scriptures has passed through several stages of transmission, and whatever the period of the actual discourses, the legends by which they are accompanied are in no case contemporary. Some of the scriptural legends, such as the descent from heaven, and the miracles of the birth and death, are just those which show most clearly the growth of apocryphal additions, as well as the development of a dogmatic system of belief about the person and functions of Buddha. Another development is that which makes Buddha the son of a king, and the descendant of a line of ancestors going back to the first king of the present cycle....The only firm ground from which we can start is not history, but the fact that a legend in a definite form existed in the first and second centuries after Buddha's death.
>
> Edward J. Thomas, *The Life of Buddha*

Buddhists themselves are not troubled about the possibility of historical inaccuracies in the account; they emphasise the messages the life story conveys. They feel that the point of the Buddha's life story is to learn lessons from it.

The significance of the Buddha

The significance of the Buddha for Buddhists is quite different from that of Jesus for Christians, or Mohammed for Muslims. Paul Williams explains:

> The Buddha is thought by Buddhists to be one who has awakened fully to the final truth of things, and thus freed, liberated, himself once and for all from all forms of suffering. He is also one who, out of supreme compassion, has taught others the way to attain liberation themselves. Buddhas are not born that way, and they are certainly not thought to be eternal gods (or God). Once (many lifetimes ago) they were just like you and me. They strove through their own efforts, and became Buddhas. A Buddha is superior to the rest of us because he 'knows it how it is'. We, on the other hand, wallow in confusion, in ignorance. Thus we are unhappy and suffer.
>
> Paul Williams, *Buddhist Thought*

Was the Buddha the founder of a new religious teaching?

Buddhists do not consider that the Buddhist teachings were invented by Shakyamuni Buddha. Richard Gombrich explains:

> Outsiders see him as the founder of Buddhism; for Buddhists the matter is slightly more complicated. As they see it, the Truth is eternal, but not always realized. Time has no beginning or end but goes through vast cycles. Every now and again there arises in the world a religious genius, a Buddha, who has the infinite wisdom to comprehend

the Truth and the infinite compassion to preach it to the suffering world, so that others too may attain Enlightenment. Gotama is the most recent teacher in the infinite series of Buddhas.

Richard Gombrich, *Theravada Buddhism*

The Dharma is considered an eternal truth that does not belong to anyone in particular. However, if we refer to Buddhism not as a teaching but as a historical development, then it is fair to say that the Buddha was the founder of the religion that began in India.

Buddha Shakyamuni is not the only buddha

The historical Buddha, whose life is described above, is one of many different buddhas who have and will come to teach people here on earth. According to some Buddhist traditions, there have been countless buddhas in ages prior to our current human history, and there will be many more in the future. Some accounts say there will be 1,002 buddhas in this age. The next buddha will be called Maitreya, and Edward Conze estimates that he will appear about 30,000 years from now after the teachings of Shakyamuni have declined. Like Shakyamuni before him, he resides in Tushita heaven until the time comes for him to be born a human being.

Is the Buddha human or supernatural?

The two main traditions of Buddhism, Theravada and Mahayana, have different understandings of the nature of the Buddha's humanity, and this is explained in Chapter 4. The Buddha himself always declared he was neither divine nor a prophet. Yet his life story contains many instances of extraordinary powers and events. For Buddhists, these illustrate the qualities and powers that come from enlightenment or from being very close to enlightenment. They are powers that can be developed by anyone who becomes fully awakened.

Questions

1 Identify three religious experiences of the Buddha, and assess how they can be described in the language of Western philosophy of religion.
2 'Stories of the Buddha's life show that he must have been a supernatural figure and not an ordinary human being.' Discuss.
3 Examine the influence that luxury and asceticism had on the subsequent life and teachings of the Buddha.
4 What lessons can Buddhists learn from the Buddha's life story? What is the significance of his death?
5 Compare Buddhist beliefs about the Buddha and Christian beliefs about Christ.

Chapter 2

The Indian context

Buddhism did not develop in a vacuum. The Buddha lived and taught in northeast India some 2,500 years ago, and the development of Buddhism as a religion was influenced by this historical context. In this chapter, we will explore the main factors that influenced the Buddha's thinking and shaped the way the religion developed after his death. In particular, the origins of Buddhism are closely connected with the origins of Hinduism.

The cultural history of northern India

Indian civilisation is one of the oldest continuing cultures in human history, along with that of China. Some scholars, such as Klaus K. Klostermaier, believe that India was already culturally advanced as early as 6000 BCE, but we have little evidence relating to this period. However, in the 1920s, archaeological excavations of the ancient cities of Mohenjo-Daro and Harappa in northwest India and Pakistan revealed the existence of an urban civilisation dating back to 2500 BCE. This is called the Indus Valley civilisation.

Evidence indicates it was extensive and had strong central government. Artefacts show its religion to be related to the forces of nature — for example, the worship of a mother goddess, sacred trees and fertility symbols. No temples have been found, indicating that religion was largely a domestic matter. Many scholars believe that elements of this ancient religion continued uninterrupted, and that the roots of Hinduism lie here.

From around 1500 BCE new ideas were brought into India by Aryan invaders from what is now northern Iran and southern Russia. It seems this was a peaceful invasion, but one which had a profound and long-lasting impact on the religion, language, society and political organisation of northern India. The Vedic culture of the Aryans was the other key root of Hinduism.

Vedic religion

The Aryans introduced the Vedic religion, based on a group of scriptures called the Vedas. *Veda* is a Sanskrit word meaning 'knowledge'. The Vedas have no

named human authors but are ascribed to ancient sages who, in certain intuitive states, 'heard' the truth of how things are. The truth of the Vedas is therefore considered to be a universal and timeless truth.

There is no one creator God but many different gods (and a small number of goddesses) related to natural forces. Central to the Vedic religion was the sacrifice of animals, carried out in public by priests in order to please the gods or ask them for favours, such as children, prosperity or a good harvest. The goals of this religion were often worldly, but fundamentally the priests were responsible for maintaining the good order of the world. In early times, they would sometimes take the hallucinogenic drug soma to induce altered states of consciousness for their rituals.

Vedic language

The language of the Vedas is Sanskrit, and this became the sacred language of India, equivalent to Latin in Western Europe. The sacred texts of Hinduism, Buddhism and Jainism — the three native religions of India — are mostly in Sanskrit.

Vedic society

The Aryans brought with them a hierarchical social structure, the origins of which they traced to their oldest scripture, the *Rig Veda*. This means they believed their social structure to be part of the order of the universe, and not man-made. This is one reason why the caste system that developed from it has been so resistant to change and still continues in modern India.

In the Hymn of the Cosmic Man (*purusha shukta*), the universe is said to have been created from a huge male figure, compared to a cosmic man. Verse 12 says, 'His mouth became the brahmin, his arms were made into the warrior, his thighs the people, and from his feet the servants were born.' The cosmic man is equated with society, and society is seen as an organic whole. Each social ranking is symbolised by a part of the body of cosmic man, and a natural hierarchy of rankings is therefore evident. It follows that there were four main social classes or *varnas*:

- priests or brahmins
- warriors and kings, or *kshatriyas*
- farmers or *vaishyas*
- servants or *shudras*

These were hereditary groups and there was no 'social mobility' between them. Each man's duty was to follow the profession suitable for his social class. It is relevant to note that India may be the only civilisation in the world ever to have placed religious priests unequivocally above kings.

Political organisation

Political organisation in Aryan culture was hierarchical and centralised. This usually took the form of monarchies. However, kingdoms could vary considerably in size, and 'kings' were sometimes no more than village rulers.

For many centuries up to and including the time of the Buddha, Indus Valley and Aryan influences co-existed side by side in northern India. So, for example, in the sixth to fourth centuries BCE, there were both kingdoms and democratic republics in the region. These were not democratic in the modern sense, but had leaders elected from and by a small group of elders. Scholars believe this was significant for the development of Buddhism, since the Buddha chose a democratic model for his monks, with decisions made by consensus.

By this time social class and religion were intimately connected, and only the three higher classes were allowed to practise the Vedic religion. The servants or *shudras* were religious outcasts and considered morally impure; they were not allowed to participate in rituals and had to live in separate settlements at the edge of the village. Priests or brahmins were so important and so powerful that the culture and religion are usually called *brahminical*.

The status of women is unclear. Socially, a woman's class would be determined by her birth, just as for men, and she would marry within her class. However, women did not directly wield political power, and it is possible that in the Buddha's time women did not have equal access to religious rites.

Society at the time of the Buddha

Between the seventh and fifth centuries BCE, the intellectual life of India was in ferment. It has been pointed out many times that this period was a turning point in the intellectual and spiritual development of the whole world, for it saw the earlier philosophers of Greece, the great Hebrew prophets, Confucius in China, and possibly Zoroaster in Persia. In India this crucial period in the world's history was marked on the one hand by the teaching of the Upanishadic sages…and on the other hand by the appearance of teachers who were less orthodox than they, and who rejected the Vedas entirely. It was at this time that Jainism and Buddhism arose, the most successful of a large number of heterodox systems.

Ainslie T. Embree, *Sources of Indian Tradition*

In the lifetime of the Buddha, economic developments had begun to destabilise the brahminical order. The introduction of iron plough shares and other tools produced agricultural surpluses which led to prosperity and strong trade. The period is characterised by the growth of large towns and the first use of money. One of the effects of these changes was the creation of new professions, such as state officials and traders, which had no place in the ancient class system. As Richard Gombrich writes in *Theravada Buddhism*, 'in the Buddha's day the dominant strata of urban society were not catered for, not even recognized, by brahminism'. So it is not surprising that evidence has been found that the Buddha's message appealed especially to town dwellers and the new social classes.

Gombrich makes two further points about the impact of urban development on Buddhism. First, it is possible that the high population densities of the new towns made illness and death seem more prevalent and widespread than they would seem in a small village. This may be one reason behind the Buddha's experience of the Four Signs, and may also explain why his teachings on suffering, illness and death in the Four Noble Truths became acceptable to people when they did.

Second, the large populations of towns and cities became crucial to the economic development of monastic communities. Monks and nuns depend on ordinary householders for their food and material needs, and small villages would not have been capable of sustaining monastic groups of any size. It is therefore arguable that urban development was a pre-condition for the growth of Buddhist monasteries.

Not all scholars agree with Gombrich. Some argue, for example, that suffering, disease and death have always been present in human society and there is no good reason to suppose that economic conditions made the Buddha's teachings more relevant in his day than they would be in any other place and at any other time. Some thinkers do not see the need to emphasise socioeconomic factors to explain what is, they say, a universally applicable religion.

In the Buddha's time, a relatively small population lived in the Ganges plain compared with today. Most people lived in small villages but a growing number of people were gathered in newly formed towns and cities. These settlements were surrounded by untouched forests, in which wild animals such as tigers, monkeys and elephants lived.

Box 2.1	
Comparative dates	

All dates are BCE and approximate

2650	Oldest Egyptian pyramid
2500	Indus Valley civilisation
2000	Abraham, first Hebrew patriarch
1290	Moses
1200	The Vedas begin to be composed
950	King Solomon builds first temple in Jerusalem
900	Homer composes the *Iliad*
700	Hesiod writes major work on Greek gods
600	The Upanishads begin to be composed
563–483	The Buddha
527	Traditional date for the death of Mahavira, Jain leader
551–479	Confucius in China
450	Lao Tzu in China
428–348	Plato
384–322	Aristotle

Religion in India at the time of the Buddha

Scholars usually set the Vedic religion in the period between 1500 and 500 BCE. The Buddha lived at the end of the Vedic period, at a time of enormous change. The three main religions of ancient India all took root between the seventh and fifth centuries BCE.

- Modern **Hinduism** was beginning to evolve from the Vedic religion, the indigenous folk religions and other ascetic trends. There are no precise dates for the beginning of Hinduism, partly because it is not a single unified religion, but many characteristic elements can be traced back to around 700–500 BCE.

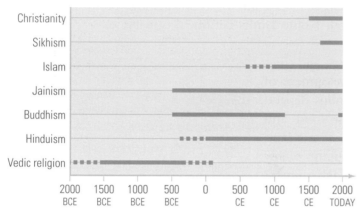

Figure 2.1 **The development of religions in India**

- **Jainism** emerged at almost exactly the same time as Buddhism. The Buddha and Mahavira, the Jain leader, are known to have been contemporaries. Jainism developed from one of the most influential groups of ascetics who rejected the Vedic religion.
- **Buddhism** developed between the sixth and fourth centuries BCE, and involved a reinterpretation of asceticism and folk religions, and a rejection of the Vedic religion.

Hinduism

In the last century or so of the Vedic period, a new set of scriptures began to be composed called the Upanishads, also known as Vedanta or 'conclusion of the Vedas'. Although based on the Vedas, these scriptures emphasise the personal rather than the public dimension of religion, and replace the animal sacrifice with the inner sacrifice of our ego and selfish emotions. The Upanishads speak of one divine energy called Brahman, the impersonal spirit of the universe, and the goal of religion is the union of the 'soul' or *atman* with the universal Brahman. The methods used to reach this union include meditation, contemplation of nature, yoga, reflective reasoning and dutiful action in society. The Upanishads introduce the ideas of reincarnation and karma.

Hinduism as we know it today evolved from the later Vedic period, and is strongly influenced by the Upanishads. Animal sacrifice was gradually discontinued, and the religion became based on prayer and devotion to a pantheon of gods and goddesses. The social class system developed into a more elaborate

system of castes, and the Vedas are still considered authoritative scriptures by Hindus. It is difficult to say whether the transition from the Vedic religion to Hinduism occurred before or after the Buddha. It is likely that the changes had already begun before the Buddha's birth and were continuing during his lifetime and beyond. A feature of developing Hinduism was a greater willingness to see the ultimate principle of the universe in personal, rather than impersonal terms. Scholars generally agree that, from the time of the Buddha onwards, there was mutual influence between Hindus and Buddhists. Just as Buddhism reinterpreted some key concepts found in the Upanishads, so later Hindus borrowed from Buddhist ideas. This dialogue continued for over 1,000 years.

Vedic religion	**Upanishads**	***Shramanas*: forest dwellers**	**Folk religions**
Vedic scriptures, which are authoritative, sacrifice of animals, social castes, *soma*, nature gods, focus on this life	Vedic scriptures, which are authoritative, inner sacrifice of ego, meditation, yoga, one impersonal God: Brahman, human soul: *atman*, religion unites the soul with God, karma determines after-life	Rejection of social and material values, asceticism, meditation, yoga, live in isolation, some accept the Vedas	Local nature spirits, rituals for the dead, spells and charms, divinations

Hinduism
- The Vedas and Upanishads, which are authoritative
- Social castes
- Nature gods and many other gods and goddesses
- No sacrifice of animals
- One impersonal divine energy: Brahman
- Human soul: *atman*
- Meditation, yoga, devotion, reflective reasoning
- Rebirth
- Karma
- Seven stages of life: leaving society in old age to practise religion

Figure 2.2
The origins of Hinduism

The Buddha's period saw several other movements away from orthodox Brahminism. Many adults (probably almost all men) chose to give up their jobs and families and live in solitude or in small groups in the forests to pursue their religious goals. These people, called *shramanas*, or ascetics, developed a number of different sects following a range of approaches and methods. It was one such person that the Buddha met on his fourth trip out of the palace, and it was this ascetic life that he lived for 6 years.

The ascetics began as social drop-outs, but as Hinduism developed it included this individual pursuit of religious goals as an accepted part of the religion. The ascetics who would be considered Hindus are those who followed the Vedas and the Upanishads. Hindu devotees living and meditating near the roadside can

still be seen in India today. Generally it is older people who adopt this life, once their social obligations have been met.

Hinduism did not spread beyond India's borders until the twentieth century, when it came to Britain and a few other countries through immigration. Today there are 900 million Hindus in the world, including 80% of the Indian population and 400,000 Hindus living in Britain.

Jainism

Mahavira, the Jain leader, lived further east than the Buddha. Although the two leaders never met, there are a number of Buddhist scriptures that refer to conversations between the Buddha and some of Mahavira's disciples.

Jainism emphasises austere asceticism, moral restraint and control as the way to free the transmigrating soul from the bonds of matter, reincarnation and suffering. Everything, even material objects, has a *jiva* or life principle that is distinct and individual — unlike the *atman* of the Upanishads, which is impersonal and can merge completely with Brahman.

Mahavira also taught the law of moral causation or karma based entirely on actions, not intentions — so killing an insect unintentionally carries all the painful consequences of deliberately taking a life.

It is estimated there are 4 million Jains worldwide today, 100,000 living outside India. Their strict moral values have led Jains to choose particular jobs for their livelihood, and many become doctors, lawyers or publishers. Both men and women are generally well educated. Jainism did not spread beyond India until modern times, when it came to Britain and other countries through immigration, but it is not a religion that seeks converts and it remains self-contained.

Folk religions

Alongside these trends, the ancient folk religions of India continued, especially at village level. These involved beliefs in local nature spirits and demons. Folk religions had various magical practices, such as fortune-telling, palmistry, prophecies, charms and spells, propitiating spirits of various kinds and the interpretation of dreams. These practices were accessible to ordinary people and, before the Buddha's time, some of them had begun to be appropriated by the Brahmin priests and incorporated into the Vedic religion.

It was the ordinary village people following these religions who, probably around the time of the Buddha, began to portray Brahman as the one creator-God who cares for us all. In those Upanishads composed before the Buddha, Brahman is the supreme reality and seen as impersonal. It is therefore possible that the idea of Brahman as it evolved in Hinduism originated from pre-Aryan folk religion. The personal form of Brahman was given the name Brahma.

What did the Buddha reject or adopt?

The teachings of the Buddha developed against a background of strong Vedic influence, but possessed an equally strong rejection of it. In terms of the three religions of ancient India that survive today, Hinduism continued the Vedic tradition with substantial modifications, whereas Buddhism and Jainism rejected the Vedic scriptures, the class system and many other elements of 'orthodox' religion. The Buddha, then, was not a lone dissenting voice. He belonged to a widespread movement that questioned the old values, systems and beliefs. This movement was one that attempted to establish a religion more adapted to society at that time, and one that gave prime importance to personal religious freedom. For Buddhists, of course, the Buddha was concerned with teaching a truth that is universal and timeless, not merely a truth that is bounded by history and context.

By identifying what the Buddha rejected from the society and religion of his time, and considering what he adapted from them, we can see more clearly what was new and radical about his teaching.

Rejected concepts

- The Buddha rejected the authority of the Vedic scriptures.
- He rejected animal sacrifice.
- He rejected the use of intoxicants such as *soma* because they disturb our mental clarity and control.
- He refused to follow the class system. Although he was born into the kingly or *kshatriya* class, he decided to lead a religious life which was not the prescribed activity of his class. The story of Sunita illustrates that he accepted the lowest social outcasts as his followers. He argued that it is how a person thinks and behaves that really counts, not his or her social status.

Box 2.2

Religious movements in India at the time of the Buddha

The following ascetics rejected Brahminism and developed their own teachings:

- **Purana Kassapa** taught that there is no such thing as moral causation; whatever one does brings no virtue or sin.
- **Makkhali Gosala** taught a form of fatalism or pre-destination. Rebirth occurs again and again through destiny and nature, and nothing we can do will make any difference to our future.

- **Ajita Kesakambali** taught materialism: there is no life after death, humans are merely physical and their bodies return to nature at death. There is no merit in good deeds.
- **Sañjaya Balatthaputta** was a sceptic who taught that human knowledge of the ultimate, including what happens after death, is impossible.
- **Vardhamana Mahavira,** the twenty-fourth Enlightened Conqueror (Jina) taught what became Jainism.

- He rejected the hierarchical structures of Aryan society.
- He rejected extreme asceticism. After experiencing it first hand, he found it did not lead to personal liberation.
- He rejected any religion or philosophy that undermines morality. He taught that there is a law of moral causation, and that good deeds do make a difference — we can change our future.
- He rejected materialism on the grounds that it renders life meaningless and morality pointless.
- He taught the doctrine of rebirth.
- He rejected scepticism. He called sceptics or doubters 'eel-wrigglers'. They sit on the fence and never follow their wisdom, which implies that they cannot act on decisions they have not taken. Their approach leads to an impasse.
- He rejected the solitary aspect of the life of an ascetic, and advised his monks always to live in groups and communities. He found that living alone for long periods can sometimes have a detrimental effect on the mind.
- The Buddha rejected the ideas of Brahman and *atman* as found in the Upanishads, on the grounds that there is no empirical evidence or logical reason that proves their existence.

Accepted and reinterpreted concepts

- The Buddha accepted the idea that we are born again and again, which was introduced in the Upanishads and taught by various ascetic groups. However, his doctrine of rebirth is a complete reinterpretation of the idea and develops it in greater detail.

Upanishads	Shramanas	Folk religions
Idea of personal, inner religion, meditation, karma, rebirth, the ultimate truth is beyond words and expression	Meditation, yoga, self-discipline, value of abandoning social obligations	Nature spirits, gods and goddesses, divination, rites for the dead

Buddhism
- Emphasis on working on one's own mind
- Karma determines rebirth
- Ultimate truth is beyond words and expression
- Meditation is the key method, but Buddhism develops the method
- Self-discipline in everyday life; moderation is encouraged
- Monasticism reflects the value of giving up family and class-based obligations
- Buddhist monasticism is radically new: creation of communities
- Tolerance of folk beliefs and rituals
- Elaborate development of rites for the dead
- Doctrine of no God and no soul, i.e. no Brahman and no *atman*

Figure 2.3 Religious influences on the Buddha's thinking

- The Buddha accepted the law of karma or moral causation, which was introduced in the Upanishads and also taught by some *shramanas*, but he was the only teacher to separate moral action and social duty and to ethicise the concept. His explanation of how karma works was more detailed than in any other religion.
- The Buddha accepted the general Indian idea that suffering is related to ignorance, and that the goal of religion is to free ourselves from both of these. This idea is also developed in the Upanishads and in Jainism.
- He accepted the Upanishadic move towards a personal religion, concerned with working on one's own mind and emotions.
- He tolerated folk religions but devalued their importance. Brahma, spirits and so on are seen to exist, but are not as powerful as folk religions would have us believe, because they cannot help to liberate us from suffering. Monks were forbidden to engage in spells and charms, but lay people could do so if they wished. From its beginnings until today, Buddhism has happily coexisted with folk beliefs in every country to which it has spread.
- The Buddha was inspired by the democratic model of social organisation developed by the north Indian republics, and adapted this in his monastic communities.

It is important to note that, although the Buddha rejected many of the social and political values of his day (class, hierarchy and so on), he never took up a political position, nor did he advocate political opposition. He never sought confrontation. On the contrary, the Buddhist approach is to respect the laws of the country where one lives and, if any laws are considered wrong, to oppose them non-violently.

Buddhism, Hinduism and Jainism

Buddhism shares a significant amount of common ground with Hinduism and Jainism. Together, these three religions are the basis of Indian thought and Indian religion.

- All three value the principle of non-violence, *ahimsa*, the concern not to harm others or to take life.
- All three believe that we live again and again, and that our moral actions determine the outcome of each after-life.
- All three characterise life as one of suffering due to ignorance, and identify the goal of religion as liberation or emancipation from suffering and ignorance. Knowledge and wisdom therefore play an important part in the liberation process.
- All three religions have their own reasons for teaching tolerance of other religious beliefs and philosophies.

The common ground shared by Indian religions is clearly different from that shared by Judaism, Christianity and Islam. If we are aware that the basic way of thinking in Indian religion is different, we may be able to question assumptions about religion in general, since current ideas in Western philosophy of religion are based solely on Judaism, Christianity and Islam.

Questions

1 What are the social and religious factors that led people to become followers of the Buddha during his lifetime?
2 Give an account of the social and religious conditions in northern India at the time of the Buddha.
3 What were the major influences on the thinking of Gautama the Buddha?
4 To what extent did the Buddha reject or accept the religious ideas of his time?

Chapter 3

A brief history of Buddhism

Buddhism is a vast and varied phenomenon: its history goes back over two and half millennia and its geography spans a large part of the globe. It has found expression in a score of languages and has stimulated a great variety of art styles. It has deeply shaped a great part of humanity past and present.

Klaus K. Klostermaier, *A Survey of Hinduism*

This chapter provides a general overview of how Buddhism has grown to become a world religion. It falls into three main sections: Buddhism in India; the spread of Buddhism through Asia; and the spread of Buddhism to the West.

The three main traditions of Buddhism

There are three main traditions of Buddhism. They developed gradually in India over the first 1,000 years after the Buddha and are still all practised today. Although they all share the same fundamental principles of the Buddha's teaching, such as the Four Noble Truths, there are many differences in emphasis and in interpretation between the traditions. The three traditions are Nikaya Buddhism, Mahayana Buddhism and Tantric Buddhism, and each is examined in detail in Chapter 4.

Nikaya Buddhism

This term refers to the so-called 18 'schools' or *nikayas* which developed in India from earliest times, and of which only Theravada survives today. *Nikaya* also means 'collection' and is the term used for the collections of scriptures used by these schools. Sometimes this tradition is called Hinayana Buddhism, but this term is derogatory and was coined by Mahayanists who were critical of this approach. *Hinayana* means 'lower vehicle' as compared with *Mahayana* which means 'great vehicle'. The term Nikaya Buddhism is neutral.

Theravada means 'the way of the elders'. It is often claimed that Theravada holds the original teachings and discipline laid down by the historical Buddha. The Theravada scriptures are generally acknowledged to be a record of the teachings collected together at the First Buddhist Council. For this reason many Theravadins believe their tradition represents orthodox Buddhism and that later traditions have modified the Buddha's original teachings, swayed by the views of their various founders.

Mahayana Buddhism

Mahayana is an umbrella term which describes a number of different schools, the earliest of which apparently emerged between the first century BCE and the first century CE. Mahayana is seen by modern scholars as a new movement which developed its own vast collection of scriptures between approximately the first and fifth centuries CE. It is characterised by different interpretations of the Buddha's teachings, for example by its understanding of the nature of the Buddha and of enlightenment. Some Mahayana schools developed new forms of devotional worship, which are unknown in Theravada.

Mahayana gave rise to two main philosophical schools in India: Madhyamaka and Chittamatra. Over the centuries, as Mahayana spread to other countries, further schools developed which had not originally existed in India, such as Ch'an (Zen), Pure Land Buddhism and Nichiren, which developed in China and Japan and are still practised today.

Tantric Buddhism

In the sixth and seventh centuries CE, a new form of religion called Tantra became widespread in India. Tantra, which means 'thread' or 'continuity', influenced the development of both Buddhism and Hinduism. Tantric Buddhism is associated with rituals and relies upon visualisation, the chanting of mantras (sacred formulae) and devotional practices. It has its own body of scriptures. It is colourful and vibrant, and so had popular appeal.

Buddhism in India

Western scholars analyse the development of Buddhism in India in various ways, and each identifies different historical periods for the phases of its development. In general, we can say that Indian Buddhism developed in four phases:
- 484–268 BCE: slow growth, localised in north India
- 268 BCE–250 CE: ascendancy and spread
- 250–500 CE: classical period, flourishing
- 500–1200 CE: gradual decline

The first of these periods is relatively unknown because there is little or no historical evidence of events from that early time. Our knowledge is based largely on accounts in the scriptures, which were written down several hundred years later. From the accession of the Indian emperor Ashoka (268 BCE) onwards, however, many events are documented through historical records and the picture is clearer and more precise.

The first 200 years after the Buddha

According to the scriptures, the Buddha died confident that his teaching was firmly established. He had been teaching and advising his followers for 45 years, and there were hundreds of enlightened *arhats* who were able to guide the community after his death. He did not appoint a successor. Instead, he told his disciples that they should follow the Dharma, the body of teachings that he left behind.

Universal Buddhist tradition claims that shortly after the Buddha's death there was an authoritative gathering of 500 *arhats* in Rajagaha, a village in the modern state of Bihar, northern India, who collected together all the authentic teachings of the Buddha. This gathering is known as the First Buddhist Council.

Upali and Ananda, both senior monks, recited the teachings and the assembly memorised them. Upali recited the Vinaya or material on monastic discipline, while Ananda recited the suttas or discourses on meditation and wisdom. The Dharma continued to be transmitted orally, from one generation to the next, for several centuries. It was not written down because writing was virtually unknown in India at that time, so the teachings were transmitted orally by communal chanting.

During the first centuries after the Buddha, Buddhism quietly established itself alongside India's other religions in the towns and villages of northern India. The monastic community was organised in small, self-contained units with no centralised authority, and the monks would wander from village to village for alms. Over the years they grouped themselves in monasteries so that they had a fixed place to live. This grouping had started in the Buddha's time, when the monks had no fixed home for most of the year but took shelter together in one place during the monsoon in July, August and September, when the violent rains made it difficult to travel. Gradually, after the Buddha, these shelters became permanent and were used year-round, and were known as *viharas* or monasteries.

Given the lack of centralised authority, it is not surprising that different schools of practice and thought emerged over time. At first, the differences related only to points of monastic discipline, but later there were divergent interpretations of the suttas as well. Although modern descriptions of these developments use

terms such as 'disputes', 'schisms' and 'sects', it is important to note that Buddhism as a whole was tolerant of these divergences and monks with different philosophical views could be found living side by side in the same monastery. The differences may well have been irrelevant to most lay Buddhists.

In order to resolve these differences, most Buddhist sources agree that a Second Buddhist Council was held roughly 100 years after the Buddha, possibly in 350 BCE, in the city of Vesali. The result of this council was a split between the School of Elders, which was the forerunner of the Theravada school, and the Mahasanghikas or 'Great Assembly', a school regarded by some scholars as the forerunner of the Mahayana tradition.

Predictably, perhaps, the Theravada account of the reasons for the council is quite different from that of the Mahayana. Theravadins refer to points of discipline, while the Mahayana tradition emphasises differences in doctrine.

- The Theravadins claim that the Second Council was called because many monks had become lax in their discipline. In particular, the monks were accepting money instead of food as alms and eating after noon (both forbidden in the Vinaya).
- Mahayana accounts claim the Second Council debated the nature of *arhats*. A monk named Mahadeva cast doubt on the perfection of those who claimed to be *arhats*: he said they had not fully conquered their passions because they still had wet dreams; they were not omniscient because they often had to ask for directions; they were still subject to doubts; they had learned their knowledge from others and not from their own experience; and they would exclaim out loud during meditation.

Further divisions occurred within each of these wings of Buddhism. Tradition has it that there were 18 different groups or 'sects' in the first few centuries of Buddhism in India, of which only Theravada survives today. Some scholars have suggested the real number of groups could have been as high as 30.

Figure 3.1 The Buddha and his main disciples, from left to right: Ananda and Maudgalyayana, the Buddha, Shariputra and Subhuti

How reliable are the scriptural stories of these first centuries? Some modern scholars have doubts about the First Council because the details vary in the accounts of different Buddhist schools. Although Buddhist tradition accepts that the early scriptures were standardised at the First Council, there were subsequent changes and additions in the versions of the scriptures adopted by each school.

Some scholars consider that the memory required to recall the entire body of scriptures would be so extraordinary that it is hard to believe such an exercise was possible. However, other scholars are less sceptical. Variations in detail may be due to the very nature of oral communication and do not necessarily mean the First Council is a fabrication. Even after writing was introduced, memorisation and oral transmission remained sacred activities. Even today there are Buddhists in Asia who can recite entire volumes of scripture from memory.

Emperor Ashoka: Buddhism's ascendancy

The development of Buddhism in India was revolutionised by Ashoka, who is famous as Buddhism's most powerful patron. He came to power in 268 BCE probably by assassinating the claimants to the throne of Magadha, in northern India, including his own elder brothers. He expanded his empire through military conquest until it covered roughly the territory of modern India except for the extreme south. Ashoka is therefore equally famous in Indian history as the first ruler to unite almost the whole subcontinent in a single empire.

After a number of brutal campaigns Ashoka became sickened by violence and converted to the non-violent values of the Buddhist religion. He was instrumental in the spread of Buddhism throughout India. Hundreds of commemorative stupas were built, especially in the holy places connected with the Buddha's life; stone pillars were erected on which were engraved decrees and edicts encouraging Ashoka's people to lead a moral life; numerous Buddhist monasteries were funded.

Ashoka transformed Buddhism from one of the many non-Vedic groups in India into the 'state religion' of one of the greatest empires on earth. At the same time, he initiated a climate of religious tolerance, and supported not only Buddhist institutions but those of Hinduism and other religions. He encouraged religious freedom and innovation. In addition, Ashoka sent missions far and wide — to Egypt, Syria and Macedonia — 'to conquer according to Dharma', and effectively turned Buddhism into a world religion. Under Ashoka, Buddhism became firmly established in Sri Lanka and Kashmir.

According to Sri Lankan sources, Ashoka convened a Third Buddhist Council to clarify certain doctrinal disputes. The Theravada sources claim that the Third

Council validated the conservative teaching of the elders. There is no record of this council in Mahayana sources.

See Chapter 19 for a more detailed presentation of Ashoka and his significance for the development of Buddhism.

The flourishing of Buddhism

Despite its internal divisions and the fluctuations of Indian politics, Buddhism spread rapidly throughout India; by the third century CE it was the major faith of India. Jainism, Vedic Brahmanism, and Hindu cults of Shiva and Vishnu all existed more or less equally as secondary religions. It was not until the fourth century CE that Hinduism began its ascendancy.

There was an intense flourishing of scholarship, and new scriptures and philosophical treatises were composed. The flourishing of Buddhist culture is reflected by its great universities such as that of Nalanda, which was established possibly as early as the second century CE. By the fifth century, Chinese pilgrims record that Nalanda housed several thousand monk-students and its library occupied a large three-storey building. The ruins of Nalanda can be seen today in Bihar state.

Many reasons have been given for the popularity of Buddhism in India.

- The Dharma is universally applicable, and is not restricted to a particular tribal or cultural group.
- Buddhism was attractive to travellers and merchants, who were detached from traditional beliefs and social structures and who played an important role in spreading Buddhism on their travels.
- Buddhism was accessible to the masses, unlike Brahmanism which was restricted to a small class of initiates. In particular, Buddhist teachers used local languages and not Sanskrit, which was the sacred language of India but was understood only by the educated elite.
- The monastic community was well organised and provided a good example of a spiritual way of life.
- The teaching itself was attractive to intellectuals for its systematic analysis, and to ordinary people for its values of non-violence and compassion.
- There were many aspects of life that the Buddha did not pronounce upon, so people were free to continue with traditional customs if they wished. Buddhism was flexible.

Decline and revival

Between about 400 and 1000 CE, Buddhism and Hinduism developed closely together, with many points of mutual influence. From 700 CE onwards, Buddhist monasteries in central Asia and northwest India were gradually destroyed by

invasions of Muslims and Turks. Over the following centuries Buddhist monasteries, universities and libraries in all parts of India were destroyed by the Muslim advance, and Buddhists were persecuted and massacred. By the twelfth century Buddhism survived in a handful of pockets in the extreme south, east and north of the subcontinent, where Muslims were not dominant, but it subsequently disappeared from India altogether.

How can we account for the collapse of Buddhist institutions which a few centuries earlier had been so strong and vibrant? A number of reasons have been given for the decline of Buddhism in India.

- The flexibility of Buddhism can mean that it becomes almost indistinguishable from surrounding religions, and it has been argued that Tantric Buddhism in particular became indistinguishable from Hinduism.
- Buddhist values of peace and non-violence make it vulnerable to military force.
- The dependence on patrons and donors makes the monasteries economically vulnerable when those in power withdraw their support.
- Monasteries and robed monks are an easily identifiable target, and with their destruction Buddhism loses the core of its identity. The importance of the monastic community or Sangha means that when monasteries are destroyed and monastic life is disrupted, it is difficult for Buddhism to survive.

Buddhism had been so successfully eradicated from the Indian consciousness that when the British ruled India in the nineteenth century no one was aware that the Buddha had been an historical figure. He had become a character of myth and legend. It was thanks to the efforts of colonial archaeologists that historical remains were found which substantiated the story of early Buddhism as we know it today: texts, stupas, Ashoka's pillars and stone edicts, the ruins of Nalanda, and the Mahabodhi temple in Bodh Gaya are some examples of what was uncovered.

Following the restoration of numerous sites and buildings connected with Buddhism, the religion experienced a revival in India through the twentieth century. There are three main factors behind this. The first is the role played by refugees from Tibet, who brought their Buddhist faith with them when they fled into exile after the Chinese Communist occupation of their homeland in 1959. They have established refugee communities in India and neighbouring Nepal, practise Buddhism freely and visit the main pilgrimage sites. In Bodh Gaya, for example, Tibetans organise several prayer festivals each year, at which tens of thousands of Buddhists congregate.

A second factor is international religious tourism. Every year thousands of Buddhists from countries such as Japan, Sri Lanka and Thailand, and from Europe and North America, visit the land of the Buddha's birth on pilgrimage.

This has helped to bring awareness of Buddhism back into the Indian consciousness.

A third factor is the influence of Dr B. R. Ambedkar (1891–1956) from Maharashtra state, who encouraged many members of the lowest 'untouchable' classes to convert from Hinduism to Buddhism. Ambedkar was himself an untouchable but gained a good education and became a lawyer. From the 1920s he worked for the emancipation of untouchables in India and became a minister in the first post-independence government. He was attracted to Buddhism because of its emphasis on love, equality, freedom and tolerance.

Today there are around 4.5 million 'Ambedkar' Buddhists in India. After conversion, they report an improvement in self-esteem, a greater sense of dignity, and a determination to become well educated as a means for social advancement.

The spread of Buddhism in Asia

As we have seen, Buddhism began to spread to other Asian countries under Ashoka, from 268 BCE onwards. The schools of Nikaya Buddhism were established in Sri Lanka, Kashmir and central Asia. There is evidence that Mahayana Buddhism also spread to central Asia, possibly around the same time or a little later, and was introduced to China by traders plying the Silk Route in the first century CE.

As Buddhism spread throughout Asia, each country followed one or more specific traditions, but only in India were all traditions and schools present. Figure 3.2 shows the approximate date at which Buddhism was first introduced into each Asian country, and the approximate date at which it ceased to be practised, if applicable.

Today, each Asian country is associated with a particular tradition of Buddhism. This has had an impact in modern times, when Asian immigrants to the West have brought their religious traditions with them. Thus, Chinese and Japanese immigrants have introduced Mahayana Buddhism to the West, while immigrants from Sri Lanka and Thailand have introduced Theravada Buddhism, and Tibetan refugees have brought Tantric Buddhism.

Sri Lanka and southeast Asia

Buddhism was introduced into Sri Lanka in approximately 250 BCE by a mission sent by Emperor Ashoka. Sri Lanka thus claims the most ancient verifiable continuous practice of Buddhism in the world. It is considered the homeland of Theravada Buddhism and has produced some of the most important historical chronicles of early Buddhism and several major commentaries on the Buddhist scriptures.

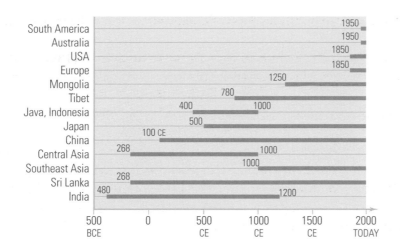

Figure 3.2 The spread of Buddhism

Ashoka sent a mission led by his son, the monk Mahinda. It met with the royal prince Tissa, who subsequently, through his alliance with Ashoka, was recognised as the first historical king of the whole island. Later Ashoka's daughter, the nun Sanghamitta, is said to have brought to Sri Lanka a cutting of the original bodhi tree under which the Buddha attained enlightenment. The tree that grew from this can still be seen today in Anuradhapura, and many other cuttings from this tree have since been planted all over Sri Lanka. These trees have often been turned into outdoor shrines decked with prayer flags.

Buddhism in Sri Lanka enjoyed state protection and financial support from the outset, and this relationship continues to the present day, when prominent monks have considerable political influence.

The ruins of impressively large monasteries bear witness to the flourishing and the strength of Buddhism in Sri Lanka. However, political upheaval, sectarian rivalries and famine weakened Buddhism so much in 43–17 BCE that Sri Lankan monks decided to preserve the Buddhist oral scriptures in writing to ensure they would not be lost. This first systematic recording of the scriptures in writing was completed in around 17 BCE: it produced the Pali Canon.

Further political disruptions and Hindu invasions from India meant that by around 1070 CE it was necessary to invite monks from Burma to revive monastic ordination in Sri Lanka; the ceremony requires a minimum of ten ordained monks to be present to give ordination to new candidates. It appears that the ordination of nuns had lapsed completely by that time and has only recently been revived, in 1998, with the help of nuns from Korea and Taiwan. Later on, in 1741, when Sri Lanka was under Dutch rule, monks were invited again, this time from Thailand, to revive monastic ordination on the island. This shows how weakened Buddhism became at certain times in the island's history.

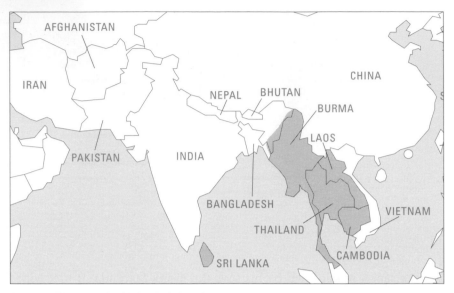

Figure 3.3 Theravada Buddhism in Asia today

Nevertheless, it survived persecution and reform from successive waves of Portuguese, Dutch and British colonialists, and remains the majority religion of Sri Lanka today.

It is possible that Ashoka sent a mission to Burma, but this has not been verified. The existing Theravada traditions in Thailand, Burma, Cambodia and Laos were established from Sri Lanka in the second millennium. The earlier Mahayana influences in the region mostly gave way to Theravada, except in Vietnam, where Mahayana flourished from the first century CE. In 580 CE Ch'an (Zen) Buddhism was introduced to Vietnam from China by the monk Vinitaruci, and has remained strong for centuries.

Laos became a state in 1353, and from that time until the present day it has followed Theravada Buddhism, introduced from Cambodia. Between the fifth and eleventh centuries CE, the Malay peninsula, Sumatra, Java and Indonesia followed Mahayana Buddhism, which they received from China and India. After the eleventh century, Buddhism was replaced as the dominant religion by either Hinduism or Islam.

In the twentieth century some Buddhists played a supportive role in southeast Asia's Communist movements, and as a result southeast Asian Communism has not been particularly anti-religious. In Vietnam, for example, Buddhism was part of the identity which Communist independence movements were trying to reassert. Buddhism continues to be practised and even to flourish throughout the region.

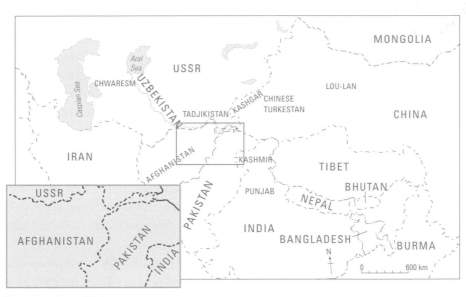

Figure 3.4 Central Asia

Central Asia

Buddhism was present in central Asia from the second century BCE. From east to west, this region covers present-day Chinese Turkestan, Kashmir, northern Pakistan, Tadjikistan and Afghanistan. It is not a unified area, politically or geographically, but throughout this region Buddhism flourished for roughly 1,000 years until Muslim conversions caused monasteries to be deserted. By around 1000 CE, what was left of Buddhist culture in the area was buried under the desert sands, not to be rediscovered until the nineteenth century.

Buddhism spread to this region from northwest India, and also from China along the trade road known as the Silk Route. Nikaya Buddhism, Mahayana Buddhism and Tantric Buddhism were all present in the region, making it particularly rich in Buddhist art, architecture and manuscripts. Among the most internationally known artistic expressions of Buddhist culture in central Asia are the monumental standing statues of the Buddha carved out of cliff faces in Afghanistan. They briefly attracted media attention during troubles in that country, when the ruling Taliban publicly defaced and destroyed all the statues.

Some important discoveries were recently made in Afghanistan, when researchers found ancient Buddhist texts in some of the meditation caves that are carved out of the cliff face near the large stone statues in Bamiyan. These texts include Mahayana scriptures, and they are among the oldest Buddhist manuscripts that have survived until today. One copy of the Prajñaparamita Sutra has been dated to the second century CE. Many of these texts are now preserved in the British Library and in the Schoyen Collection in Norway.

China

Buddhism was introduced into China in the first century CE. According to the traditional story, the Han Emperor Ming, who ruled 58–75 CE, dreamed of a divine being in the shape of a golden man. He was told this must be the foreign god called Buddha, and so he sent envoys to India, who returned with one or two Indian Buddhist masters, a white horse, and a text of the Sutra in Forty-Two Sections. The Emperor later founded the Monastery of the White Horse near Lo-yang.

Modern scholars are more comfortable with accounts which attest to the intro-duction of Buddhism through two separate routes, first, in the first century CE, from central Asia by foreign merchants plying the Silk Route, and, second, by at least the third century along the southern route from Sri Lanka to Indo-China, Canton and the lower Yangtse.

In China, Buddhism encountered an advanced and literate civilisation with highly developed religious, philosophical, social and political systems of its own. The story of Buddhism in China is therefore different from that of its spread to most other countries. Buddhism never replaced these systems, but grew alongside them. The two main influences on Chinese Buddhism were Confucianism and Taoism.

Figure 3.5 Mahayana Buddhism in Asia today

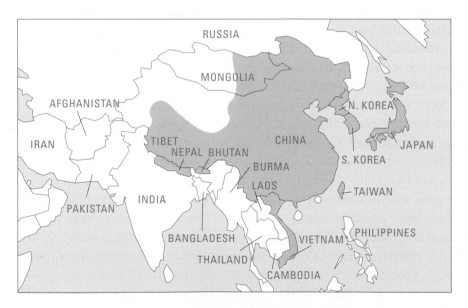

Confucianism

Confucius (551–479 BCE) established the main system of ethical behaviour in Chinese culture, which continues to be followed by Chinese communities today. It consists of guidelines for the behaviour of individuals, of the family and of

society as a whole. The fundamental virtues are considered to be respect for others, courtesy, hard work, social concern and honouring one's parents. Moral behaviour is motivated by a sense of genuine loving kindness towards others, and results in the best possible benefit for all. The Golden Rule of Confucianism is: 'Do not do to others what you would not like them to do to you' (usually rendered in English as: 'Do as you would be done by').

Confucianism is concerned with the best and most harmonious way of living this life, and contains no speculation about an after-life. It is therefore called a 'this-worldly' system, as opposed to an 'other-worldly' system. Human beings are seen as one point in a triangle of forces: earth, man and an impersonal heaven. The emperor is the mediator of the three forces and so is worthy of the greatest respect. This gives rise to a hierarchical social and political system, in which everyone knows their place and must pay respect to their superiors for harmony to prevail.

Confucius did not mention any reward or punishment for moral behaviour in an after-life, so the benefits of morality seem to be the tangible benefits arising from a healthy and harmonious society. T'ien or heaven is where one can place one's trust when things go wrong on earth, but it is not for human beings to speculate about heavenly matters.

Confucians developed these ideas in a religious or humanistic way in the fourth and third centuries. Well before the Common Era, Confucianism had developed the classic *I Ching*, which is a manual for divination, now well known in the West, based on maintaining harmony between the two principles of yin and yang. Yin stands for darkness, passivity and femininity, while yang stands for light, activity and masculinity. The balancing of these principles can be applied to medicine, to diet and even to feng shui (the art of positioning objects — graves, buildings, furniture — for a balanced, propitious flow of the chi (energy) of the environment and the user).

Under the Sun dynasty (960–1279 CE), Confucianism became the official state cult. It is known as Neo-Confucianism because it was heavily influenced by Taoism and Buddhism. All government officials or civil servants had to take exams based on knowledge of the Confucian classics, so this system of thought remained the dominant influence on the ruling classes until the Communist take-over in 1949.

Taoism

Taoism (pronounced Dow-ism) is said to have been founded by Lao-tzu in the sixth or fifth century BCE, but there is doubt about his historical existence. The ideas of Taoism are found in two foundational texts: the *Tao te Ching* and the *Chuang tzu*. They speak primarily of the unity that underlies all existence and

that can be experienced in nature and through quiet contemplation. Taoism therefore tends to emphasise qualities and aspects of life that are quite different from those prized by Confucianism: natural and spontaneous behaviour rather than formal etiquette; the simplicity of nature rather than the sophistication of government or imperial courts; the value of the individual rather than that of society; the benefit of withdrawing from society, living close to nature and engaging in contemplation as opposed to active social and economic engagement. Taoism emphasises peace and quiet and shuns the violence that often comes with politics. Its main virtues are humility, compassion and effortless naturalness. Many of the ideas of Taoism are embodied by Pooh Bear in the A. A. Milne stories, as pointed out in the popular book *The Tao of Pooh*.

Taoism was vague about life after death and simply considered life to be a dream, and death a natural change. By the second century CE it had combined with folk religions to form a Taoist religion with nature divinities, temples, rituals and priests. The emphasis of this religion was the quest for immortality, healing and the forgiveness of sins. In practice, the Chinese incorporate both Confucianist ethics and Taoist beliefs and attitudes into the way they view the world.

Socio-political context

The Chinese ruler was thought to be sanctified by the mandate of heaven and to maintain the cosmic equilibrium of man, earth and heaven by performing perfectly his ritual, ethical and administrative duties. In principle, the authority of the emperor and of the imperial government was unlimited and all-inclusive. They had the power to rule over both public and private life.

Chinese society was highly structured and hierarchical. Its prevailing style was authoritarian and paternalistic. There was an immense difference between rich and poor, between the educated elite and the uneducated peasantry, and this gap was accepted as part of the social order. The basic social aims were pragmatic and secular: maintaining law and order, peace and harmony. The assumption was that the emperor and the government must maintain overall control for this to be possible.

Buddhism in China

The introduction of Buddhism to China brought about a clash of cultures. It was not immediately successful for several reasons. First, the Buddhist teaching was difficult to accept.

- It was considered foreign and therefore inferior.
- It was seen as morbid, stressing suffering rather than happiness, and death rather than life.

- It was seen as selfish, because it did not follow the Confucian values of contributing to society through hard work.
- It introduced strange new beliefs unknown in China before this, such as rebirth.

Second, the Confucian-influenced state found Buddhist monasticism unacceptable and questioned its right to exist.

- Initially, monks would not bow to the emperor, since in India the religious or priestly class had always been above the ruling class.
- Monks were organised independently — they had their own rules and their own system for punishing monks who disobeyed the rules — and this was seen as threatening social cohesion. Monks did not consider themselves liable to government supervision.
- Celibacy was seen as an unnatural violation of the sacred laws governing family behaviour; it undermined the family as the basic social unit.
- Monasteries were economically autonomous — they were supported by believers and expected to be exempt from state taxes. This was seen as politically unacceptable and potentially dangerous.
- Monks were accused of being unproductive and socially useless — twentieth-century Communists later called them 'social parasites'.
- Some monks had no fixed place to live, and wandered from village to village begging for alms. The state disliked this way of life because it is impossible to control.

Despite all these factors, Buddhism gradually attracted growing numbers of Chinese. Between the second and third centuries CE the first Buddhist scriptures were translated into Chinese. The turning point came when the Han dynasty (206 BCE–220 CE) broke up, and in the turmoil that ensued, Buddhism filled the cultural vacuum. From that point its development is traced in terms of the Buddhism in northern China and the Buddhism in southern China.

In northern China, Buddhism was popular but was under the control of the ruler. This sometimes meant patronage and sometimes meant persecution (in 446 and 574–577CE). By the sixth century there were 30,000 Buddhist temples in northern China, indicating the tremendous popularity of the religion. Initially, it attracted small traders, clerks, copyists and people with limited education, but by the end of the fourth century it started to penetrate the upper classes.

In southern China, Buddhism was more intellectual from the start, appealing to the educated classes. It was independent of the political rulers and allied itself with Taoism.

The Golden Age of Buddhism in China was from the sixth to ninth centuries CE, under the Sui and T'ang dynasties. Buddhism was the dominant religion of the

people, although rulers varied in their favours. It was the dynamic stimulus of intellectual and cultural life. It is said, for instance, that China invented wood-block printing in the eighth century in order to print Buddhist images and texts. This alone would mean that Buddhism made an enormous social contribution.

Some village temples were quite small, with just one or two monks who worked among the local people, while other monasteries grew large, enjoyed official patronage and, as a result, became even more powerful and wealthy. Peasant families and serfs were allocated to large monasteries to work in the temple fields, so they had regular, tax-free incomes. Monasteries functioned as study centres and temples, hospitals, guest houses and banks. Many owned mills and oil presses, used by the local population for a fee. Monks helped to build roads, bridges and irrigation projects and to plant trees as a way of engaging in socially useful work.

From this brief description it can be seen that Chinese Buddhism made significant adaptations to the national culture. There were several other important developments.

- Monks engaged in economic activities.
- Monks were given an 'ordination certificate' showing their 'spiritual genealogy', that is, who they received ordination from. This echoed Chinese respect for family lineage.
- Chinese ancestral worship was incorporated into Buddhism: ancestors could be cared for by transferring one's good karma to them.
- The Mahayana *bodhisattva* of compassion, depicted as a male in India, assumed a female form in China. She is called Kuan-Yin and symbolises the motherly qualities of compassion.
- Yama, the ruler of the hells, was depicted as a Chinese magistrate, who decided on each person's rebirth by weighing up his or her good and bad deeds.

The decline of Buddhism in China came as a result of political jealousies and rivalries prompted by the wealth of the monasteries. In 715, the government confiscated all copper and bronze religious statues to turn them into cash. In the eighth century, civil war impoverished the state, so Emperor Wu-tzung (841–847) finally decided to break Buddhist dominance.

In 845, there was a tremendous backlash against Buddhism. All Buddhist establishments were destroyed, monks and nuns were secularised, and all temple lands and property were confiscated. Monastic Buddhism was suppressed throughout the empire and never recovered its dominance.

Decline was steady and gradual. Most of the different schools of Chinese Buddhism disappeared, and intellectual life went back to Confucianism. Under

the Ming dynasty (fourteenth to seventeenth centuries), for example, state officials were forbidden to be Buddhists. This meant that the best minds in the country were no longer drawn to the Buddhist debating halls but to the Confucian classics required for state examinations.

The two main schools of Chinese Buddhism to survive were Ch'an and Pure Land. The approach of these schools meant that neither depended on large institutions or vast libraries of scriptures, and they therefore succeeded in continuing after the persecution. Although monasteries were destroyed, Buddhism was still practised by lay people right up to the Cultural Revolution of 1949. It had become confined to being a popular religion rather than a religion of the educated elite. Buddhism was severely persecuted during the Cultural Revolution but, since the 1990s, it has seen a significant revival in mainland China, and monasteries have once again been established.

Japan

Buddhism spread from China to Korea and from Korea to Japan. It was introduced into Japan in the sixth century CE along with other elements of Chinese civilisation. At that time Japan had no strong institutions of its own, so there was no opposition to Buddhism. In 538 or 539, a Korean ruler sent a deputation to make an alliance with a Japanese ruler, and the delegation included Buddhist monks, scriptures and Buddha statues. From that time some of the Japanese ruling class began to follow Buddhism, which was later supported by Prince Shotoku (574–621), who is considered the father of Japanese Buddhism. He was a generous patron, built monasteries and temples, and made Buddhism virtually a state religion.

Shinto

The main religion already present in Japan at that time was Shinto. Shinto is related to the forces of nature and is concerned with creating good circumstances here and now. It is based on the belief that the gods are immanent in nature and do not live somewhere else, in some transcendental sphere. The deities of Shinto are called kamis, the spirits of mountains, trees, waterfalls and other powerful forces of the world. There is no chief kami corresponding to the idea of God. The kamis are considered to have an influence on human life, so this is why prayers and offerings are made to propitiate them. Shinto is practised mostly outdoors with local shrines in nature, although families may have a 'kami shelf' in their homes where symbols of the kami are kept.

When Buddhism arrived, Shinto had no written scriptures or strict doctrines, so it did not present an intellectual challenge in the way Confucianism or Taoism did in China. Furthermore, Shinto had no iconography — the kami were

not represented by images but by symbols such as a mirror, sword or jewel. Over the centuries Shinto and Buddhism coexisted peacefully in Japan and influenced each other. People still see them as complementary.

Buddhism in Japan

Japanese Buddhism is unique and characterised by its extensive secularisation. Apart from the Pure Land school it is not so concerned with escape from the endless cycle of life and death, or with transcendental states and realities; it focuses more on this-worldly questions — on the importance of finding oneself and realising enlightenment here and now. This is reflected in the way Buddhism pervades cultural life: in painting, in gardening, in flower arranging, in calligraphy and in drama. Each of these arts was developed on the basis of Buddhist meditation and contemplation. In addition, Japan developed a unique form of Buddhist clergy, which is highly secularised. The largest sect, Jodo-shinshu or True Pure Land, abandoned monastic celibacy altogether in the thirteenth century and created a priesthood, whose priests can marry, can take ordinary paid jobs and will pass responsibility for their temples from father to son. As part of modernisation and Westernisation, in the late nineteenth century the emperor decreed that monks could marry.

There are three features that make Japanese Buddhism unique:

1 **Buddhism and authority:** Buddhism was first accepted by the ruling classes and was then disseminated throughout Japan from the top down. Buddhist faith is connected with absolute devotion to a leader — for example, to the founder of a sect. Most sects developed a close connection with the central government of the time.

2 **Magic powers:** Buddhism is associated with magic powers, and this is one reason why it was accepted by the authorities. Buddhist monks were requested to use their powers to prevent disease, maintain peace, bring rainfall and good harvests, and so on. Buddhism was given the role of 'pacifying and protecting the state'.

3 **Buddhism and Shinto:** Buddhism did not attempt to replace Shinto but amalgamated with it. It recognised the Shinto gods as manifestations of the buddhas. From the fourteenth century onwards, the buddhas were often seen as manifestations of the kamis.

Between the seventh and tenth centuries several different schools of Chinese Buddhism became established in Japan. The most influential was the Tendai school, which incorporated a 12-year programme of study, meditation and monastic discipline with Tantric Buddhist practices. However, by the tenth century many of the monasteries had become decadent and a period of social, religious and political chaos ensued. Two far simpler forms of Buddhism

Corel

Figure 3.6
Influenced by
Taoism and by
Shinto, Buddhist
temples in Japan
were designed to
be in harmony
with nature

emerged from this time, which continue to be strong today: Zen and Pure Land, both of which are more adapted to the common people.

Between the twelfth and sixteenth centuries there were periods of military conflict between rival Buddhist monasteries. These battles were waged by hired troops or sometimes by armed monks. Jodo-shinshu developed fortified temples and was known to lead peasant uprisings. The sect founded by Nichiren (1222–83) set out to attack all other forms of Buddhism in Japan, denouncing them as misguided and doomed, and caused considerable chaos. Two powerful warlords put an end to military monasteries in the sixteenth century, and Zen, Pure Land and Nichiren were the main forms of Buddhism that survived.

In the nineteenth century, Japanese nationalism reacted against European colonialism and Christian missionaries (Christianity was banned in Japan in the seventeenth century) and declared Shinto to be the state religion with Buddhism as the secondary religion. Most Japanese people today combine both religions.

The Himalayan region

The last Asian region to which Buddhism spread was the Himalayan region. Buddhism was established in Tibet in the eighth century CE under the patronage of King Trisongdetsen. The monk Shantarakshita introduced Nikaya and Mahayana Buddhism from India, and the yogi Padmasambhava introduced Tantric Buddhism from central Asia. It seems that Shantarakshita and Padmasambhava also visited Bhutan and established Buddhism there in the same period.

Despite a brief period of persecution confined to central Tibet in the ninth century, Buddhism remained the dominant religion of the country until the Chinese Communist take-over in 1959. The Buddhist scriptures were translated from Sanskrit to Tibetan, thus preserving many Sanskrit texts which are now lost. Buddhism inspired the entire Tibetan culture for centuries, including art and architecture, music, scholarship and political and social organisation. Buddhism was introduced to Mongolia from Tibet after the conversion of Kublai Khan in around 1250. Tibetan Buddhism is also practised in some areas of the former Soviet Union.

Figure 3.7 Padmasambhava

Modern history

Over the past 500 years, Buddhism in some Asian countries, for example in Sri Lanka and Vietnam, has suffered from European colonialism and Christian missionary activity. More recently, Buddhism was persecuted by Communist regimes in China, Cambodia, North Korea, Tibet and Mongolia. By the end of the twentieth century, however, Buddhism had begun to make a come-back in many of these countries, although Christian missionaries remain active in Sri Lanka, South Korea and Mongolia in particular. Buddhism is still strong in many parts of Asia and especially in Japan, South Korea, Taiwan, Laos, Thailand, Burma (Myanmar), Sri Lanka and Bhutan.

Buddhism in the West

India and Europe in ancient and medieval times

Although Buddhism has become established in the West only recently, contacts and cultural exchanges occurred between Europe and India from the earliest times. In 334 BCE Alexander the Great marched into India but he only went as far as the Indus Valley and did not reach the Buddhist heartland. After that, there were constant diplomatic exchanges between Greece and India. The first documented exchange with Buddhism is that of Menander, one of the generals in the Greek army of Demetrius, who invaded India in 182 BCE. Menander became a Buddhist, and it is he who engages in dialogue with the monk Nagasena in the Theravada scripture, *The Questions of King Milinda*.

The Indian emperor Ashoka sent missions westwards to Egypt, Syria and Macedonia around 250 BCE, but we have no evidence that they arrived in these countries.

After the time of Christ commerce between Asia and the Roman empire was strong, and Buddhist ideas were known in Europe. A small number of Indians, including Buddhist monks, settled in Athens and Alexandria. There is considerable evidence of cross-cultural exchange: for example, many of the Jataka Tales (stories of the Buddha's previous lives) were retold as Aesop's Fables. Several early Christians such as Origen and Basilides believed in reincarnation and in freedom from suffering through knowledge, showing similarities with Buddhist ideas. However, with the fall of the Roman empire contacts with Asia were lost and so was knowledge of Indian religions.

During the Middle Ages the popes sent several missionaries to Asia, who came back with information on Buddhism and Hinduism. William of Rubruck and Marco Polo went to Mongolia in the thirteenth century. Their accounts were sympathetic, but Christians at this time were generally intolerant of all non-Christian religions.

European colonialism

European powers expanded into Asia between the sixteenth and nineteenth centuries. Portugal, for example, occupied parts of Sri Lanka as early as 1505. As a result, Europeans came to know about Indian religions once again. In the eighteenth century, Europe was particularly receptive to new ideas and in the nineteenth century this led to a new academic discipline: the comparative study of religion. What brought about this openness?

- The Enlightenment brought a belief in reason and science which weakened the authority of revealed Christianity.
- Some people began to believe in 'natural religion', a fundamental truth that is common to all humankind and that is cross-cultural.
- Scientific evolution theory seriously weakened the biblical account of creation.

By the end of the nineteenth century there was a vogue for Buddhism in Europe. People were attracted by its ideas of self-help instead of dependence on God or priests, its similarities with science in that it is based on experience, and its belief that the universe is ruled by laws, and that humans are not radically distinct from other species. Buddhism was more than science: it also had mysticism and, paradoxically, appeared to bring together faith and reason.

In the nineteenth and early twentieth centuries, therefore, interest in Buddhism was primarily intellectual and mainly touched the cultured elite.

Scholars began to translate Buddhist scriptures. The German philosopher Arthur Schopenhauer (1788–1860) was strongly influenced by Buddhist ideas; the editor of the London *Daily Telegraph*, Sir Edwin Arnold, wrote a life story of the Buddha in verse, published in 1879 as *The Light of Asia*; and Herman Hesse wrote *Siddhartha* in 1922.

Spiritualism was in vogue at this time, based on the belief that the spirits of the dead communicate with the living, especially through mediums. Madame Blavatsky and Colonel Olcott founded the Theosophical Society in New York in 1875, offering a mix of esoteric religions influenced more by Hinduism than by Buddhism. This movement spread to London and succeeded in introducing many key concepts to the British public, such as karma and rebirth. Then, in 1924, a British lawyer, Christmas Humphreys, founded a Buddhist Lodge in the Theosophical Society, which in 1943 became an independent charity called The Buddhist Society. This society played an important role in introducing Buddhism to the upper classes and now provides information on all Buddhist groups in the UK to the general public.

Many of the nineteenth- and early twentieth-century writers and scholars of Buddhism have since been criticised for inventing their own version of Buddhism rather than studying the subject with Buddhists themselves. They have been accused of both over-rationalising and over-romanticising Buddhism, and creating an exotic image of it in the minds of the general public. Certainly they related to Buddhism not as a religion that could be lived and practised, but as an intellectual system.

The role of migrant communities

At the same time as Westerners were travelling to Asia, Asian immigrants steadily settled in North America and Europe. Chinese immigration to the USA and Canada was strong by the 1860s and 1870s, and Japanese immigration began in 1868. These migrants took their Buddhist faith with them and built small temples in their communities. However, there was little or no spread of Buddhism from these Asian communities into society at large. There are a number of Chinese and Japanese Buddhist centres in North America, Brazil and Europe today, but most of their adherents are of Chinese or Japanese descent. Although Buddhists of Asian origin account for well over 50% of all Buddhists in the UK, they remain self-contained. Since 1975 Europe has welcomed refugees from several other Buddhist countries, such as Vietnam, Laos and Cambodia, but there is not much spread of Buddhism from these communities into the general population.

A change in this pattern came in the 1960s and 1970s with the arrival of Tibetan masters (*lamas*) and Japanese Zen masters (*roshis*) in Europe and the USA. This

was a time when young people belonging to the hippy counter-culture were interested in all things Eastern. They were attracted by the colourful rituals of Tibetan Buddhism and the simplicity and aesthetic of Zen. Many Westerners came to know about Buddhism when they went on the 'hippy trail', travelling overland to India and Nepal. In the UK, Theravada also attracted a significant number of followers during that period. The big difference between that period and the earlier interest in Buddhism was that Westerners wished to practise it themselves as a religion, not simply to learn about it from a distance, and both Tibetan and Japanese masters were willing to take Western students seriously.

The present day

From the 1960s to the present day numerous Buddhist centres have been established throughout Europe, North America, South America and Australia, and the majority of their members are Westerners. They come from all walks of life and include ordinary people, scholars, professionals and film stars. In the USA, UK and France alone there are now around 6 million Buddhists, and the numbers are growing steadily.

What is unique about the way Buddhism has expanded into the developed world is that so many different traditions and schools of Buddhism are being introduced almost simultaneously and coexist side by side. Whereas in Asia Theravada and Zen, for instance, were geographically circumscribed and virtually unknown to each other, in the West a new pan-Buddhist understanding is emerging together with a new appreciation of the value of each form of Buddhism in its own right. Nikaya Buddhism, Mahayana Buddhism and Tantric Buddhism are all now being practised in the West. The precise pattern of establishment was initially dependent upon colonial and diplomatic connections, so in the UK, for example, there are Theravadins from Sri Lanka and Thailand, whereas in France there are Mahayana followers from Vietnam and Cambodia. The forms of Buddhism that can be found relatively evenly throughout the Western world today are Tibetan Buddhism, Zen and Theravada.

Questions

1 Analyse the factors which facilitated the establishment of Buddhism in either China or Japan.
2 Evaluate the claim that Buddhism changed radically in the process of its expansion in China and Japan.
3 Do you agree that Ashoka's contribution to the development of Buddhism was on balance a positive one?
4 Give an account of how Buddhism has spread to the West.

Chapter 4

The Three Vehicles

To do no harm whatsoever;

To cultivate good to perfection;

To tame this mind of ours:

This is the teaching of the buddhas.

Dhammapada 183

What are the Three Vehicles?

During his lifetime the Buddha taught for some 45 years and spoke to many different types of people: old and young, men and women, kings, peasants and untouchables, educated and uneducated. It is therefore reasonable to expect that as a good communicator he found different ways of expressing the teaching according to the needs of his audiences. This is the logic behind the idea that the Buddha's teaching can be categorised into three different 'vehicles' or *yanas*, meaning three approaches or methods that serve as a means to help different kinds of people on the path to enlightenment.

These Three Vehicles are known as:

- **Hinayana** or **Nikaya Buddhism**, the Common Vehicle
- **Mahayana** or the Great Vehicle
- **Vajrayana** or the Diamond Vehicle, sometimes also known as Tantra or Tantrayana, that is, Tantric Buddhism

The term *Hinayana*, meaning 'lower vehicle', was coined by Mahayanists as a derogatory term, indicating that Mahayana was a greater approach than that of the 18 or so schools of Buddhism that preceded it during the first few hundred years after the Buddha. These days such bias is considered unacceptable, and the term Nikaya Buddhism is preferred, as it is neutral. Alternatively, it can be called the Common Vehicle in English, since its teachings form the basis of the teachings of all vehicles. The scriptures of this vehicle are organised into collections or *Nikayas*.

Nikaya Buddhism has been flourishing ever since the Buddha died, so it is undoubtedly the oldest public tradition of Buddhism. Mahayana Buddhism

appears to have gradually emerged in India somewhat later, possibly as early as the second century BCE or between the first century BCE and the first century CE. Vajrayana emerged in India around the fifth century CE. So, broadly speaking, there is a chronological order for the historical emergence of these vehicles.

Theravada, the only surviving school of Nikaya Buddhism, flourishes in south and southeast Asia. Theravadins do not accept the model of the Three Vehicles since they do not accept that the teachings of Mahayana and Vajrayana were given by the historical Buddha. The model of the Three Vehicles is therefore a Mahayana and Vajrayana model.

The Mahayana and Vajrayana both generated several different schools or traditions of Buddhism, so they are umbrella terms which include the various schools relating to each. Mahayana Buddhism is present in southeast Asia and the far east today, while Vajrayana Buddhism is present in Tibet, Mongolia, the Himalayan region and Japan. There are now followers of all Three Vehicles in the West.

One way of characterising the Three Vehicles is to relate each one to a line of the summary that the Buddha made of his own teaching in the *Dhammapada* (quoted at the start of this chapter).

1 **To do no harm whatsoever** is the emphasis of Nikaya Buddhism: the principles of non-harming and non-violence (*ahimsa*), the ethics of refraining from harmful actions, and the practice of overcoming negative emotions through meditation, mindfulness and loving kindness.

2 **To cultivate good to perfection** is the emphasis of Mahayana Buddhism: perfecting virtuous actions so that they become totally selfless (the *paramitas*), developing the positive qualities of our buddha nature, and devoting our lives to the benefit of others.

3 **To tame this mind of ours** is the strength of Vajrayana Buddhism: working with the mind and its perception of the world, and transforming it from confusion to enlightenment through meditation and visualisation.

It is important to note that all three aspects of the Buddha's summary are present in every vehicle, so the difference between them is only one of emphasis.

In examining the features of these three approaches we need to identify their similarities and differences. We will focus particularly on Theravada, representing Nikaya Buddhism, and the core doctrines of Mahayana, concentrating on the following themes:

- buddhology, or the study of who the Buddha was
- the goal of the Buddhist path
- the main features of the Buddhist path
- other core principles

A summary of these topics will be followed by a detailed explanation.

Theravada and Mahayana: a summary

Buddhology

Theravadins recognise only the historical person of the Buddha and the teachings believed to have been given by him during his lifetime. Mahayanists believe that the Buddha can appear and teach great masters in visions and dreams, and they accept that the Buddha can communicate in Sambhogakaya form — the Sambhogakaya (literally 'body of joy') is a dimension of energy and light that is visible in special meditative states but intangible, like a rainbow. Theravada does not accept the existence of the Sambhogakaya.

The goal of the Buddhist path

In Theravada and all schools of the Common Vehicle the goal of the Buddhist path is *nibbana* (nirvana): the extinction of the Three Poisons of ignorance, craving and aggression, freedom from karma and rebirth, and liberation from suffering. *Nibbana* brings liberation from samsara, the cycle of conditioned existence. It is considered that *nibbana* has no beginning and no end, and is a state that is outside of time. When one attains *nibbana* one is called an *arhat*, someone who has conquered the mental poisons.

In Mahayana the goal of the Buddhist path is complete buddhahood. *Nibbana* is acknowledged to be freedom from samsara but is viewed as only a stepping stone on the way to complete enlightenment. Mahayana claims that the difference between *nibbana* and buddhahood is that there are some subtle mental veils remaining in *nibbana* that perpetuate a subtle level of ignorance; these are removed by means of the Mahayana path, enabling the practitioner to attain the omniscience of full enlightenment. When one attains the goal of the Mahayana path one becomes a buddha, an enlightened one. Anyone following the Mahayana path is called a *bodhisattva*.

Main features of the Buddhist path

In Theravada, the path is called the Noble Eightfold Path and is taught as the fourth of the Four Noble Truths. Its eight elements are as follows:

1 right view
2 right attitude
3 right speech
4 right action
5 right livelihood
6 right effort
7 right mindfulness
8 right concentration

These eight elements can be grouped into the Three Higher Trainings (see Figure 4.1):

● moral discipline (3, 4, 5)

- meditation (6, 7, 8)
- wisdom (1, 2)

All Buddhists follow the Eightfold Path, whether they are monastics or lay people, although different guidelines apply to each group.

The Eightfold Path

Moral discipline	**Meditation**	**Wisdom**
Right speech	Right effort	Right view
Right action	Right mindfulness	Right attitude
Right livelihood	Right concentration	

Figure 4.1 The Eightfold Path

The Mahayana path is called the *Bodhisattva* Path. It is divided into ten stages or *bhumis* (literally 'grounds'), on each of which specific qualities are perfected. These are called the ten *paramitas* or 'perfections':

1 generosity
2 moral discipline
3 patience
4 diligence
5 concentration or meditation
6 wisdom (*prajña*)
7 skilful means
8 strength/power
9 aspiration
10 primordial wisdom (*jñana*)

After the tenth stage one attains buddhahood. A *bodhisattva* is someone who follows the path in order to attain enlightenment both for themselves and for all other beings. The *bodhisattva* reaches his or her goal by arousing *bodhichitta*, the awakened mind, and taking the vows of a *bodhisattva*.

Other core principles

Some of the other core principles of Mahayana, which are not found in Theravada, are as follows:

- The belief that every single being has the 'buddha nature' (*tathagatagarbha*) or potential for enlightenment within, so that enlightenment is not a matter of attaining a distant and inaccessible state but rather of discovering, uncovering, revealing and expressing who we actually are.
- The ethical principle of skilful means (*upaya*) — see Chapter 12.
- The distinction between conventional truth and ultimate truth, known as the Two Truths: conventional truth refers to what we accept as true in the everyday world, while ultimate truth refers to truths that are beyond words and that we understand only through meditation and study. Conventional truth is how things appear; ultimate truth is how they really are.

Theravada and Mahayana in detail

Buddhology

The key to understanding how the Buddha is seen, according to the Three Vehicles, is the Buddhist doctrine of the Three Bodies of the Buddha, or Trikaya doctrine. The word 'body' as a translation of *kaya* does not mean a physical body; it does not mean that the Buddha had three separate 'bodies' in this sense. Rather, it has the collective meaning the word sometimes has in English in expressions such as 'a body of literature' or 'a body of knowledge', that is, a collection of qualities and characteristics. The three *kayas* refer to three aspects of buddhahood, or three dimensions of the enlightened mind. These three aspects are:

- **Dharmakaya:** the body of truth
- **Sambhogakaya:** the body of enjoyment
- **Nirmanakaya:** the body of manifestation.

The **Dharmakaya** refers to the enlightened mind itself, the complete realisation of the truth of all things. It is purified consciousness, totally free from all defilements, and beyond even the distinction between pure and impure. In fact, the Dharmakaya is beyond words and cannot be described in ordinary language.

The **Sambhogakaya** refers to the dimension of energy and light in which enlightened beings can choose to dwell. In their Sambhogakaya form, buddhas and advanced *bodhisattvas* are intangible but visible, like a rainbow. All the pure realms of the buddhas, including the Sukhavati Pure Land of Buddha Amitabha, are Sambhogakaya realms, and the beings that dwell there are in the Sambhogakaya dimension. This is a form of existence that allows beings at advanced meditative levels to communicate with the buddhas; indeed, all religious experiences involving visions are understood as meditative perceptions of Sambhogakaya beings.

Buddhas and *bodhisattvas* may choose to remain in Sambhogakaya form out of compassion, in order to remain accessible to suffering beings. This explains why Mahayana Buddhists are able to pray to them for support and guidance, and why the path of devotion is seen as such a powerful one. The Vajrayana practice of visualisation is a method that refines our perception so that we are able to see this dimension of reality for ourselves.

Figure 4.2 The three tiers of monastery roofs symbolise the three *kayas*

The **Nirmanakaya** refers to the physical manifestation of an enlightened being, and in the case of Shakyamuni it refers to the historical Buddha, whose life story we learn. From the Mahayana perspective, the Buddha was already enlightened before he was born as Siddhartha, and his decision to take physical form was a voluntary one. Buddhas have the power to manifest in any physical form they wish, in any part of the universe and even in several universes at once. This means that buddhas manifest as animals to guide animals, as human beings to guide humans and so on, and they may also manifest as the religious teachers of other religions.

The three *kayas* are related to each other in that the Dharmakaya gives rise to the Sambhogakaya, and the Sambhogakaya gives rise to the Nirmanakaya. The Dharmakaya is the ultimate truth, and both Sambhogakaya and Nirmanakaya exist in relation to it. One image used to evoke the Dharmakaya is that of a clear and cloudless sky, or infinite space. An image for the Sambhogakaya is of the brilliant sun in a cloudless sky, and an image used for the Nirmanakaya is that of the warmth of the sun's rays, which touch everyone everywhere.

The *kayas* not only describe aspects of enlightenment; they are cosmic principles that describe the way mind transforms into light and energy, and how light and energy transform into matter. This Buddhist principle can be used to explain how the universe arises. Some modern religious leaders have drawn parallels between the Trikaya doctrine and that of the Christian Trinity, with God the Father being similar to the Dharmakaya, the Holy Spirit to the Sambhogakaya, and God the Son to the Nirmanakaya.

Figure 4.3 Green Tara. Tara embodies the feminine aspect of compassion and exemplifies a deity in Sambhogakaya form

The goal of the Buddhist path

The Lotus Sutra is a Mahayana scripture which teaches the superiority of the Mahayana goal in relation to that of Nikaya Buddhism, and which also claims that the Buddha actually taught 'only one single vehicle' (*ekayana*), not two or three, in the sense that all vehicles of Buddhism ultimately lead to the same goal, which is buddhahood. According to this view, the teachings of Nikaya Buddhism are preliminary instructions for those with little spiritual maturity, and their goal

of nirvana (*nibbana*), although a very worthy one, is only a temporary resting place on the long road to buddhahood.

This view is based on the idea that the Buddha adapted his teachings to the needs of his audiences, so he chose to offer nirvana as a goal for those with intense suffering, whose deepest wish was to find a way to be free from suffering. The prospect of a mental state in which suffering and its causes are totally eliminated is effective in motivating such people to follow a spiritual path. However, for those whose suffering is less intense, whose karma is somewhat purified and who have already lived many virtuous lives, there is a greater goal which embraces not only the elimination of suffering for oneself, but the ability to lead others to enlightenment. The *bodhisattva* following the Mahayana path is motivated by *bodhichitta*, the genuine and heartfelt aspiration to become a buddha for the sake of others.

The principle of the *ekayana* is illustrated by the parable of the phantom city in the Lotus Sutra. A group of people are travelling along a road through a wild and deserted region to reach a place with many rare treasures. The road is long and difficult and they became disheartened, frightened and exhausted. They feel like turning round and going back, but their compassionate leader, who knows the road well, encourages them to carry on and describes a city which is not far ahead, an oasis of calm and rest. Everyone is overjoyed and they reach the city. Once they are well rested, the leader explains that the place they are in is only a phantom city that he created, and they need to go a little further to find the treasures, which they accept they must do. In the same way, nirvana is a resting place that inspires those who are weary of suffering to begin on the spiritual journey to buddhahood.

The difference between nirvana and complete buddhahood is a subtle one. Nirvana is freedom from samsara and the cycle of rebirth. This attainment is based on the realisation of *anatta*, the principle that there is no essence or inherent entity that constitutes identity; there is nothing that I can truly call 'me', there is no 'self' there. Mahayana extends this realisation of *anatta* and applies it not only to persons but to all phenomena. This gives rise to the realisation of *shunyata*, 'emptiness', the lack of inherent existence in all things, without any exception. Realising *shunyata* as the nature of all things brings the omniscience of buddhahood.

The main features of the Buddhist path

1 The Eightfold Path

In the Common Vehicle, the path is described as the Eightfold Path and contains eight different elements, depicted in the eight-spoked wheel which symbolises the Buddhist religion (see Figure 4.4). These elements are not sequential; all work together and reinforce each other.

- **Right view** refers specifically to understanding the Four Noble Truths, and intuitively grasping their meaning. In other words, right view is a correct understanding of how things actually are, the highest wisdom that sees ultimate reality. At a preliminary level, right view is explained as accepting the importance of generosity and moral actions, and accepting rebirth.
- **Right attitude** includes thoughts such as selfless renunciation, detachment, love and compassion for others, non-violence and equal-mindedness.
- **Right speech** is refraining from lying, backbiting, idle gossip and harsh words.
- **Right action** refers to honest actions that do not harm others.
- **Right livelihood** is abstaining from any work that involves harming others.
- **Right effort** is the energetic will, enthusiasm and diligence to prevent unwholesome states of mind and the actions that result, and to cultivate wholesome states of mind and virtuous actions.
- **Right mindfulness** is continual awareness of the activities of one's body, what one says, and the thoughts and feelings in the mind.
- **Right concentration** is the mental concentration developed especially by *shamatha* meditation and is an antidote to distraction.

Robert Beer

Figure 4.4 The eight-spoked wheel

Moral discipline is motivated by right view and made possible by effort, mindfulness and concentration. Similarly, meditation is aided by discipline because, if one leads an unruly or unvirtuous life, one will not be able to meditate. Examples of this are trying to meditate with a hangover, or failing to find peace of mind because one feels guilty about what one has done. In this way, all aspects of the Eightfold Path support each other and strengthen each other in a constant 'cycle of happiness'.

The ethical virtue of giving or generosity (dana) is emphasised at every stage of the Theravada Path and for lay people it is the chief way of accumulating merit.

2 The *Bodhisattva* Path

The path followed by the *bodhisattva* in Mahayana is similar to the Eightfold Path in that it, too, includes the Three Higher Trainings of moral discipline, meditation and wisdom. The first four *paramitas* or perfections fall under

discipline (generosity, discipline, patience and diligence); the fifth is meditation; and the last five relate to wisdom (wisdom, skilful means, power, aspiration and primordial wisdom). The main difference is the motivation of *bodhichitta*, and the understanding that even virtuous actions are ultimately 'empty' of inherent existence.

Generating the motivation of *bodhichitta* is in itself a tremendous achievement, which requires great merit and wisdom. Mahayana practitioners usually take a formal '*bodhisattva* vow' to mark their conscious commitment to the *Bodhisattva* Path. The vow is taken in the presence of a Mahayana master or simply in the visualised presence of the buddhas and *bodhisattvas*. In contrast to monastic vows, which are taken only for the duration of the present life, the *bodhisattva* vow is taken with the aspiration that one will follow it throughout present and future lives and until the point of reaching enlightenment. The vision of this path is therefore vast. The great eighth-century Indian poet-scholar Shantideva expresses the aspiration of a *bodhisattva* in these words:

> For as long as space exists
> And sentient beings endure,
> May I too remain
> To dispel the misery of the world.
> > *Bodhicharyavatara* 10.55

The *Bodhisattva* Path begins with a tremendous experience of joy arising from the glimpse one has of the ultimate truth. On this basis one gradually perfects each of the transcendental actions of the path, one by one, with the wisdom of *shunyata*, emptiness, pervading all the *paramitas* at least to some degree. This is why perfected actions are not self-conscious and have no ulterior motive. In the case of generosity, for example, the *bodhisattva* realises that neither the gift, nor the giver, nor the beneficiary, actually exist; all are empty of true existence.

Once the *bodhisattva* has accomplished the sixth *paramita* of wisdom, he or she is free of rebirth caused by karma, and is able to take rebirth deliberately in different realms to help suffering beings. All actions of body, speech and mind are so many skilful means to help others. At the eighth stage of the path, the ability to 'transfer merit' is fully mastered, so that if anyone prays to him or her the *bodhisattva* is able to transfer a store of tremendous merit — the result of good actions — to uplift that person and transform his or her situation. At the ninth stage, the *bodhisattva* has the power to teach all beings according to their needs, and at the tenth stage he or she reaches the Sambhogakaya level and dwells in the Tushita heaven, from where fully enlightened buddhas may manifest and take birth as human beings. Buddhahood is attained at the eleventh stage.

Table 4.1 The *Bodhisattva* Path

The *bhumis* or stages	The *paramitas* or qualities perfected
1 Complete joy	Generosity
2 Without stain	Discipline
3 Giving out light	Patience
4 Dazzling with light/radiant	Diligence
5 Difficult to overcome	Concentration
6 Advancing/knowing clearly	Wisdom (*prajña*)
7 Gone far	Skilful means
8 Immovable	Strength/power
9 Perfect intelligence	Aspiration
10 Cloud of Dharma	Primordial wisdom (*jñana*)
11 Buddhahood	

We have said that Mahayana is an umbrella term denoting a number of different schools; some of these began in India while others developed elsewhere, in China, Japan and Tibet in particular. There were two main Mahayana schools of philosophy in India which have had a far-reaching impact: the Madhyamaka school and the Chittamatra school.

Madhyamaka philosophy was founded by the Indian scholar Nagarjuna in around the first century CE. Madhyamaka literally means 'the middle way', and refers to a middle way between the extreme views of believing that things really exist and believing that nothing exists at all. Philosophically, these views are termed eternalism and nihilism. Nagarjuna argued that things do not exist

Figure 4.5 Nagarjuna

Figure 4.6 Asanga

Figure 4.7 Vasubandhu

Origins
- Origins are unclear
- Separate Buddhist Council?
- Secret transmission in India?
- Mystical revelation of new scriptures?
- Rise of the laity?
- Emerges in India between second century BCE and first century CE

Geographical spread
- India until twelfth century
- Pakistan, Afghanistan
- China, Korea, Japan
- Indonesia
- Tibet, Mongolia, Bhutan
- Europe, North and South America, Australia in twentieth century

Characteristics
- The goal is full buddhahood, not merely nirvana
- Motivation to follow path is for oneself and others
- Enlightenment is omniscience and *bodhichitta*
- Those on the Mahayana path are *bodhisattvas*
- The path has ten stages (*bhumis*)
- Bodhisattvas develop six or ten *paramitas*
- Enlightenment is possible for monastics and laity, men and women
- *Trikaya* doctrine of the Buddha

Mahayana Buddhism

Madhyamaka
- Founder: Nagarjuna, first century CE
- Prajñaparamita Sutras (Heart Sutra)
- Two Truths: (a) Conventional: things exist as accepted conventionally; (b) Ultimate: emptiness (*shunyata*) is not non-existence: it means things have no essence, are not independent or unchanging
- Neither wholes nor parts exist ultimately

Ch'an or Zen
- Traced to Buddha, who holds up a flower; Kasyapa understands meaning without words
- Perhaps secret transmission in India
- Founder in China: Bodhidharma (fifth to sixth centuries CE)
- In Japan, two schools develop:
  Rinzai (founder Eisai, 1141–1215), sudden enlightenment (*satori*), use of *koans*, dramatic methods, martial arts
  Soto (founder Dogen, 1200–53) zazen (meditation), simple life, discipline, gradual path
- Little study (mainly Lankavatara Sutra)

Main schools
India:
Madhyamaka, Chittamatra
China, Korea, Japan:
Zen, Pure Land

Chittamatra
- Founders: Asanga and Vasubandhu, fourth century CE
- Lankavatara Sutra, Samdhinirmocana Sutra
- Criticise Madhyamaka, saying their interpretation of emptiness is nothingness
- Three natures: *parikalpita* (thought-constructed), *paratantra* (what we experience), *parinispanna* (reality as it is).
- Eight aspects of consciousness: eighth is *alaya*, which continues after death and stores karmic seeds
- *Tathagatagarbha*: buddha nature or potential in everyone

Pure Land
- Traced back to Indian scripture; story of monk Dharmakara, who upon his enlightenment becomes Amida Buddha (Buddha Amitabha) and vows to take his devotees to his heaven or Pure Land, *Sukhavati*
- Begins in China in fifth century, Japan in tenth century
- Two schools in Japan: Pure Land (Honen) and True Pure Land or Shin Buddhism (Shinran)
- Main practice: *nembutsu* and devotion to Amida
- Emphasises other-power for this degenerate age

Figure 4.8 Mahayana Buddhism

inherently, but this does not imply that they do not exist in any way; they do appear to us, and Buddhists do not deny the obvious fact of empirical experience, so they acknowledge that things exist on a conventional level. Yet, on an ultimate level, under analysis, their nature is seen to be 'empty' of true existence; things are entirely interdependent; nothing exists independently and permanently, not even the minutest particles from which objects are made. The ultimate truth of Madhyamaka is therefore emptiness (*shunyata*) or interdependence (*pratityasamutpada*), and the main framework of analysis is called the Two Truths: conventional and ultimate, addressing respectively how things appear and how they are.

Chittamatra literally means 'mind only' and was founded in the fourth century CE by the brothers Asanga and Vasubandhu. This school considers that everything we perceive is a projection of the mind, and the way we see the world is totally dependent upon the characteristics of our human senses, and does not give us an objective view of how reality is 'out there'. For example, animals of different species each perceive the world differently. I see you as a human with a head, two arms and two legs, but a spider might perceive you as a vast undulating landscape that it could crawl around. Likewise, for humans water is something to drink, but for fish it is a home to live in. It would be arrogant on our part to imagine that the way human beings perceive the world must be the only objectively true way. The world of our experience is therefore a mental construct, hence the name of the school. Only through wisdom can we perceive how things truly are, the ultimate truth being the realisation that subject and object are not two separate entities but one in nature.

Chittamatra developed the theory of buddha nature or *tathagatagarbha*, the principle that all sentient beings in samsara, from the smallest insect to human beings, have the potential to become fully enlightened if they can apply themselves to the spiritual path. Like gold buried in the earth, this potential is hidden from view by all our defilements but, once we have removed these, it naturally shines. Most importantly, this buddha nature can never be spoiled by our mental poisons or harmful actions, which are only like dust collecting on a mirror. The mirror itself remains intact and clear; the dust is only superficial and when wiped away reveals the mirror to be what it has always been.

Figure 4.8 is a mindmap which presents the main features of Mahayana, including an outline of four Mahayana schools. Some points are explained in later chapters.

The Vajrayana

The view and methods of Vajrayana are based on Mahayana, both on the principles of Madhyamaka and those of Chittamatra. The aspiration of *bodhichitta* is the same, and the goal that is being sought is also the same.

The difference between them lies in the methods used, which include visualisation and mantra recitation and, most importantly, devotion. The core practice of Vajrayana is known as 'guru yoga', merging one's mind with that of the spiritual master or *guru* in Sanskrit, until there is no difference between student and teacher. Devotion is considered fundamental to this process, and a skilful way of helping the student give up any sense of 'I' or ego.

Vajrayana requires that the practitioner has already reached a degree of spiritual maturity, so that he or she has strong trust in the Dharma and in the

teacher as well as a mind that is clear and focused enough to practise visualisation. It is said that the Vajrayana Path is more powerful and more effective than those of the two previous vehicles and that it will enable the practitioner to reach enlightenment much faster. It is believed that the Vajrayana Path is particularly appropriate in this morally degenerate age, when only the most powerful of methods are able to cut through the thick clouds of ignorance engulfing our minds. Its methods are seen to enable us to access and communicate with the Sambhogakaya dimension of reality.

Questions

1 Critically examine the stages and perfections of the *Bodhisattva* Path.
2 In what sense do the Theravada and Mahayana understandings of enlightenment differ?
3 'There is only one vehicle'. Examine this quotation from the Lotus Sutra and assess its significance for Mahayana teaching on enlightenment
4 Compare and contrast the *arhat* and the *bodhisattva* as Buddhist ideals.
5 'Mahayana Buddhism is so different from Theravada Buddhism that it is hardly the same religion.' Examine the main differences between Theravada and Mahayana Buddhism. To what extent do you agree with this statement?
6 Which teachings do Theravada Buddhism and Mahayana Buddhism have in common?

Chapter 5

The Buddhist scriptures

Composition of the Buddhist scriptures

As soon as we look at its scriptures we realise how different Buddhism is from all other world religions. Buddhists have a totally different way of understanding the nature, value and role of scripture. It is one of the few world religions to reject the theistic idea of 'revealed scripture', because it does not believe in God. The scriptures contain the words of the Buddha, and these words are considered authoritative only because he gained the supreme wisdom and compassion of enlightenment. So, for a Buddhist, the scriptures can only be called 'revealed' texts insofar as the Buddha 'revealed' to us truths that we were previously unaware of, due to our confusion and ignorance. The role of a buddha is to explain the truth to the unenlightened.

In spite of this rejection of the idea that scriptures contain a truth revealed by God, Buddhism has the largest number of scriptures of all religions. Not only is the collection of scriptures enormous in terms of the number of titles it contains, but many of them are extremely long. If the Chinese Buddhist scriptures were translated, they would fill over half a million pages of print. So, when we speak of scripture in Buddhism, we are not talking about a single sacred book, like the Torah, the Bible or the Qur'an, but about a vast body of texts.

Buddhism is unique in that it has not one but several separate collections of scriptures, each of which is considered authoritative. Such a collection of scriptures is called a **canon**. This situation arises from the way Buddhism developed in India without any centralised authority and therefore without any institution which could claim that some scriptures were 'orthodox' while others were heretical. These various collections exist side by side. The Buddhist canon today is in four main languages: Pali, Sanskrit, Chinese and Tibetan. Most of

the Pali Canon has now been translated into English, but the majority of the Sanskrit, Chinese and Tibetan texts have not yet been translated into Western languages.

How Buddhists relate to their scriptures

Given their sheer volume, it may not be surprising that ordinary Buddhists would never be expected to read and study all these books. They rely on monks to tell them the essence of the main scriptures in an accessible way. Even among the monks, only the most scholarly study the scriptures in a comprehensive way.

But there are some stories and sayings from the scriptures that every Buddhist would know. For example, stories of the life of the Buddha found in the Pali Canon are part of Buddhist culture. The advice on meditation is still followed today. And some passages from the scriptures are recited either every day or on festival days as part of the morning and evening chanting. In other words, the most well-known parts of the scriptures are a living part of the Buddhist faith.

Copies of the scriptures are treated with great respect. In ancient times, when each text was copied by hand, the scriptures would be rare and hard to find. Pilgrims would travel many thousands of miles to find a text they wished to study. This is one reason for the respect shown to the scriptures. Indeed, it is claimed that the Chinese invented printing in the eighth century CE in order to reproduce Buddhist scriptures more easily. As a mark of this respect, religious texts are placed high up off the floor and sometimes on a Buddhist shrine. Scriptures are occasionally placed inside stupas. The reason for this respect is that the scriptures represent not only the Dharma, the Buddha's teachings, but also, more universally, wisdom and truth.

Questions about authority of the scriptures for Buddhists are addressed more fully in Chapter 17. It is important to note here that the approach to scripture in Buddhism encourages a critical reading of texts rather than an uncritical acceptance of the truths they contain. In other words, Buddhists are not expected to believe in truths simply because they were spoken by the Buddha. The Buddha encouraged his disciples to reflect on his words in order to come to their own personal conviction that they are true. According to the Pali scriptures, this is the advice he gave his monks:

> O monks and wise men,
> Just as a goldsmith would test his gold
> By burning, cutting and rubbing it,
> So must you examine my words and accept them
> But not merely out of reverence for me.
> *Kalama Sutta*

In Buddhism, the truth of the scriptures needs to be tested, first, against one's experience of life; second, against logical reasoning; and, third, against meditation experience. If any argument fails this process — that is, if it is contradicted by experience and/or by logic — then it will not be accepted as true.

The implications stemming from the idea that Buddhist scriptures are not divinely revealed are very far-reaching. One of the most important consequences is that they are held to be humanly accessible, that is, it is possible for human beings to understand them. The scriptures do not contain unfathomable mysteries. If one applies the correct process of studying, reflecting and meditating on the scriptural texts, it is possible, in time, to come to the same realisation of the truths they contain as the Buddha did himself.

The Pali Canon

The Pali Canon contains the scriptures followed by the Theravada tradition. Pali was a language spoken in the Buddha's time, which was probably similar to the language he would have known himself, Old Magadhi. Buddhists believe that the Buddha spoke many different local dialects and not just one language, and Theravadins believe that the Buddha spoke Pali; their scriptures are therefore said to contain the original words of the Buddha.

Modern scholars accept that the Pali Canon contains some of the oldest texts of all the Buddhist scriptures and is probably close to the teachings originally recited in the First Buddhist Council. Having been transmitted orally, by communal chanting, for generations, the canon was first written down in Sri Lanka in the first century BCE.

The Pali Canon is divided into three sections, or 'baskets', known as the *Tipitaka* (Pali) or *Tripitaka* (Sanskrit). They are called 'baskets' because the early scriptures were written on palm leaves which were stored in baskets; baskets formed their ancient filing system. The three sections are Vinaya, Suttas and Abhidhamma.

- The **Vinaya** consists of the code of discipline for monks and nuns. The Theravada Vinaya contains a total of 227 rules for monks. But it is far more than a list of rules. The Vinaya contains stories about the situations that prompted the Buddha to make each rule. For example, the rules for helping the sick were made after the community neglected to care for a sick monk. Likewise, the monastic rule of celibacy was formalised as Buddha's response to an occasion when a particular monk visited his ex-wife because she wanted a son. The purpose of the Vinaya is to maintain harmony within the community. It also acts as an aid to a disciplined and mindful lifestyle, free from the distractions of lay life, where energies can be focused on spiritual

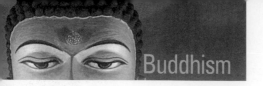

development. Monastics learn the Vinaya by heart and recite it together as a group once a fortnight.

- The **suttas** (Sanskrit **sutras**) are the 'discourses' of the Buddha, that is, the talks and teachings he gave over 45 years. Each sutta states the village or town in which the teaching was given and the names of the individuals involved, but there is no dating. The suttas contain all the central teachings of Buddhism and they run into the hundreds. They make up the five nikayas or collections of the Pali Canon.
- The **Abhidhamma** (Sanskrit **Abhidharma**) texts contain philosophical analysis of the Buddha's teaching. The underlying doctrinal principles presented in the suttas are organised into a systematic framework. These texts address topics such as human psychology and the relationship between mind and matter. Some Buddhists believe that the Buddha himself explained this analysis, while others assert the Abhidhamma was composed by later Buddhist scholars. For the former the Abhidhamma is authoritative, but for the latter it may not be.

Two Theravada scriptures are particularly popular: the *Dhammapada*, which contains a series of brief verses summarising the main principles of the Buddha's teaching, as found in more detail in the suttas; and *The Questions of King Milinda*, a dialogue between the Buddhist monk Nagasena and the Greek King Menander, setting out key Buddhist arguments on a number of topics (this dialogue took place in the second century BCE, when Greek armies had crossed central Asia and reached India). Both are readily available in English translation.

The Mahayana scriptures

The scriptural corpus

Modern scholars believe that the Mahayana scriptures were composed between the first century BCE and the fifth century CE in India, since there is no evidence to support the idea that they derived from an oral tradition that had continued from the time of the Buddha. It would seem that, unlike the Pali Canon, these scriptures were first written, not oral. However, recent discoveries of Mahayana scriptures in Afghanistan dated to the second century CE may require us to revise this account of the early history of Mahayana Buddhism (see Chapter 3). The earliest Mahayana manuscripts we have might be just as ancient as the earliest existing Theravada manuscripts.

The origin of the Mahayana scriptures is a much debated topic and until these recent finds there were a number of differing views, even among Buddhists themselves.

- Some claim that because they emerged so many centuries after the Buddha, with no evidence of their existence beforehand, the Mahayana scriptures can only have been written by later Buddhist scholars, giving their interpretation of the Buddha's teachings. They do not represent the teaching of the Buddha himself. This view is held by most Theravadins.

- Some followers of Mahayana claim that there was another Buddhist Council held in parallel to the First Buddhist Council, at which the Mahayana teachings were recited. These teachings were then transmitted orally for generations until they were written down. It is argued that the lack of evidence for this claim is due to the secrecy with which Mahayana was guarded, because it was considered an advanced teaching and was not communicated widely and publicly.

- Others explain that, although the historical Buddha did teach Mahayana during his lifetime, it was too advanced for people; they did not fully understand or appreciate it. So teachings such as the Prajñaparamita Sutras were magically hidden and given to mythical sea serpents called *nagas* for safekeeping until human beings were ready for them. (*Nagas* are sometimes depicted rather like mermaids.) Several centuries after the Buddha, the Mahayana teachings were mystically rediscovered by Buddhist masters such as Nagarjuna (first century CE) and written down by them during states of religious inspiration.

Theravadins do not consider the Mahayana scriptures to be authoritative, but Mahayana followers do. They consider that their scriptures represent the word of the Buddha, albeit the word heard by Buddhist masters in special states of meditation.

Do the Mahayana scriptures fall into the same three sections as the Pali Canon? Not exactly.

- There is no Mahayana Vinaya. Mahayana monks and nuns follow one or other of the Vinaya codes of discipline belonging to the Nikaya traditions.

- Most of the Mahayana scriptures are sutras. Some of these sutras present the words of a disciple of the Buddha — not the Buddha himself — who speaks in the Buddha's presence and is inspired by him. At the end of the disciple's discourse the Buddha confirms that what he said was correct and true. Mahayana extends the authority of the Buddha beyond that of the historical Buddha to include any Buddhist with enlightened insight.

- Some Mahayana works contain Abhidharma analysis. For example, some texts explain the psychological process of meditation, or the different qualities and powers of enlightenment. However, many of these texts are believed to be inspired not by Buddha Shakyamuni but by Buddha Maitreya, the next buddha who is due to come down to the human world and teach the Dharma in the future.

While the Theravada scriptures were written in Pali, the majority of the Mahayana scriptures were originally written in Sanskrit. Many of these Sanskrit texts are now lost, so these scriptures survive mainly in translation. Original Sanskrit texts from India were translated into Chinese and Tibetan, and subsequently the Chinese Canon was translated into Japanese and the Tibetan Canon into Mongolian. The Chinese and Tibetan Canons include texts of Nikaya Buddhism as well as the Mahayana corpus.

A number of Mahayana sutras became especially popular or important in Asia.

- The **Prajñaparamita Sutras**, or Discourses on the Perfection of Wisdom, set out the Mahayana understanding of *shunyata* or 'emptiness', the idea that nothing in the universe exists independently, permanently and inherently. The shortest of this series is called the **Heart Sutra** and is often recited today in Japanese and Tibetan monasteries. These sutras are the foundation of the Madhyamaka school.

- The **Lankavatara Sutra** sets out the theory of buddha nature or *tathagata-garbha*, the idea that we all have a seed of enlightenment within us which simply needs nurturing and developing for us to become buddhas ourselves. This sutra is important in the Chittamatra school and in Ch'an/Zen.

- The **Lotus Sutra** is seen by some schools of Buddhism in the far east as the expression of the Buddha's definitive teaching. It is therefore regarded as the most important sutra of all, and some schools, such as Nichiren in Japan, have developed a ritual cult around it. The Lotus Sutra emphasises the idea that Mahayana is superior to Nikaya Buddhism; it illustrates the *bodhisattva* ideal and the idea of skilful means.

How do Mahayana followers relate to their scriptures?

Mahayana schools vary significantly in the importance they give to the Buddhist scriptures.

- Some schools refer to one or more sutras as the foundational texts of their philosophy or religious practice. This applies to the Prajñaparamita Sutras for Madhyamaka and the Lankavatara Sutra for Chittamatra. But, at the same time, these schools continue to read and respect all the other scriptures too.

- Some schools focus entirely on one scripture, which they consider supreme, and do not place value on the study of other scriptures. This applies to the Lotus Sutra for Nichiren Buddhism in Japan, and the Sukhavati Sutras for Amida Buddhism (Pure Land).

- Other Mahayana schools discourage the study of all scriptures on the basis that meditation practice is more effective for attaining enlightenment than

intellectual study. This is the case for Ch'an (Zen) Buddhism. In practice, however, Zen teachers do study some scriptures, especially the Lankavatara Sutra, the Diamond Sutra and the Heart Sutra.

The Tantric scriptures

Vajrayana Buddhism follows all the Mahayana scriptures outlined above and in addition has its own distinctive collection of scriptures called **tantras**. The earlier tantric texts appeared in India and other regions of Asia around the sixth century CE. They describe various rituals and visualisation practices, and present tantric teachings on the nature of the mind and on the various world systems.

The tantras are written in cryptic language, which is extremely difficult for the uninitiated to understand. Vajrayana generally lays particular emphasis on the importance of following a master or guru, and in the case of scriptural study this is vital because without individual tuition the student would be unable to understand the tantras. The tantras are found in both the Chinese and Tibetan canons, as well as in the Japanese and Mongolian canons.

Conclusion

There is no set way in which all Buddhists relate to their scriptures. To begin with, followers of each school or tradition regard a different set of texts as the authentic body of scripture they consider authoritative. In other words, the scriptures that Buddhists refer to vary from one tradition to another. Second, there is a broad range of approaches in terms of the respect for scripture. Attitudes vary from the extreme of honouring one single text (Lotus Sutra, Nichiren) to the other extreme of according little value to the study of any scriptures at all (Zen). Most Buddhist schools follow a moderate and more relaxed path in between these extremes: people with scholarly inclinations study a broad range of scriptures, while those who are unable to do this simply learn the main points and try to apply them in their lives.

Many of the key points we have seen in connection with the Buddhist scriptures stem from the basic idea that they are not divinely revealed. Because of this, scriptural words do not have a special status for Buddhists as the *qur'ans* do for Muslims. For Buddhists, words, even those of scripture, are not divine but conventional and part of human language. The highest truths cannot be put into words. This is why scripture has a value only insofar as it helps human beings transform themselves from ignorance to enlightenment, from suffering to freedom. Ultimately, scriptures do not have intrinsic value, only instrumental value.

Buddhism

1 How significant are the scriptures for Buddhists of different schools of thought?

2 Select one scripture and explain the religious beliefs about the revelation or inspiration of this scripture.

3 On what basis do Mahayana Buddhists consider their scriptures to be authoritative?

Chapter 6

The Three Refuges

Just about every Buddhist tradition includes taking refuge in the Buddha, the Dhamma and the Sangha. These three provide a focus for our commitment and for our reflections on the practice.

Ajahn Sumedho, *The Mind and the Way*

The meaning of the refuges

When anyone formally decides to become a Buddhist, he or she recites what is called the Three Refuges, three times each:

I take refuge in the Buddha,
I take refuge in the Dharma,
I take refuge in the Sangha.

This 'refuge formula' was developed by the Buddha himself and in its ancient Pali form the words are:

Buddham saranam gacchami
Dhammam saranam gacchami
Sangham saranam gacchami.

These three principles of Buddha, Dharma and Sangha are sometimes called the Three Jewels because they are considered so precious and valuable. Other English terms for the Three Refuges include the Threefold Refuge and the Triple Refuge — they all mean exactly the same. To put it simply, a Buddhist commits himself or herself to: following the Buddha as teacher; what he taught, the Dharma, as guidance; the community of fellow practitioners, the Sangha, as companions through life.

There are two ways we can talk about the Three Refuges: one is to describe what each of them is according to common Buddhist practice and according to the scriptures; the other is to explain the meaning behind the refuges. With the first approach, we examine Buddhism as an outsider looking in, and with the second approach we try to understand what the refuges mean from the point of view of a Buddhist. Let's take the second approach first.

Why do Buddhists take refuge? What meaning does the refuge have for a Buddhist? Ringu Tulku, a contemporary Tibetan Buddhist teacher, explains:

> The concept of 'refuge' is fundamental in Buddhism. It's connected with something that I think also applies in a way within every spiritual tradition, and even to every individual person: our need to find a purpose in our lives.
>
> What is it that I really want? What is the highest goal that I want to realise? What is my ultimate dream? Asking myself these kinds of questions can enable me to identify my purpose, whatever it is that I want most to achieve, that would benefit myself and others.
>
> Ringu Tulku, *Refuge*

There are two points to make here.

- First, by taking refuge a Buddhist is consciously identifying enlightenment as his or her ultimate aim. This means accepting the Buddha's analysis of what true happiness is and committing oneself to finding happiness, not in anything external, such as a good job, money, love, friends, music and so forth, the way many people do, but through inner development and transformation.
- Second, the basic meaning of taking refuge is that an individual is making a personal commitment to follow the Buddha's teachings and put them into practice. This includes following the external manifestations of the Buddhist religion — the scriptures, the practices, the festivals and so forth. Taking refuge is deciding on Buddhism as the religious path one chooses to follow in order to attain one's aim in life.

The notion of a 'refuge' here does not mean a place to hide or a place to escape to. Taking refuge in the Buddha, for example, does not mean that we are pleading or praying for the Buddha to save us. Rather, taking refuge is more like making a decision based on the conviction that we have the potential for enlightenment within us, and that it is possible to awaken this potential: one decides that one does indeed want to awaken this potential and one makes a commitment to take that as one's life goal. The Buddhist teacher Trungpa Rinpoche puts it another way: it is as though Buddhists see themselves as 'refugees' from samsara, the endless cycle of suffering. By taking refuge they are trying to make their new home in nirvana and find a life of peace that is free from all suffering.

So, while taking refuge in the Buddha, Dharma and Sangha is a way of expressing one's reliance in these three principles, the fundamental understanding is that one is ultimately placing one's reliance and trust in one's own enlightenment potential, which is called 'buddha nature' in Mahayana. Refuge is not so much a relationship of dependence on external principles as a

commitment to following the way to one's own enlightenment. From the Buddhist point of view supreme happiness is to be found not in anything outside us, but deep within us. The Buddha says in *Dhammapada* 380: 'One is one's own master, one's own refuge.'

The Buddha advised his disciples to be 'a refuge unto themselves' because dependence on anyone else is always unsatisfactory in the end. Each person needs to work with himself or herself in order to attain nirvana. The Buddha, the Dharma and members of the Sangha can all help to show us the way to follow, but we have to tread the path ourselves. Going for refuge gives Buddhists a sense of direction and meaning in life. It offers them the goal of ultimate happiness as well as the practical means of finding that happiness. And it is a way of developing inner strength.

In terms of how Buddhists lead their everyday lives, the most important commitment entailed by taking refuge is not to cause harm; this means making every effort not to harm others or ourselves in any way.

How Buddhists take refuge

There are two main ways in which Buddhists take refuge. The first takes place in a refuge ceremony, during which one takes refuge for the very first time. Generally, such ceremonies are held in a local monastery in the presence of several monks, who serve as witnesses to one's recitation of the refuge formula. In Buddhist countries, children generally take refuge in this way when they are around 7 years old. The intention in participating in a refuge ceremony is to follow Buddhism until enlightenment is attained. However, if a Buddhist decides later to change religion, he is free to do so and there are no sanctions against it.

In the Tibetan tradition, the individual is given a refuge name, in much the same way as a Catholic is given a name at confirmation. In the case of lay people, a small lock of hair is cut, symbolising that one is giving up vanity to prioritise spiritual values.

The second way in which Buddhists take refuge is by reciting the refuge formula each day as a reminder of their original commitment. For example, morning and evening prayer ceremonies begin with three recitations of the refuge formula.

The Buddha

Theravada understanding

When Theravadins take refuge in the Buddha, they acknowledge his historical role in communicating the Dharma and express their respect and gratitude to

him. They recognise him as their ultimate teacher and guide, recalling that his life serves as an example that all Buddhists can follow. But this refuge does not entail worshipping the Buddha in any way. The Buddha is seen as an extraordinary human being, respected because he succeeded in attaining enlightenment and showed us the way to do so ourselves.

Theravada emphasises taking refuge in the historical Buddha Shakyamuni. In other words, the Buddha in Theravada is primarily understood as the historical founder of Buddhism. However, to a certain extent, this tradition also understands the refuge in terms of past and future buddhas and the principle of enlightenment. In this sense, taking refuge in the Buddha points to honouring the principle of wisdom and enlightenment within each one of us, a principle that is understood to be supremely embodied by the Buddha.

Mahayana understanding

Mahayana developed a specific understanding of who or what the Buddha is through its Three Body or Trikaya doctrine (see Chapter 4). According to this doctrine, taking refuge in the Buddha refers not only to the Buddha Shakyamuni but to other Nirmanakaya buddhas of the past and the future and, most significantly, to Sambhogakaya buddhas as well.

Mahayana is, of course, an umbrella term for many different schools, and certain Mahayana schools have unique ways of understanding refuge in the Buddha. For example, the Pure Land schools of China and Japan emphasise primarily or exclusively taking refuge in Buddha Amitabha rather than Buddha Shakyamuni. In Ch'an or Zen, the emphasis is on taking refuge in the buddha nature within rather than in Buddha as an external figure.

Vajrayana understanding

The Vajrayana schools share the same understanding of this refuge as the Mahayana schools. In addition, Vajrayana practitioners take refuge in their spiritual master (*guru* in Sanskrit, *lama* in Tibetan). This is because the master is seen as a living embodiment of the qualities of the enlightened mind and of the essence of all of the Three Refuges. The master represents the Buddha since he is one's guide and teacher; his words express the truth of the Dharma; and as a human being he is also one's closest spiritual friend in life. In this way he is considered to embody all the refuges in one.

In the Tibetan tradition it is said that in one way the master or lama is even kinder than the Buddha himself because he is physically present to train and guide us according to our individual needs. He also has the ability to make the Dharma accessible to us, so we know how to apply it to our own situation and to

our own mind. Without a master, enlightenment would be virtually impossible to achieve. So in Vajrayana, one takes refuge in the master first, then in the Buddha, Dharma and Sangha.

Statues of the Buddha

The statue of the Buddha has become a familiar image in our society. He is usually depicted sitting in meditation, but there are also statues of him teaching, standing up, or lying down on his right side at the moment of his death. This classic portrayal of the Buddha dates back possibly as early as the first century BCE, when Greek art had an influence upon Central Asian and Indian art. Before then the Buddha was never portrayed in human form. His enlightenment was represented symbolically, mainly by stupas. So this Greek-inspired image of the Buddha is not seen as a realistic depiction of what he looked like as a human being; it, too, is symbolic — of the wisdom, compassion, peace and perfection of enlightenment.

When Buddhists of all schools express devotion in front of statues of the Buddha in their temples and on their shrines, they do not believe they are worshipping him either as an idol or as a human being. Rather, the statue is there as a reminder of the qualities and virtues of enlightenment that Buddhists seek to attain. Many statues are so beautiful that it is believed they may inspire those qualities and virtues in those who see them.

Buddhists express their devotion to the Buddha in various ways. They may offer candles or incense; and they may bow three times. All these practices can be understood within the context of what it means for a Buddhist to take refuge in the Buddha.

In Vajrayana it is believed that great Buddhist masters can infuse a statue with transformational blessings so that the statue becomes a 'live' presence. These blessings can then benefit devotees. In Theravada, too, there are ceremonies to consecrate key statues and infuse them with the Buddha's power.

Figure 6.1 Statue of the Buddha in Bodh Gaya, India

The Dharma

Some meanings of the term 'Dharma'

The word *dharma* (in Sanskrit) or *dhamma* (in Pali) has many different meanings. The following meanings are relevant to the Buddhist refuge.

- Dharma denotes the universal truth, the laws or order inherent in nature. This truth and order has no beginning or end. It exists whether human beings or particular individuals are aware of it or not. All Indian religions share a belief in universal truth and cosmic order.
- Dharma specifically denotes the teachings of Buddha Shakyamuni, and in particular the record of those teachings contained in the various collections of scriptures. The Buddhist understanding is that what the Buddha taught was no other than the universal truth.
- Dharma is a term used for the path that one follows when one applies and practises the teachings of the Buddha. This meaning is especially emphasised in the refuges, so that taking refuge in the Dharma means above all following the Buddhist path.
- Dharma refers to the personal realisation of the truths of Buddhism attained through learning the teachings, reflecting on them and meditating on them.
- In English, Dharma is commonly used as a word meaning 'Buddhism'. Sometimes the expression 'Buddha Dharma' is used.

When one takes refuge in the Dharma, the understanding is that the Buddha's teachings are there to be heard and read, studied and understood, practised in formal sessions as well as in everyday life, and finally they are to be fully realised so that the practitioner comes to embody them.

It is possible to argue that the Dharma is the most important of the Three Refuges, especially since the scriptures quote the Buddha as saying:

> He who sees the Dharma sees me; he who sees me sees the Dharma.
>
> Samyutta Nikaya, III.120

To understand the nature and significance of the Buddha is to understand his teaching, and by understanding his teaching we will come to understand who the Buddha really is. The key that opens the meaning of all of the Three Refuges is therefore an understanding of the Dharma.

The Mahayana understanding

All schools and traditions of Buddhism share an understanding of the meaning of this refuge. The main point that differs from one tradition to another is the precise composition of what is accepted as the body of scriptures (see Chapter 5). However, in Mahayana, there is an emphasis on taking refuge in

Dharma as truth, that is, as the universal truth, and not necessarily restricting oneself to the words of the Buddhist scriptures.

Dharma as universal truth is the meaning behind the words. Indeed, the tradition of Ch'an or Zen places more emphasis on meditational experience and realisation than it does on study of the scriptures. Since the ultimate truth is beyond words, the use of words to express it can become a hindrance rather than a help to understanding. In this context, refuge in the Dharma will emphasise Dharma in the sense of practice and realisation of the teaching rather than the scriptures themselves.

The Three Higher Trainings

When the Dharma is spoken of as a path it is often presented in terms of what are called the Three Higher Trainings, namely moral discipline, meditation and wisdom. Taken together, these three trainings comprise the complete path to enlightenment, and all three are necessary to reach the goal. Nikaya and Mahayana Buddhism describe their respective paths in different ways, but both the Eightfold Path of Nikaya Buddhism and the *Bodhisattva* Path of Mahayana share the same basic structure of these three trainings. They are therefore a useful framework for understanding the Buddhist approach to enlightenment.

Respect for the Dharma

What does 'taking refuge' in the Dharma mean precisely? In the case of refuge in the Buddha, we saw it meant primarily feeling gratitude, appreciation and respect for what the Buddha achieved and gave to people. In the case of the Dharma, it is rather a matter of developing a fundamental trust in the teachings, and a personal commitment to understanding and practising them.

Buddhists are not required to have uncritical trust in the Buddha's teachings or to develop blind faith in the truth of what he said. On the contrary, they are encouraged to use their intelligence to think through the arguments for themselves, and put the teachings to the test by reflecting and meditating on them. In this way every individual experiences personally how true these truths are. Taking refuge in the Dharma includes a commitment to engaging in this process of discovery.

This is why taking refuge in the Dharma is not seen as a form of escapism. The Buddhist approach is not to surrender one's intelligence and ability to reason and escape into a blind belief in dogmatic truths. Refuge in the Dharma entails personal effort and discipline, and a willingness to learn and to change. It is an active process, not a way of avoiding responsibility.

The Sangha

The Fourfold Sangha

In the West, our idea of Buddhist monks tends to be that they sit in meditation virtually all day long. Most people think that monks remain within the monastery walls and have little or no contact with the rest of the community. Because they do not take ordinary jobs and earn money we think there is nothing for them to do but meditate. In addition, many people in the West imagine that all Buddhists are monks. It is surprising how many people believe that to be a Buddhist you have to give up your possessions and all your attachments to life — which means becoming a monk. Some students even think that if you want to become a Buddhist you have to give up sex entirely. All these views are mistaken.

Sangha is the word for the community of those who follow the Buddhist path. Often, Sangha refers to the monastic community — the monks and nuns who have abandoned a worldly life to lead an exemplary life of virtue. But these days the term refers to lay people as well, ordinary people who follow a religion but who have jobs, families and other social responsibilities. This is known as the Fourfold Sangha: monks, nuns, lay men and lay women. So, in every country where Buddhism is practised, a follower has the choice of being a householder or taking the special commitment of becoming a monastic. Buddhists include both monastics and lay people.

The role of monastics

Monks and nuns play an extremely important role in Buddhist societies. The practice of ordaining people into monastic life was initiated by the Buddha, and the rules monastics follow were set out by the Buddha in what later became the Vinaya scriptures. The authority of monasticism as an institution is therefore linked to its antiquity and to the authority of the Buddha himself.

First and foremost, monastics maintain Buddhism as a living religion. They study the scriptures, practise meditation every day, teach Buddhism to others, perform ceremonies and rituals, and offer advice according to Buddhist values. In their personal lives they are expected to uphold the ethical values of Buddhism and manifest the qualities that are to be developed on the path. In other words, monks and nuns are living examples of the religion. Buddhists usually consider that, without monastics, their religion would be reduced to a collection of words in books.

It follows that by taking refuge in the Sangha a layperson is acknowledging the vital role that monastics play, not only for the continuation of the religion as a whole but for the welfare of the community.

Being of exemplary conduct, members of the Sangha are worthy of respect and of gifts. Indeed, they are thought of as an excellent 'field of merit'. Merit or virtue is gained by any act of generosity, but, just as a seed planted in better ground yields better fruit, so a gift made to a virtuous person brings greater merit. The idea of merit also includes the power of good actions to bring about good results naturally. Buddhists take refuge in the Sangha because they appreciate the way monastics benefit the world by offering this special opportunity to gain abundant and purifying merit. This is especially the case because, strictly speaking, the Sangha into which one goes for refuge contains those who have had some glimpse of nirvana.

From a practical point of view, lay people take refuge in the Sangha by honouring the monastics with respectful behaviour, with gifts of food, clothing, medicines and so on, and by relying on them for advice and encouragement.

The Mahayana understanding

Refuge in the Sangha is understood and practised quite differently in Mahayana, and there is variation in practice from one Mahayana school to another. Mahayana generally accepts the classification of the Fourfold Sangha, and the distinction is made between monastics and lay people. Even though Mahayana is said to place more emphasis than Nikaya Buddhism on the status of lay people, nevertheless, in practice, monastics have tended to be more highly respected than lay people in most Mahayana communities.

The big difference in Mahayana concerns the nature of monasticism: the role of monks, their way of life, the discipline they follow and their relation to the larger community. In China, and especially in Japan, the Vinaya evolved and changed as Buddhism became established. In Japan some Buddhist schools such as True Pure Land have no monks at all and instead have priests who are allowed to marry and have families, take jobs and earn money. They live as householders and perform their priestly duties on certain occa-sions only. They are therefore integrated into the community in quite a different way from a Theravadin monk. In Soto Zen, monks may live a communal life of poverty and simplicity akin to the lifestyle of Theravadin monastics, but in both Soto and Rinzai Zen, Buddhist teachers have the option to marry.

The other key difference in the Mahayana understanding of refuge in the Sangha is that Sambhogakaya buddhas and *bodhisattvas*, in whom one can take refuge, are included within the idea of Sangha. The practitioner aspires to emulate them and become like them, developing their particular enlightened qualities, and prays to them for help and protection.

Summary of main points

Which of these Three Refuges is the most important? One answer is that all three are equally important. However, we can analyse the relationship between Buddha, Dharma and Sangha in different ways, to establish arguments that show that one or other of the Three Jewels has primacy over the others.

For example, according to one argument, the Buddha must be the most important refuge, because if it were not for him we would have neither the Dharma nor the Sangha. This logic establishes the Buddha's importance on the basis of the historical development of Buddhism. On the other hand, a different argument points out that, in terms of someone's experience of the Buddhist religion, the Dharma is the most important refuge. The Buddha himself has passed away, and the core of the religion is now his teaching. The Sangha are those who follow that teaching. This reasoning is made from the point of view of a person encountering Buddhism now and whose conviction will be based on what he or she sees as the truth of the teaching and the good example of those who follow it.

Similarly, according to a third argument, we might consider that the Sangha is the most important refuge because it preserves and passes on the Dharma from one generation to the next and keeps it alive.

There is no single correct answer to this question from the Buddhist point of view, and it is very much up to individual Buddhists to choose the reasoning they prefer.

- All Buddhists express commitment to their religion by taking refuge in the Buddha, Dharma and Sangha — the Three Jewels.
- Taking refuge in the Buddha means expressing gratitude and respect for his enlightened teaching.
- Taking refuge in the Dharma is an undertaking to study, practise and fully embody the Buddha's teaching.
- Taking refuge in the Sangha means primarily honouring the role and authority of the monastics, and in Mahayana extends to honouring Sambhogakaya buddhas and *bodhisattvas* as well.
- The inner meaning of taking refuge is a commitment to developing one's inner strength and potential for enlightenment.
- The practical implications of the refuge for daily life are a commitment not to harm oneself or others and to develop trust in the truth wherever one finds it, whether within oneself or in the world.

Questions

1 Explain what is meant by taking refuge in the Dharma and assess to what extent taking refuge in the Dharma is sufficient to gain enlightenment.

2 'All Buddhists, regardless of tradition, take refuge in the Three Jewels of Buddha, Dharma and Sangha. So, although Theravada Buddhism and Mahayana Buddhism are described as different vehicles, they do in fact share many common features.' What do Buddhists mean when they say, 'I go to Buddha for refuge'?

3 'Buddhism is based on faith in the Buddha.' How far do you agree with this view?

4 Is taking refuge really a form of escapism?

5 Explain the meaning and teaching of the Three Refuges. Evaluate the claim that the refuges are the essence of Buddhism.

Chapter 7

The Four Noble Truths

The Four Noble Truths are the very foundation of the Buddhist teaching, and that is why they are so important. In fact, if you don't understand the Four Noble Truths, and if you have not experienced the truth of this teaching personally, it is impossible to practise Buddha Dharma.

The Dalai Lama, *The Four Noble Truths*

Introduction

What did the Buddha teach? The theme of the very first teaching he gave after his enlightenment is known as the Four Noble Truths. On that occasion he spoke in a place known as the Deer Park in Isipatana (modern-day Sarnath) near Benares, to five ascetics who had previously been his companions in the forest. After that he taught about the Four Noble Truths again and again, and we find presentations of them in many different suttas in the Pali Canon.

The Four Noble Truths, sometimes translated as the Four Holy Truths, are the foundation of all the different teachings the Buddha gave over his 45-year ministry. They offer a framework into which everything fits. They are taught in every tradition and school of Buddhism in the world, even though there can be variations in emphasis and interpretation.

The Four Noble Truths are:
- the truth of suffering (*dukkha*)
- the truth of the causes of suffering
- the truth of the cessation (or end) of suffering
- the truth of the path leading to the cessation of suffering

Briefly, the Buddha teaches the following.

1 Suffering is universal and is experienced by every living creature, yet nobody wants suffering, and we all long to find happiness.

2 The root causes of suffering lie within our own minds. They are craving, aggression and ignorance — known as the Three Poisons. On the basis of these we engage in actions which, through the laws of karma, cause harm to others as well as ourselves. The suffering we experience only prompts us to react even more aggressively or blindly to the next situation.

3 It is possible to put an end to suffering by putting an end to the causes of suffering. If we transform our actions and our minds and become selfless we can find true and lasting happiness, known as nirvana or enlightenment.

4 The way out of the vicious circle of suffering is to follow the Buddhist path of moral discipline, meditation and wisdom.

The Four Noble Truths should not be seen as a set of dogmatic truths in which all Buddhists must believe. In this sense, they are not the equivalent of the Christian Creed or the Five Pillars of Islam. The word 'truth' in this context refers to 'reality', the way things are, rather than to truths with which we are free to agree or disagree. Suffering, for example, is a universal fact of life that applies to everyone, whether Buddhist or non-Buddhist. The Four Noble Truths are realities that we discover for ourselves through hard experience.

It follows that the Four Noble Truths are not the core of Buddhist dogma but a framework for understanding Buddhist thought. Many teachings in Buddhism are preserved as numbered formulae: the Four Noble Truths, the Three Marks of Existence, the Six Paramitas and so on. These should be seen simply as convenient ways of memorising the Dharma, especially in a context in which followers retain teachings by heart. The Buddha said that no words or formulae could really capture the truth and experience he was trying to share, because the ultimate is beyond words. Buddhists should not see the Four Noble Truths in a rigid way, as though there were precisely four 'truths' out there to understand, but rather as a tool to help them see the Buddhist vision of the world.

The logic of the Four Noble Truths

The Buddha began his teaching life by addressing the universal problem of suffering. Everyone suffers in life. Although each of us longs to be happy, somehow we rarely find the lasting happiness we seek. And when we look beyond our own situation, and see just how many people in the world are going through far greater suffering than we are, the pain can feel overwhelming. Nowadays we only have to switch on the television to see this: wars, natural disasters, starvation, disease, violence, betrayal, poverty, death. Suffering seems endless and nobody is spared.

When the Buddha left his palace he set out to find a solution to suffering and this teaching is the fruit of his search. In the Four Noble Truths he describes the

problem, explains what is causing the problem, finds that the problem can be solved, and sets out the method for solving it. One image often used to illustrate this teaching is that of a wise doctor tending a patient. Suffering is the patient's condition; the causes of suffering are the doctor's diagnosis of that condition; the cessation of suffering is the good news that the complaint is curable; and the path is the treatment prescribed by the doctor to bring about a cure. In this analogy, the Buddha is the doctor and each Buddhist is a patient.

Some doctors can exaggerate the seriousness of an illness, while others might lack the experience to know just how serious it is. But the Buddha is a wise doctor, whose analysis of the situation is objective and accurate. This is why Buddhists believe that the Buddha's teaching is neither pessimistic nor optimistic, but offers a realistic appraisal of the human condition. It shows us who we are, what our world is, and what actions are effective in bringing about change.

Table 7.1 The logic of the Four Noble Truths		
First pair	Suffering	Effect
	Causes of suffering	Cause
Second pair	Cessation of suffering	Effect
	Path	Cause

The logic of the Four Noble Truths can be analysed in different ways from different points of view. For example, if we take them purely rationally, they can be seen as two sets of pairs. Each pair consists of a cause and an effect, as in Table 7.1.

If we follow this logic we could present them in a different order, taking the second truth first, then the first truth; and taking the fourth truth next, then the third. This is because we usually think that causes come before their effects. This pairing of the Four Noble Truths highlights the contrast between them: the first pair describes how our lives are at the moment and what lies at the root of the suffering we experience. The second pair describes how things could be if we changed: how, by following the path of moral discipline, meditation and wisdom, we can turn things around and create the causes of nirvana, where suffering ceases altogether. So the first pair describes samsara and the second pair is related to nirvana.

It is important to note that ultimately speaking nirvana is unconditioned and not caused or produced by anything. However, it is fair to say that on a conventional level, the path is followed because it eliminates the causes of suffering and therefore leads to nirvana.

On the other hand, we can approach the Four Noble Truths from the point of view of personal experience and take them in the order in which they are usually given. Our experience of suffering is the starting point. If we did not suffer at all, we would have no wish to follow a spiritual path to change the situation. When we do undergo painful experiences, we naturally ask ourselves why. Why is this happening to me? Why do I have to go through this? Why did

things go wrong? We instinctively look for an explanation of the reasons for our predicament. If we find an explanation, it usually entails some understanding of how to end our suffering in the short or long term. Finally, we have to make the necessary changes to put an end to our suffering.

The man wounded with a poisoned arrow

One of the most striking things about Buddhism is the way that the Buddha began teaching by talking about everyday reality rather than the grand philosophical questions that we usually associate with religion. Every other religion offers answers to the big questions of life, such as how the universe began, why we are here, whether our souls survive after death. The Buddha considered such answers to be vain metaphysical speculation, because they are questions that can never be satisfactorily answered. He insisted that religious teaching must be practical. It should not aim at satisfying intellectual curiosity, but should lead us to complete freedom from suffering. If a religious teaching does not do this, then it is of little value.

Some of the Buddha's disciples did not appreciate his approach, and there is a well-known story of one disciple, named Malunkyaputta, who complained that the Buddha had not given him the answers he was looking for. He accused the Buddha of failing to answer his questions because he did not in fact know the answers. The ten questions on which the Buddha was silent are:

1 Is the universe eternal?
2 Is the universe not eternal?
3 Is the universe finite?
4 Is the universe infinite?
5 Is the soul the same as the body?
6 Are the soul and the body two separate things?
7 Does the Buddha continue to exist after death?
8 Does the Buddha no longer exist after death?
9 Does the Buddha both exist and not exist after death?
10 Is the Buddha both non-existent and not non-existent after death?

Malunkyaputta challenged the Buddha to answer the questions if he knew the answers, and said that if he did not know them he should be honest enough to admit it. He then threatened that he would stop being his disciple if the Buddha did not respond to his satisfaction.

The Buddha replied by pointing out that he had never promised any of his disciples that he would give them answers to such questions, and therefore he could not be accused of misleading them. He went on to tell the story of the man who is wounded with a poisoned arrow. The wounded man's relatives take

him to a surgeon, but he insists that he does not want the arrow to be removed until he has established who shot it, what social background the assailant came from, his name and what he looks like. And on top of this, he insists he needs to know what sort of bow was used, what sort of arrow and what wood the arrow was made from. Only then will he accept treatment. In such a situation, said the Buddha, the man would surely die before all this information could be gathered. Likewise, one might well die before finding any answers to these ten metaphysical questions. Malunkyaputta was convinced by this, and remained a monk.

According to the Buddha, one does not need to depend on such answers to lead a religious life. Whatever opinions we may have about the beginning of the universe, the nature of the soul and eternity, they will not help us to understand our suffering nor will they help us to overcome it. From the Indian point of view at least, the whole point of religion is to eliminate suffering. This is why the Buddha taught the Four Noble Truths, because they are useful and practical in this precise respect.

Another way to understand the Buddha's silence on these questions is from the point of view of logic. Take the fifth question as an example: the way it is phrased means that neither a 'yes' answer nor a 'no' answer would be satisfactory from the Buddha's point of view. This is because the question rests on the assumption that there exists something called a soul that we can talk about and define in relation to the body. However, for the Buddha, the very existence of the soul is an assumption that needs to be questioned, and this makes question 5 unanswerable as it stands. Each of Malunkyaputta's questions rests on a similar assumption.

The middle way

The Buddha characterised his approach to the religious life, as set out in the Four Noble Truths, as 'the middle way'. This expression is now commonly used to describe the Buddhist approach in general. The Buddha distinguished his middle way from other approaches that promote extreme positions. Such approaches need not only be religious ones — they can include any vision or method for finding happiness, however that is defined.

For example, one extreme pointed out by the Buddha is 'devotion to the indulgence of sense pleasures, which is low, common, the way of ordinary people, unworthy and unprofitable'. He had had first-hand experience of this way of life from his years of luxurious indulgence in the royal palace. Clearly, 'ordinary people' does not simply refer to the poor but rather to anyone, of whatever social or educational background, who is satisfied with the everyday

pleasures of this life and does not yearn for higher things. Such a hedonistic outlook is associated with materialism, because it leaves no room for spiritual goals and values and denies any form of after-life.

Another extreme mentioned by the Buddha is that of self-mortification. This is the opposite of indulgence in sense pleasures: deliberately subjecting one's body to extreme pain and discomfort with a view to freeing the spirit from the shackles of the body and finding lasting peace and happiness. Once again, the Buddha had experienced this approach at first hand when he lived as an ascetic in the forest. He describes self-mortification as 'painful, unworthy and unprofitable'; it causes one to suffer, to lose one's dignity, and does not lead to the desired goal.

The Buddha continues by saying that it is by avoiding both these extremes that he has realised a middle path, which 'gives vision, gives knowledge, and leads to calm, to insight, to enlightenment, to *nibbana* (nirvana)'. The Buddha assures us that this path of moderation and balance really does lead to the happiness we seek. It is this 'middle way' approach that gives rise to the qualities of non-violence, tolerance and compassion for which Buddhism is known.

Summary of main points

The Four Noble Truths encapsulate the essence of Buddhism. They present the Buddhist understanding of suffering and its causes as well as the Buddhist method for overcoming suffering and attaining nirvana. Buddhists claim this path leads to realisation of ultimate reality, to complete freedom and happiness, to peace, compassion and wisdom, in this life.

When a Buddhist engages with the Four Noble Truths in practice, each truth is applied in a different way.

- The first Noble Truth, suffering, must be understood.
- The second Noble Truth, the causes of suffering, must be abandoned.
- The third Noble Truth, the cessation of suffering, is that which has to be realised.
- The fourth Noble Truth, the path, should be followed.

We can see from this that, for Buddhists, mere knowledge of the Four Noble Truths is not enough to attain nirvana. It is vital to apply that knowledge by changing attitudes and behaviour and by adopting a wholesome way of life. Like other religions, Buddhism is not simply about holding certain beliefs but about adopting particular practices in life. The Thai master Ajahn Chah explains how we pass from knowledge to action:

> What is this going beyond suffering all about? What should we do to escape from suffering? It's necessary for us to do some study; we need to study the thinking and

feeling in our hearts. Just that. It is something we are presently unable to change. We can be free of all suffering and unsatisfactoriness in life by changing this one point, our habitual world view, our way of thinking and feeling. The authentic Dharma of the Buddha is not something pointing far away. It teaches self.

Ajahn Chah, Being Dharma

The Four Noble Truths help us to understand ourselves and how we can change. Each one of them is explained in the following chapters under the headings in the table below.

Table 7.2 The Four Noble Truths and coverage in this book

The Noble Truths	Topic	Chapter of this book
Suffering (*dukkha*)	Three Marks of Existence	Chapter 8
	Dependent origination	Chapter 8
Causes of suffering	Rebirth	Chapter 9
	Karma	Chapter 10
	Samsara and Wheel of Life	Chapter 11
Cessation of suffering	Nirvana	Chapter 11
	Religious experience	Chapter 18
Path to the cessation of suffering	Eightfold Path	Chapters 4 and 12
	Bodhisattva Path	Chapters 4 and 12
	Buddhist ethics	Chapter 12
	Meditation	Chapters 14 and 15

- The Four Noble Truths form a framework for understanding the whole of Buddhism.
- The Buddha called this approach 'the middle way' because it encourages moderation and discourages the extremes of indulgence and asceticism.
- The main analogy used to describe the Four Noble Truths is that of a patient with an illness seeing a doctor who offers a diagnosis and a cure.

Questions

1 What 'extreme' ways of life can you identify within our society today? What is the underlying assumption or understanding of each about the nature of happiness? Do these ways of life succeed in bringing about their respective forms of happiness or not? How can you tell?

2 Modern society has many different explanations for the causes of suffering; for example, in terms of psychology, psychoanalysis, psychotherapy, sociology, politics, economics, religion and genetics. Consider some of these accounts and assess their validity.

Chapter 8

The Three Marks of Existence

Introduction

The Three Marks (or 'characteristics') of Existence encapsulate the basic Buddhist world view: in a nutshell, everything that exists in our ordinary world is conditioned, impermanent, causes suffering and is interdependent with everything else. Buddhists hold the Three Marks of Existence to be so important because people do not usually realise that the world is like this, and it is this basic ignorance of their condition that is the root cause of their suffering. To attain enlightenment and realise the unconditioned, we need to dismantle our false ideas so that we understand how things really are. We have to see through the false images we have of ourselves and connect with who we truly are. The entire Buddhist path is about freeing oneself from a distorted view of reality and the suffering it brings.

Box 8.1
The Three Marks of Existence
1 *Anicca*: impermanence
2 *Dukkha*: suffering
3 *Anatta*: 'no-self'

The Buddhist teachings present these Three Marks in a detailed and systematic way. Because they are so fundamental to Buddhist thought, we will examine all the main categories in order.

Anicca: the impermanence of all things

The Buddha found that everything in the world is impermanent and changing, which implies that there is nothing whatsoever that is permanent. We could say that change (*anicca*) is a fact of life. This truth might sound banal, but the Buddhist view is a radical one because it does not allow for any exceptions. It covers everything from the book in your hand to the solar system and more. In the moment a book begins to exist, its impermanence is assured. This is because it is composed of many different parts, and all compound things must have a

beginning, middle and end. If they are compound they must be produced; they only exist when certain factors come together, and at some point in time those factors will naturally separate and disperse and the compound thing will cease to exist.

Box 8.2
Analysis of the Three Marks of Existence

1 Impermanence — *anicca*
  a Gross impermanence
  b Momentary change

2 Suffering — *dukkha*
  a Ordinary suffering
  b The suffering of change
  c The suffering of conditioned existence

3 'No-self' — *anatta*
  a The 'no-self' of phenomena or inanimate objects
  b The 'no-self' of the person or animate objects

Although we all know that things change, in practice most of us believe there are some things in life that are permanent and lasting; or at least we behave as though they are. For example, there may be some values we believe are universal and eternal: justice, peace, truth or beauty, for instance. Those who follow a religion other than Buddhism might believe there is an eternal God, an everlasting soul and an eternal heaven. Even in terms of everyday life, when we have a crush on someone we think it will last for ever. We relate to ourselves as permanent; we make plans as though we were always going to be healthy and young, and when death approaches we regard it as a failure, a shock or a surprise.

The Buddha questioned all the things people regard as permanent and came to the conclusion that there is nothing that is not subject to change. He explained that change, or impermanence, operates on two levels, the gross and the subtle.

The gross level of change

The gross level is the obvious physical level of change: things we experience, such as the weather, the seasons, the way things decay or get broken, the way people grow up and age and die. This gross level also applies to historical change, social change, geographical change and so on; in fact, the Buddha said it applies to all areas of life and the world. This is what we commonly call change — a phenomenon that we can usually observe with our own eyes and that does not require special scientific or philosophical methods to be discovered. Buddhists consider that change in this sense is undeniable.

Momentary change

The subtle level of change is sometimes called 'momentary change': this means that everything is in a perpetual process of flux from moment to moment. Although objects like tables and chairs might look the same today as they did

yesterday, in fact they are continually changing in each moment. If we use a specialised microscope we will see that the atoms and molecules that objects are made of are in perpetual motion and are continually changing their configurations. So, even though at the gross level objects appear to remain the same for a certain length of time before they are broken, decay or are destroyed, nevertheless at the subtle level they are subject to the change process all the time. It is on account of this subtle level of change that things eventually change visibly at the gross level: we don't suddenly grow old on a certain day or even in a certain year; it's a gradual process. Visible changes like ageing or the change of the seasons do not happen as one special event, but result from the accumulation of millions of smaller changes.

Momentary change cannot be observed by the naked eye. Nowadays we can relate to the idea by referring to modern science and the use of microscopes, but the Buddha, of course, did not have any microscopes nor did the Buddhist scholars who wrote the philosophical treatises of the Abhidharma. They made their observations of momentary change through the special insight they developed in meditation. It seems that this is a point on which modern science and Buddhism might converge.

You might think that radical impermanence makes no sense, because things don't change all the time and there *is* some continuity. If we could not recognise our friends from one day to the next because of change, life would be chaotic. Clearly, this is not the case: we do recognise people from one day to the next, even from one decade to the next. So does this mean that Buddhists have got it wrong?

All philosophers have grappled with the problem of the relationship between continuity and change. The way Buddhists account for this relationship is by explaining that momentary change happens as a continuum of linked moments. Each moment is so short that we don't notice it (a moment is sometimes defined as one sixtieth of a second). That is why we have the impression that life is continuous. It is rather like the frames of a film going through the projector at just the right speed to give us the illusion of a continuous sequence. But, if we check the film reel, we see that each frame is separate.

This continuum of moments does not happen haphazardly: I cannot be a human being in one moment and in the next moment become an elephant. The continuum happens in an orderly fashion because one moment produces the next, and a moment can only produce another moment that is similar to it because there are causal connections between each of the factors that make up a situation. For example, if we imagine change in slow motion, the process is rather like looking at a dancer in a night club under stroboscopic light. Each

time the light flashes we see one dance pose, and although we cannot see what happens between the flashes we know that each dance pose is produced from the previous one. There is a causal connection between the situation we see in each flash of light.

Finally, even if we agree that impermanence affects all inanimate and animate objects in the world, what of our abstract ideas of permanent things? What about beauty, truth and God? Why does the Buddha deny that these things are permanent? The very definition of all these terms includes the notion of permanence: God would not be God if he were not eternal.

Here, Buddhists make a distinction between the ideas we have about things and the reality to which our ideas refer. They say that the bare fact we have an idea that something exists is no proof that it exists in actuality. It is clear we can have quite convincing ideas and images of the existence of things or people that do not exist: unicorns are the classic example of this, but we could add modern examples such as hobbits or Spiderman. The Buddhist view is that none of our *abstract* concepts corresponds to something that objectively exists; they are only human ways of interpreting experience. Beauty, truth, justice, God and enlightenment are all instances of human beings creating an idea in order to understand and communicate experience — but they are not real. The same goes for the idea of permanence. The first Mark of Existence is telling us that there is no such thing as a permanent existent. To say that anything exists permanently is a contradiction in terms.

Graham Price

Figure 8.1 Statues of the Buddha passing away are used as reminders of impermanence and death. This statue is at Polinaruura, Sri Lanka

It is one thing to agree with the philosophical reasoning on impermanence, but it is quite another to accept it in practice because we are so habituated to our own views. This is why change is one of the first themes on which a Buddhist will meditate. Flowers are often used as a focus of meditation because their beauty does not last long and they therefore symbolise impermanence. The other image that is often used is that of the Buddha lying on his right side passing into *parinirvana*, because this is a reminder that everything, even the people we value the most, are subject to death. By contemplating and reflecting on impermanence we may come to a deeper acceptance of the truth of change.

This reflection makes us realise that change is not always a reason to be sad. On the positive side, it is because we change that we are able to learn and make progress. It is because we are subject to impermanence that it is possible to change a negative situation into a positive one, or transform a negative emotion into a positive one. The main benefit of reflecting on change is that it loosens our attachment to things. If we realise deeply that things come and go, that everything in our experience will eventually come to a natural end, this helps us to stop hanging on to things. We will grasp at things less and it will be easier to let go when the time comes. Accepting that change is a natural part of life will make us happier because we can then 'go with the flow'. The Buddha taught that much of our suffering is caused by grasping at things or craving for things or desiring things that are not, ultimately, real.

Dukkha: the nature of things is suffering

> The end of craving is the end of sorrow.
>
> *Dhammapada* 354

All too often we cannot go with the flow; we don't want certain things to change. We cannot let go of our desire and craving. We fail to see the transitory nature of the things and people we are attached to most, and when they do change we experience pain and suffering. *Dukkha*, which is the First Noble Truth as well as one of the Three Marks of Existence, is usually translated as 'suffering' in English, but the word is inadequate to convey the full meaning of what Buddhists mean by *dukkha*. Walpola Rahula explains:

> It is true that the Pali word *dukkha* (or Sanskrit *duhkha*) in ordinary usage means 'suffering', 'pain', 'sorrow' or 'misery', as opposed to the work *sukha* meaning 'happiness', 'comfort' or 'ease'. But the term *dukkha* as the first Noble Truth, which represents the Buddha's view of life and the world, has a deeper philosophical meaning and connotes enormously wider senses. It is admitted that the term *dukkha* in the first Noble Truth contains, quite obviously, the ordinary meaning of 'suffering',

but in addition it also includes deeper ideas such as 'imperfection', 'impermanence', 'emptiness', 'insubstantiality'. It is difficult therefore to find one word to embrace the whole conception of the term and so it is better to leave it untranslated.

Walpola Rahula, *What the Buddha Taught*

Buddhism distinguishes three types of suffering, and by looking at these the variety of meanings of the term *dukkha* will become clear.

Ordinary suffering

The first type of suffering includes experiences that human beings universally identify as obvious forms of suffering, regardless of whether they follow a religion or not: experiences such as giving birth and being born, old age, illness and disease, and dying. The common quality of these experiences is that they are painful. This type of suffering also includes the grief of being separated from those we love or from places we feel at home in; the distress of not getting what we want; and the pain of having to watch the suffering of people we love.

The suffering of change

The second type of suffering includes the many types of distress and anxiety that result from changes in our life situation. As the first Mark of Existence showed, everything in the world is impermanent, and because either we don't realise this fact or don't want to accept it, we suffer when things change beyond our control. Even happy feelings or happy situations do not last forever, although we wish they would, so when they change they bring about suffering. Examples of this are marriage break-ups and divorce; bereavement; losing one's job; even having to move house.

Sometimes it is we who change rather than our circumstances. For example, the music you love at one time you might later find rather boring, and then you look for something new to bring you pleasure in an endless cycle of frustration and lack of contentment. Consumerism and advertising are based on this very impermanence of our likes and dislikes, and they feed the cycle. This fluctuation in our feelings about things is one reason why people who seem to have everything can still feel bored and unhappy.

The suffering of conditioned existence or conditioned states

The suffering of conditioned existence refers to the background dissatisfaction we have with life, a latent anguish or *angst* which arises from a sense of insecurity, the frustration we feel at our own limitations and at our powerlessness to control our life and our world. We often find we don't fully understand

why things are the way they are, we don't know where our actions will lead or what the future holds in store. And when we consider that, whatever we achieve ends with our death anyway, life itself can feel pointless. So this is not a dramatic form of suffering or one that is sparked by any event in particular, rather it is a more fundamental and more subtle background feeling of unease.

This third type of suffering may be more difficult to understand than the first two because it is based on philosophical analysis. While the first two types of suffering are self-evident; the third type is unique to the Buddhist understanding of *dukkha*. According to Buddhism, everything and everyone in the world exists only in dependence on other things, which means to say that there is absolutely nothing that has independent and permanent existence. It is for this reason that we sometimes feel that things are insubstantial, that life is like a dream, that even things we really value — like love, for example — are not ultimately real. More to the point, perhaps, is the fact that we ourselves are constantly changing, and the identities we create for ourselves are not who we really are.

We might be asking ourselves the big question: is there anything at all in the world that *is* real? A Buddhist answer to this question is that none of the things or people of our everyday experience is ultimately real. To understand what is meant by this, we need to look at the other two Marks of Existence, the other two factors that describe what our world is like.

So, *dukkha* covers pain, suffering, grief, frustration, dissatisfaction, unease, anguish and so on. This characteristic of existence implies that everything can at some point become a cause of suffering. Even happiness is seen as a cause of suffering because when it comes to an end there is pain and misery.

However, this does not mean that Buddhism is gloomy and pessimistic, or that the Buddha did not value life and the pleasures it can bring. Sometimes Buddhism is misunderstood as a religion that sees 'all life as suffering'. In fact, the Buddha acknowledged that there are both material and spiritual forms of happiness. For example, in one Theravada sutta he lists several types of happiness, such as that of family life and that of monastic life; the happiness of sense pleasures and that of renouncing sense pleasures; the happiness of being attached to what you love and that of being detached; physical happiness and mental happiness; and so on. But all these states are included in *dukkha*. Even high states of meditation are included in *dukkha*; this is simply because they are all subject to change and, as the Buddha said, 'whatever is impermanent is *dukkha*'.

> **Box 8.3**
>
> **Mind**
>
> In English we differentiate between inanimate and animate objects on the basis of whether they are alive or not. In Buddhism an animate object, termed 'sentient being', is defined as one that has a mind, and an inanimate object as one that does not have a mind.

This is not a pessimistic view, however, since the Buddha went on to say that there is an alternative. He said that true happiness — the lasting happiness we are all looking for — is *nibbana* (nirvana) or enlightenment, a state free from suffering and the causes of suffering, a state that is not conditioned by anything else and is beyond change because it is beyond time. Until we reach this state, however, our experience is marked by suffering, change and the insubstantiality of things.

Anatta: no-self

The Buddhist notion of impermanence is developed philosophically as *anatta* or 'no-self' (Sanskrit *anatman*). This is a difficult principle to understand and is unique to Buddhism. Whatever common ground we can find between all world religions, this is one point on which Buddhism differs from the others.

Basically, radical impermanence implies that nothing has an unchanging essence or 'self'. Buddhist thought makes no distinction between the core or essence of a thing, which is unchanging and has *ontological* existence, and its secondary qualities which may change and have only *contingent* existence. Instead, everything is process, and things are simply made up of a lot of constantly changing parts and particles. Rupert Gethin puts it this way:

> Buddhist thought understands change not in terms of a primary substantial essence remaining constant while its secondary qualities change, but solely in terms of the causal connectedness of different qualities. There is no primary substance to remain constant.
>
> Rupert Gethin, *The Foundations of Buddhism*

This is radically different from Plato's theory of forms, for example, where the perfect form of each thing exists unchanged in a separate dimension from that of empirical experience.

Let's take an example of what these ideas might mean. If we believe that things have an unchanging essence and that change affects only their secondary qualities, then if we chop a large branch off a healthy tree we will still consider that the tree remains the same tree. Its existence as a particular tree does not depend on the continued existence of all its parts. Likewise, in the case of a human being, if over time I find that my moods, thoughts and feelings change, I could consider that such mental change has no effect on who I really am. I continue to be me, whatever my psychological state might be; my identity has not changed; the true me is not dependent on the existence or non-existence of particular states of mind.

There are problems with this view for both Buddhist and non-Buddhist philosophers. If we take the example of the tree again, how much of a tree can

you chop down before it ceases to be a tree? Two branches, three, all the branches, the trunk? And how much change can my body or mind undergo before you might say that my identity has changed?

The 'no-self' of inanimate objects

Anatta, usually translated as 'no-self', means 'no essence', 'no inherent existence'. This idea is linked to the Buddhist understanding of causality, the fact that everything in the universe — and the universe itself — comes into existence through the power of certain causes and conditions. A causes B, X causes Y, and so on; also, A causes B and B causes C, and so on. This is what is meant by *conditioned existence*: everything arises from causes and conditions. It is important to note that for Buddhists nothing ever arises from a single cause, but from a combination of causes and conditions.

The implication of conditioned existence is that everything must therefore be impermanent. Why? If there is a chain of causes and effects this logically means that causes must exist before their effects; and if this is so it means that effects begin to exist from a particular point in time and before that point they do not exist.

We can illustrate this in a simple table, where T is a moment in time, and A, B and C are objects.

B does not exist at T_1, nor does it exist at T_4, so the existence of B has a clear beginning and end. It exists from the moment it is caused by something else until the moment it produces its own effect.

Table 8.1 Conditioned existence

A	$\rightarrow$	B	B	$\rightarrow$	C
T_1		T_2	T_3		T_4
Cause		Effect	Cause		Effect

Let's apply the model to a particular situation. A could be a cherry seed; once planted, watered and fertilised, A produces B, a young sapling. Later, when all the growing conditions have been good, B produces C, a cherry tree. When the tree is fully grown the seed and sapling no longer exist. At T_1 when only the seed exists, the sapling and the tree do not yet exist. This shows how, if things are caused by other things, they have to have a beginning and an end and are therefore impermanent. In other words, conditioned things are necessarily subject to time.

But the Buddhist analysis goes one step further than this. Impermanence in itself is not enough to prove non-inherent existence because it could be argued that change only applies to a thing's secondary qualities and not to its essence. Buddhists must show why they do not think there are essences. They do this through what can be called a process of reductionist analysis, that is, by logically breaking things down and reducing them to their parts, and by reaching the conclusion that things are merely the sum of their parts. Buddhists argue that the existence of a thing can be fully accounted for by its parts without the need

for positing an unchanging essence. Furthermore, an essence is something we cannot perceive and of which we have no experience, so its existence cannot be justified either logically or empirically.

Example of the chariot

The classic example of this is found in *The Questions of King Milinda*. The monk Nagasena asks King Milinda what mode of transport he used to come and meet him. The answer is a chariot. Nagasena uses the chariot as an example to explain the principle of *anatta*. He asks the king what a chariot is. Is it the axle, the wheels, the wooden frame, the yoke or the reins? Naturally, the answer is that none of these things on their own constitutes a chariot. So, if none of the parts is the chariot, where is the real chariot? The king replies:

> It is in dependence on the pole, the axle, the wheels, the framework, the flagstaff, etc., that there takes place this denomination 'chariot', this designation, this conceptual term, a current appellation and a mere name.

Nagasena completely agrees with the king's view. So what is he saying? What we conventionally call a chariot only exists in dependence upon all the parts that make it up; if some or all of those parts were missing, there would be no chariot there. Furthermore, a chariot is not something that exists over and above the sum of its parts: it is simply a concept, a word that we apply when all the parts are assembled and function together in a particular way. We can go even further and conclude that there is nothing called 'chariot' that exists in actuality; 'chariot' is simply a term used to designate a particular association of pieces of wood and metal. The corollary of this is also true; if we take all the pieces apart, or destroy them, the chariot no longer exists. Therefore chariots only have conditioned existence: they exist in dependence on certain causes and conditions coming together in a particular way, and once those causes and conditions change, chariots cease to exist.

A modern example of this would be a car. What is a car? Clearly, it is not simply the tyres, or the engine, or the bonnet on their own. We say a car exists when all its parts are assembled in a particular way so that it functions as a car. Once the car gets old and we take it to the car breakers, can we still call it a car when it has no wheels, or no windows, or no engine, or no steering wheel? At what point does a car cease being a car when we start taking it to pieces? And once we have disassembled the entire car and there is nothing left but parts, is there still an 'essence of car' that exists? And if there is, where, how, and how do you know?

The principle of Buddhist philosophy here is called *dependent origination*, *dependent arising*, *conditioned arising* or *interdependence* (*paticcasamuppada* in Pali; *pratityasamutpada* in Sanskrit), meaning that things arise or originate in

dependence on causes. Nothing exists without a cause. One of the classic formulations of this idea in the scriptures is the following:

> When this exists, that exists;
>
> From the arising of this, that arises;
>
> When this does not exist, that does not exist;
>
> From the cessation of this, that ceases.

Majjhima Nikaya, I.262–64

Box 8.4

Interdependence

The Vietnamese Zen master Thich Nhat Hanh has coined a new English word to describe interdependence: he calls it 'interbeing'. Things inter-are. In this passage he conveys the meaning of interdependence poetically.

If you are a poet, you will see clearly that there is a cloud floating in this sheet of paper. Without a cloud, there will be no rain; without rain, the trees cannot grow; and without trees, we cannot make paper. The cloud is essential for the paper to exist. If the cloud is not here, the sheet of paper cannot be here either. So we can say that the cloud and the paper inter-are.

If we look into this sheet of paper even more deeply, we can see the sunshine in it. If the sunshine is not there, the forest cannot grow. In fact, nothing can grow. Even we cannot grow without sunshine. And so we know that the sunshine is also in this sheet of paper. The paper and the sunshine inter-are. And if we continue to look, we can see the logger who cut the tree and brought it to the mill to be transformed into paper. And we see the wheat. We know that the logger cannot exist without his daily bread, and therefore the wheat that became his bread is also in this sheet of paper. And the logger's father and mother are in it too. When we look in this way, we see that without all of these things, this sheet of paper cannot exist.

Thich Nhat Hanh, *The Heart of Understanding*

Nothing is unitary — nothing is just one single thing — everything is made up of numerous parts, so the existence of an object depends on the coming together of all its parts. This analysis makes us realise that the objects of our everyday world do not exist in the way we think they do, as substantially distinct entities. This is just how they appear to us, how we perceive them. This philosophical analysis enables us to make a distinction between the way things appear and the way they really are. By reflecting and meditating on this, we break down the phenomena that make up our world until we realise that they are as insubstantial as a dream, a mirage or a rainbow.

The philosophical analysis used in Nikaya Buddhism reduces the objects of our world to their parts, and so on down to the tiniest particles that things are made of. The conclusion of this reasoning is that there are only two types of reality: the infinitely small particles that join together to produce material things, and the infinitely small moments of consciousness that join together to produce our stream of consciousness. In other words, matter is made of

spatial parts and mind is composed of temporal parts. Particles and moments of consciousness are therefore the building blocks of reality; they are the starting point of the causal chain. Logically, they are considered necessary because otherwise, if we reduced everything to its parts endlessly, the argument would be accused of infinite regress. There never would be a starting point to causation. So these two types of reality make this theory of causation possible.

A modern example of interdependence that echoes this analysis is provided by chemistry. As we know, water is H_2O; it is made of hydrogen and oxygen. There is no such thing as 'water' that exists apart from this particular combination of hydrogen and oxygen. Naturally, when its chemical parts come together in this particular way it has its own characteristic function — it flows, for example — but if, through a chemical experiment, we separate the hydrogen from the oxygen, there will be no water. If we extend this chemical model, we can also see that water is not a distinct, substantial entity that is entirely different from, say, the air or the earth. Why is this? It is because chemical analysis will show that the elements that make up water (atoms and molecules of hydrogen and oxygen) are also present in the air and the earth but in combination with other elements. Therefore everything in the world is interconnected; nothing is completely separate from anything else, even though that is not how we usually perceive things.

The 'no-self' of persons

The chariot example applies the reductionist analysis to inanimate objects, but Nagasena extends the example to cover animate objects as well, namely human beings or persons.

> Your Majesty has spoken well about the chariot. It is just so with me. In dependence on the thirty-two parts of the body and the five *skandhas* there takes place this denomination 'Nagasena', this designation, this conceptual term, a current appellation and a mere name. In reality, however, this person cannot be apprehended.

In this passage Nagasena outlines the Buddhist concept of a person. Persons have no unchanging, permanent, inherent essence or soul, they have no intrinsic identity, instead they are entirely dependent on the various processes that make them up. In fact, our names (Nagasena, Harry, Sue and so forth) do not refer to any separate reality but merely to the sum of these parts functioning in a particular way. There isn't any particular entity that can be called Dominique Side; the fact that I think there is, is, in Buddhist terms, a delusion and one of the main reasons that I am not already enlightened. We do not exist in the way we think we do. Understanding that persons lack a permanent self is perhaps the most important single attainment on the path to enlightenment.

What we call an individual or person, according to Buddhist philosophy, is a combination of ever-changing physical and mental energies, which can be divided into five groups, technically called 'aggregates' or *khandhas* (*skandhas*). These five aggregates are form, feeling, perception, mental formations and consciousness. Together they constitute the person: the body and mind of a human being.

The Buddha said that 'in short, these five aggregates of attachment are *dukkha*', and 'What is *dukkha*? It should be said that it is the five aggregates of attachment.' He clearly identifies *dukkha* with the aggregates, so suffering and these five aggregates are not two separate things. This is because each aggregate is a focus or object of our grasping and attachment and, according to Buddhism, grasping is one of the main causes of suffering. The way they function, then, is that each one of us grasps at one or other of the aggregates and identifies with it as 'me', 'I' or 'mine'. It is therefore helpful to examine what the aggregates are in order to come to a better understanding of *dukkha*.

Form or matter *Rupa*

The first aggregate is translated as form or matter, and refers to our body as well as the physical world around us. This aggregate is itself made up of the physical elements. It includes our bodies, our sense organs, and the objects we perceive in the external world.

Feeling or sensation *Vedana*

The second aggregate refers to all the sensations that are experienced through the contact of our sense organs with the external world. These sensations can be either pleasant, unpleasant or neutral. In Buddhist psychology, there are six senses and not five as in Western thought. The six senses include the usual five — sight, hearing, smell, taste and touch — plus the mind, considered as a sense organ in its own right. Each sense organ apprehends only the type of sense objects related to it, as the eyes apprehend visible forms, for example, and not smells or sounds. The particular objects apprehended by the mind are thoughts and feelings.

Box 8.5
Aggregates

The five aggregates or *khandhas*

1 Form or matter		*Rupa*
2 Feeling or sensation		*Vedana*
3 Perceptions		*Sañña*
4 Mental formations		*Sankhara*
5 Consciousness		*Viññana*

Perceptions *Samjna*

Perception is the faculty of identifying objects as mental or physical, as a table rather than a chair, and so on, and involves an initial process of conceptualising our sense data. Perceptions recognise, identify and classify, and put sensory experience into words.

Mental formations *Samskaras*

This aggregate groups together 50 different mental factors and states. The most significant cover volitional activity, that is, any mental activity that involves willpower, intention or determination. Crucially, mental formations include karma, because in Buddhism the moral effects of our actions are determined primarily by the intentions behind the actions (see Chapter 10). The aggregate of mental formations covers the mental conditioning that results from karma accumulated in previous lives, as well as earlier in this life; this colours the way we understand and react to situations, and shapes our personality and character. At the same time, this aggregate includes mental activity that produces new karmic effects — activity such as attention, determination, confidence, concentration, desire, hatred, pride and the idea of self.

Consciousness *Vijnana*

In this context, consciousness refers to a mental reaction or response that has one of the six sense faculties as its basis. For example, visual consciousness has the eye as its basis and a visible form as its object. The aggregate of consciousness is therefore connected with all the sense faculties. It does not recognise objects; it is more of an awareness of the presence of an object. So, when the eye comes into contact with a blue object, for example, visual consciousness is aware of the presence of a colour but it does not recognise that it is blue. It is perception, the third aggregate, that recognises that it is blue. Seeing is not the same as recognising.

In addition, the aggregate of consciousness plays a coordinating role between the sense faculties, so that in any given situation we perceive sights, sounds, smells and so on in an integrated picture and not separately with no connection between them. Consciousness is therefore the faculty of making overall sense of what we perceive, in collaboration with the other aggregates, and the way we do this constitutes our mentality or mind set.

How the aggregates function

There are many different ways of explaining how the aggregates work but the main point is always that we don't realise how these different factors function; instead we think we are a self that is permanent and separate from everything else. This creates tremendous anxiety and insecurity. How often do we feel lonely and isolated, lost and depressed? Such feelings come from a belief that we are separate from the world and they lead to an experience of life that is fraught with fear.

As a result we can become over-sensitive and take life very personally. One way this works is that the aggregates become objects of our attachment. So, for

example, we might identify just with our body or physical appearance and think that this is all we are. Or we might attach to and identify with ideas that other people have given us about life and who we are: for example, we might believe we are worthless or we are good, better than others or worse. Because we believe we are 'something', we hang on to these labels as a way of describing ourselves. Sometimes we can get stuck with believing in a particular self-image for a lifetime. Or we might identify with a particular experience in our past, either good or bad, in a way that colours and distorts our ability to relate to situations in the present or future.

Imagine that you are an Arsenal fan. You think it is the best and the greatest football team, following it becomes the focus of your life, you wear the T-shirt and the cap, and being an Arsenal fan becomes your identity, part of who you think you are and who others think you are. It determines how you feel and how you behave, and is the cause of the suffering you go through when Arsenal loses. From the Buddhist point of view, that is an example of the way we create false ideas of ourselves that mask the deeper reality, and of how these ideas produce suffering.

Identifying with the fourth aggregate of mental formations might take the form of accepting certain personality traits, habits or tendencies as being who we are: 'I'm like that, I can't help it.'

It may be tempting for scholars or academics to identify with the fifth aggregate of consciousness or mind. Indeed, the caricature of a university professor who cannot tie his shoe laces depicts someone who is out of touch with the aggregate of form and whose sense of identity is based mainly on his mental life.

Reflecting on each of the five aggregates in turn and seeing how we relate to them is one of the themes used in Buddhist meditation. The first benefit claimed for this is that we grow to understand ourselves better; we can distinguish between views and biases that come from our conditioning and our habits, and insights that are pure and unattached. The second benefit is that a transformation gradually takes place deep within us, and rather than identifying with the person we imagine we are, we shift our attention to pure awareness. Ajahn Sumedho, an American-born Theravadin monk living in the UK, describes the process like this:

> If we allow our personality, with its views and biases, to be the subject of our consciousness, we experience reality in terms of that personality. Because the person-ality can take any form, we can be elated or depressed — we can feel successful or feel like a failure. We live in a culture that very much emphasises personality as being oneself....If we are feeling good we are happy, if we are not feeling good, we are unhappy. That's the personality view. Any success that comes to this being is personal,

and any failure is personal. But when pleasure and pain, praise and blame, are seen from the viewpoint of the subject who is aware — rather than the viewpoint of a person — this is the awakened mind. When we contemplate more and more, we are making pure awareness the subject of our consciousness.

Ajahn Sumedho, *The Mind and the Way*

By meditating on the aggregates and on *anatta*, Buddhists start by correcting their self-image and balancing and harmonising the various factors of their personality. This leads to a personal realisation that each of us is not in fact a unitary 'person'; we are made of many interacting aspects, each of which is constantly changing. This leads to a personal conviction in 'no-self' (*anatta*). The Buddha acknowledged that philosophical analysis alone is not sufficient to convince us of the truth of *anatta*, so strong is our attachment to our own unitary existence. Unless we meditate on the five aggregates, he said, *anatta* will only be an interesting idea at best; it will never transform our understanding.

Mahayana perspective

The Mahayana schools of Buddhism accept the Three Marks of Existence but interpret their meaning differently. In particular, the Madhyamaka analysis of causation is more radical, and this leads to a more subtle understanding of no-self. In addition, Mahayana applies the paradigm of the Two Truths to suffering and therefore asserts that suffering exists on the conventional level but does not exist in ultimate truth.

The Madhyamaka analysis of causation

To put it simply, Madhyamika scholars argue that the usual explanation of causation, where a cause at T_1 produces an effect at T_2, must be mistaken. It makes no sense to say that at T_1 the cause exists but not the effect, and later at T_2 the effect exists but not the cause. If this were the case, the cause and the effect would never meet and the action of production could never take place. It follows that effects must exist simultaneously with their causes if they are to relate to each other. If this is so, then our whole notion of production occurring in linear time has to be revised.

For Nikaya Buddhism, however, interdependence based on production through causes and conditions is one of the cornerstones of Buddhist thought. As we have seen, it underpins the Buddhist understanding of impermanence (*anicca*) as well as the idea of no-self (*anatta*), and it is the cause of the third type of *dukkha*, the suffering of conditioned existence. In other words, one could say that it is the basis for all of the Three Marks of Existence. But Madhyamaka does not in fact reject interdependence, it just understands it differently.

Interdependence plays the same role within the framework of Mahayana thought as it does in the framework of Nikaya thought.

According to Nagarjuna, the great Indian scholar of Madhyamaka (second to third century CE), interdependence means *shunyata* or 'emptiness'. Things are 'empty' of inherent, independent and permanent existence; they have no intrinsic essence; everything is constantly subject to a process of change. This 'empty' quality applies to absolutely everything, even the parts and particles that make up the objects of our experience. This radical view of 'no-self' means that nothing exists that can be called a cause, and nothing exists that can be called an effect, because no unitary entities exist at all. Even atoms and particles and moments of consciousness — the unitary realities of Nikaya Abhidhamma — are themselves made of parts and are constantly changing, so when we look for causes we can never find a definite starting point for our analysis.

So how are things produced? The Buddha said that if anyone is able to answer this question fully they are already enlightened. One way of trying to understand it is to say that things come together in each moment through the mysterious interplay of dynamic energies and forces. The convergence of a particular set of factors in a particular moment gives rise to the situations and objects of our experience; and these will change from moment to moment as some energies fade and new energies and forces come into play. The process is therefore not linear and chronological but synchronic.

The concept of emptiness (*shunyata*), just like no-self (*anatta*), allows for the impermanence of things, on both gross and subtle levels, and also accounts for the suffering we experience when we try to grasp and hold on to objects, situations, emotions and so on, which are insubstantial. There is really nothing there we can hold on to, either physically or conceptually. At the same time, if we realise the emptiness of all things, we can enjoy life to the full because we will have overcome all the cravings and misunderstandings that hinder and limit our freedom to connect with the way things really are. Far from being a desperate state of nothingness, enlightenment is full of joy, love, wisdom and understanding.

Nagarjuna goes on to warn of the temptation of holding on to the idea of emptiness itself as the answer. Madhyamaka does not replace the existence of ordinary things with the existence of emptiness. 'Emptiness' (*shunyata*) is a concept like any other, and like all concepts it is simply an interpretation or intellectual fabrication; so the concept 'emptiness' is itself empty. What the concept is pointing to is interdependence; that although things appear, they are insubstantial, and although they are insubstantial nevertheless they do appear to us. Although an object appears as one thing, it includes many things within it, indeed it includes the whole universe (see Box 8.4). These statements are not contradictions.

The Mahayana approach to suffering

Mahayana distinguishes between conventional and ultimate truth (the Two Truths). Conventional truth refers to what is true in the world of empirical experience, while ultimate truth refers to the way things really are. We could also say that conventional truth appears true to those with deluded understanding, while ultimate truth appears true to those who have an enlightened understanding. How is this framework applied to *dukkha*?

From the Mahayana point of view, *dukkha* is real only to deluded beings so it can only be accepted as a truth conventionally. It cannot be an ultimate truth because it is possible to bring about the complete cessation of *dukkha*. An ultimate truth is by definition true all the time; it is not something that is true only under certain circumstances. The Four Noble Truths present the fact that *dukkha* is produced by causes and is therefore impermanent, and that it can be brought to an end completely, in which case *nibbana* (nirvana) is attained. For someone who has reached nirvana there is no suffering. *Dukkha* is therefore a conventional truth.

An example shows how this works. A child makes a fantastic sandcastle and plays with it for hours. But then the tide comes in and flattens the whole castle and the dream. The child cries and is upset, but the parents are not. The suffering of losing one's sandcastle is not real for the parents because they know from experience that sandcastles don't last and are always lost. If one has a true understanding of how things are then one does not have attachment to them and does not experience the suffering. Things are not inherently painful, they are painful when grasped.

It is in this context that one should approach the words of the Heart Sutra (see Box 8.6), one of the key Mahayana texts teaching about emptiness, when it says: 'There is no…suffering, no origin of suffering'. This does not mean that Mahayana totally rejects the Four Noble Truths of Nikaya Buddhism, nor that what Mahayana upholds contradicts the Four Noble Truths. Rather, the Heart Sutra is pointing out that suffering and the causes of suffering do not exist ultimately.

Critical evaluation

Religious arguments

When the Buddha developed his theory of *anatta* (Sanskrit *anatman*) he consciously did so as a counter to the Hindu theory of *atman*. *Atman* is often translated as 'soul' but it does not have any of the meanings that souls are given in Western thinking. According to different Western philosophers from the ancient Greeks onwards, 'soul' can refer to the intellect, to the capacity for moral

Box 8.6

The Heart Sutra

Thus have I heard. Once the Blessed One was dwelling in Rajagriha at Vulture Peak mountain, together with a great gathering of the sangha of monks and a great gathering of the sangha of *bodhisattvas*. At that time the Blessed One entered the samadhi that expresses the dharma called 'profound illumination', and at the same time noble Avalokitesvara, the *bodhisattva mahasattva*, while practising the profound prajñaparamita, saw in this way: he saw the five skandhas to be empty of nature. Then, through the power of the Buddha, venerable Shariputra said to noble Avalokitesvara, the *bodhisattva mahasattva*, 'How should a son or daughter of noble family train, who wishes to practise the profound prajñaparamita?'

Addressed in this way, noble Avalokitesvara, the *bodhisattva mahasattva*, said to venerable Shariputra, 'O Shariputra, a son or daughter of noble family who wishes to practise the profound prajñaparamita should see in this way: seeing the five skandhas to be empty of nature. Form is emptiness, emptiness also is form, emptiness is no other than form, form is no other than emptiness. In the same way, feeling, perception, formation, and consciousness are emptiness. Thus, Shariputra, all dharmas are emptiness. There are no characteristics, there is no birth and no cessation, there is no impurity and no purity. There is no decrease and no increase. Therefore, Shariputra, in emptiness, there is no form, no feeling, no perception, no formation, no consciousness; no eye, no ear, no nose, no tongue, no body, no mind; no appearance, no sound, no smell, no taste, no touch, no dharmas; no eye dhatu up to no mind dhatu; no dhatu of dharmas and no mind consciousness dhatu. No ignorance, no end of ignorance up to no old age and death, no end of old age and death; no suffering, no origin of suffering, no cessation of suffering, no path, no wisdom, no attainment, and no non-attainment.

'Therefore, Shariputra, since the *bodhisattvas* have no attainment they abide by means of prajñaparamita. Since there is no obscuration of mind, there is no fear. They transcend falsity and attain complete nirvana. All the buddhas of the three times, by means of prajñaparamita, fully awaken to unsurpassable, true, complete enlightenment. Therefore, the great mantra of prajñaparamita, the mantra of great insight, the unsurpassed mantra, the unequalled mantra, the mantra that calms all suffering, should be known as truth, since there is no deception. The prajñaparamita mantra is said in this way: TEYATHA OM GATE GATE PARAGATE PARASAMGATE BODHI SOHA (Gone, gone, gone beyond, completely exposed, awake, so be it). Thus, Shariputra, the *bodhisattva mahasattva* should train in the profound prajña-paramita.'

Then the Blessed One arose from that samadhi and praised noble Avalokitesvara, the *bodhisattva mahasattva*, saying, 'Good, good, O son of noble family; thus it is, O son of noble family, thus it is. One should practise the profound prajñaparamita just as you have taught and all the tathagatas will rejoice.' When the Blessed One had said this, venerable Shariputra and noble Avalokitesvara, the *bodhisattva mahasattva*, that whole assembly and the world with its gods, humans, asuras and gandharvas, rejoiced and praised the words of the Blessed One. Thus concludes the Sutra of the heart of transcendent knowledge.

Translated by the Nalanda Translation Committee and reproduced with permission

judgement, simply to the mind, or again to a personal, individual essence that continues after death. The characteristic of *atman*, however, is that it is an instance of the impersonal god Brahman, and at the moment of liberation the *atman* merges completely with Brahman and becomes indistinguishable from it. There are other Sanskrit terms that are used for intellect and mind (*citta*, *manas* and so on).

It is useful to bear the Hindu context in mind when we attempt to evaluate the idea of *anatta*, because it will give us a clearer idea of exactly what the Buddha was rejecting. When he taught no-self (*anatta*) he did not mean that human beings don't exist at all, or that we don't have minds, or that we don't have an intellect, or that we don't have the capacity to make moral judgements. He was specifically denying the existence of an unchanging, impersonal essence or reality, a principle that is explained by Hindus as *atman* and Brahman.

The implication of the Three Marks of Existence is that Buddhism also rejects the Christian idea of the soul. Naturally, the Buddha did not reject this explicitly because Christianity did not exist in his day, but by applying the Three Marks of Existence to the Christian idea of the soul we can see that it is not logically acceptable to Buddhism. The Buddha denied the ultimate existence of the person or individual by showing that we are merely the sum of the five aggregates. This does not mean we do not exist at all — we do of course exist as individuals in conventional reality. It means there is no over-arching personal identity that continues independently of the aggregates, either during life or after death. It follows that there can be no *personal* soul that continues after death, because by definition death is the moment when all the aggregates separate and the person is no more.

Scientific arguments

The Dalai Lama, the Tibetan Buddhist leader who has engaged in many dialogues with modern scientists, believes that science is very close to Buddhist thinking in terms of the radical impermanence of things:

> The Buddhist view of phenomena as dynamic and of momentary nature — which emerges as a consequence of the principle of universal impermanence — is quite close to the view of a dynamic, ever-changing physical universe as presented by modern physics.
>
> The Dalai Lama, *The Meaning of Life*

Nagarjuna's view of *shunyata* and interdependence as a dynamic and synchronic emergence of things, persons and situations is often compared to the theories of quantum physics, where everything exists contingently, and where even the object of an experiment depends on the person carrying out the experiment. By contrast,

the view of traditional physics based on linear causality is similar to the Abhidhammic analysis of Nikaya Buddhism.

For scientists in general, reality is that which can be perceived and experienced, so any truths that relate to ideas with no empirical basis are regarded as scientifically invalid. This is the case for the existence of souls, for example, or for the metaphysical idea of essences. The Buddhist approach is similar to this in that abstract ideas such as essences and souls, which have no basis in experience, are not accepted as true even on the conventional level. If nobody has ever seen a soul, or can describe one, or has had insight of one through meditation, or can explain its existence rationally, then in Buddhist logic it is not valid to claim that a soul has objective existence.

There is room for some discussion on this point, because certain Christian mystics like Hildegard of Bingen claim to have had visions of souls. The Buddha, however, claimed not to have had any such visions. It is possible that more clarification is needed as to what is meant by 'soul' in each case.

One of the most interesting scientific models that can help us to evaluate the Buddhist theory of the aggregates is the recent research into the neurobiology of the brain. In his ground-breaking book *Emotional Intelligence*, Daniel Goleman reports that recent research by LeDoux and Damasio shows that sense data from eyes, ears and so forth travel first in the brain to the thalamus, and then to the amygdala, which is the main brain area for emotion; then a second signal goes from the thalamus to the neocortex, which is the thinking brain. Thirdly, the prefrontal lobes function as a coordinator of data and are able to plan and organise actions towards a goal. This three-step process echoes the function of the aggregates: feelings (the second aggregate), the conceptualising intellect (the third aggregate), and the capacity to act or react (the fourth and fifth aggregates). These stages in brain activity are measured in thousandths of a second, so we are not aware of them in everyday life.

Conclusion

The Three Marks of Existence are impermanence, suffering and no-self. Although they are listed as three distinct factors, they are inextricably linked together and are like three different ways of approaching the same truth. For example, the Buddha said that impermanence is suffering, and also said that the aggregates of the person are suffering. And conversely, among the three types of suffering we find the suffering of change and the suffering of conditioned existence. All of the Three Marks of Existence, then, point to dissatisfaction with our world of experience, and reflecting on them might motivate us to try to break free from it and find something more real, more lasting and more meaningful.

Buddhism

Questions

1 Outline Buddhist teachings about the three characteristics of existence.

2 Explain the teaching on suffering (*dukkha*) in the first of the Four Noble Truths.

3 Assess the view that the Three Marks of Existence are all of equal importance for Buddhists.

4 'The Three Marks of Existence are really *anicca* described in three different ways.' Discuss.

5 Explain how the Buddha came to the conclusion that everything in this world is *dukkha*.

6 What are the five constituents (aggregates)? Discuss the significance of the belief that each of these constituents is 'impermanent and so ultimately leads to suffering'.

7 Analyse the different theories of the 'self' in Buddhism and Christianity.

8 Compare *anatta* and *atman* in Buddhism and Hinduism respectively.

9 'Mahayana Buddhism is a revolution of the Theravadin beliefs about suffering.' Discuss.

10 Compare a Buddhist view of the soul with those of Plato and Descartes.

11 'It makes no sense to talk of a person without a soul.' Discuss with reference to Buddhism.

12 Describe and assess the Theravada analysis leading to the claim that all things arise dependently.

13 Why does understanding *anatta* lead to happiness?

Chapter 9

The cycle of life and death

In the Buddhist approach, life and death are seen as one whole, where death is the
beginning of another chapter of life. Death is a mirror in which the entire meaning
of life is reflected.

Sogyal Rinpoche, *The Tibetan Book of Living and Dying*

The Buddhist understanding of rebirth

In stories of the Buddha, we learn that in the first watch of the night, when
Gautama sat under the bodhi tree in meditation, he saw with his mind's eye the
previous lives he had had over countless aeons in detail. This insight based on
meditation experience was the basis for his teaching on rebirth, the idea that
all beings are caught in a continuous cycle of life and death. Death is not the
end, it is the gateway to a new beginning.

All Indian religions (Buddhism, Hinduism and Jainism) believe that we have
a series of lives, and that death marks the end of one life and the beginning of
a new one. This continuous cycle of life and death is called samsara. It is marked
by suffering. Nobody wishes to die but the fact is that death spares no one.
Indian religions link together the principles of karma and rebirth, with the idea
that every moral and immoral action will produce appropriate fruits in this or
future lives, and that many of the experiences of the present lifetime are the
consequences of past actions performed either earlier in our present life or in
previous lives.

The ultimate goal of every Indian religion is freedom from the cycle of rebirth
or reincarnation, so karma and rebirth are profoundly connected in the sense
that if one is free from the law of karma one will also be free from rebirth. While
all three Indian religions share these points, each has a distinct way of explaining
them, so we need to define what rebirth means for Buddhism in particular.

First, rebirth in Buddhism is not the same as reincarnation in Hinduism. The Hindu idea of reincarnation is that the essence of our personal self survives without our body, continues after death and joins another body to live a new life. This process happens for an unimaginably long time until we reach liberation (*moksha*). There is therefore personal continuity from one life to the next; we can say that it is 'me' or the 'essence of me' that is reincarnated into another body. 'I' am therefore identified not with my body but with my mental self and life force.

The term 'rebirth' or 'rebecoming' is used in Buddhism, rather than 'reincarnation'. Buddhism teaches that there is no essential self (see Chapter 8) and is therefore unable to explain the process of rebirth in the same way as Hinduism. This is why rebirth is a complex process, and why Buddhists have developed elaborate theories to explain exactly what it is that continues after death if we have no essence or soul.

Rebirth should not be confused with the Christian concept of resurrection. Resurrection is a theory that assures believers that they will be 'born again' when Christ returns to earth at the final judgement. This idea entails not only spiritual continuity but physical continuity and is the reason why Christians have traditionally been buried and not cremated. It is believed that the physical body will come back to life and will be animated by the soul. In Buddhism, as in Hinduism, the physical body is considered to be subject to death; it is impermanent and after death all the elements that make it up disintegrate and scatter. This is seen as a natural process, and neither rebirth nor reincarnation ever entails the *physical* continuity of a person in another life.

What continues? Karma and rebirth

Buddhism does not have just one single answer to the question about what continues after death; there are a number of answers that vary according to which philosophical tradition one follows. However, the basic principle is common to all schools of Buddhist thought and applies to all beings in the six realms of samsara (see Chapter 11), not just to human beings.

We have seen that no unchanging self continues from life to life and yet there must be some continuity from one life to the next, otherwise we would have to say that the future life involves a different person from the one I am now, and so *I* would not be reborn. Nagasena gives a classic formulation of this in *The Questions of King Milinda*. When asked by the king whether the person who is reborn is the same as the one who died, Nagasena replies, 'Neither the same nor different'. He illustrates the principle of continuity within change with several analogies. First, if you compare yourself as a baby to the way you are

today there is obviously a big difference; physically, you might be unrecognisable yet at the same time you consider you are 'the same person'. Second, if you light a big candle in the evening and let it burn throughout the night, is it true to say that the candle flame is the same at the end of the night as it was at the beginning? The flame will change physically, beginning small and gradually getting bigger and hotter, yet we generally consider it is the same candle and the same flame. Third, Nagasena uses the example of the way milk turns into butter. Milk is allowed to separate and the cream is skimmed off. This cream is churned into fresh butter and the butter is then melted for cooking and (in India) is called ghee. Are the milk, the curds, the butter and the ghee all the same thing, or are they different?

The answer is that it is incorrect to say that all these different stages of a thing or person are exactly the same, rather each has been produced by the preceding one. We are therefore looking at a collection of successive moments of existence which are linked by causal connections. There is no 'one thing', only a series of successive moments, and it is the causal series that provides continuity without identity. There is no substance, either material or spiritual, only process.

Despite this explanation, King Milinda pursues the problem of continuity after death, because if the person who is reborn is neither the same nor different from the person who has died, is there not a loophole in Buddhist thinking which makes it impossible to have moral responsibility for actions in a past life? If the person who is reborn does not remain identical, how can he or she be held responsible for the moral consequences of past actions? This is a crucial question because, if it cannot be satisfactorily answered, problems associated with rebirth will invalidate the Buddhist theory of karma.

The dialogue is reproduced in Box 9.1. Nagasena argues that exactly the same applies from life to life as applies from moment to moment within a single life: that is, there is nothing other than a series of causally linked moments. At death the mental series continues while the physical series continues only as an impersonal physical process (the process of disintegration of the body), but it ceases to have a connection with the mental series. Death, then, is simply the separation of the mind and the body or, to be more precise, the separation of a cluster of mental processes from a cluster of physical processes.

It is helpful to mention the Buddhist understanding of conception at this point so all the causal links in the life and death cycle are clear. Just as death is the separation of the mind and the body, conception is the coming together of the consciousness with a fertilised egg. The reason why a particular consciousness joins with the fertilised egg of particular parents is primarily karmic. So the parents provide the basis of the physical body — the genes and so on — but not the basic characteristics of our mentality, which will result from our stream

of consciousness through previous lives, together with the karmic imprints embedded in that consciousness. It follows that, for Buddhists, there is a person present from conception, because conception is defined as the coming together of a consciousness with the physical basis of an embryo. Abortions are therefore seriously discouraged.

In order to answer the question about what continues after death, Buddhism seeks to define the nature of the mind that continues after death. Whatever it is that continues is mental in nature, not physical. We will consider three Buddhist theories on this matter: the Theravada response, the Mahayana response of the Chittamatra school, and the Vajrayana response of Tibetan Buddhism.

Box 9.1	
The Questions of King Milinda	
King	If there were no passing on from this body to another, would not one then in one's next life be freed from the evil deeds committed in the past?
Nagasena	Yes, that would be so if one were not linked once again with a new organism. But since one is linked once again with a new organism, therefore one is not freed from one's evil deeds.
King	Give me a simile!
Nagasena	If a man should steal another man's mangoes, would he deserve a thrashing for that?
King	Yes, of course.
Nagasena	But he would not have stolen the very same mangoes as the other one had planted. Why then should he deserve a thrashing?
King	For the reason that the stolen mangoes had grown because of those that were planted.
Nagasena	Just so, Your Majesty, it is because of the deeds one does, whether pure or impure, by means of this psycho-physical organism, that one is once again linked with another psycho-physical organism and is not freed from one's evil deeds.

The Questions of King Milinda, transl. E. Conze

Theravada response

In its analysis of the mind, Theravada asserts the existence of a subtle type of consciousness called the *bhavanga* consciousness. *Bhavanga* is the state of mind we are born in and the state of our minds in deep, dreamless sleep. It is also the state to which our minds return in the gaps between moments of consciousness. More significantly, perhaps, it is the state of mind that arises at the moment of conception in the womb, so it forms the link between the consciousness of

the past life and the consciousness of the next life. The characteristics of the *bhavanga* consciousness are unique to each individual and reproduce themselves throughout a person's life, thus defining him or her as an individual.

In Theravada philosophy, rebirth is considered to take place in the moment immediately following the moment of death. In other words, the final moment of consciousness in one life is the immediate causal link with the first moment of consciousness in the next life. The gap between the two is similar to the gap that exists between any two moments of consciousness in life. There is no intermediate state between one life and the next; the transition is immediate.

Chittamatra response

Chittamatra scholars developed a model of eight aspects of consciousness. This does not mean that we are supposed to have eight minds each; rather, the model is a way of describing eight different functions of the one consciousness. The first six aspects of consciousness are exactly the same as we have already seen in relation to the person in Chapter 8: each is related to one of the six senses. The seventh consciousness is the one that discriminates and judges according to its conditioning and prejudices, but this consciousness is also the one that can be transformed through spiritual practices such as meditation, so that it thinks positively and selflessly rather than divisively and selfishly. The eighth consciousness is called the *alaya* consciousness, sometimes translated as 'storehouse consciousness' because it is the storehouse for karmic seeds. According to this model, it is the *alaya* consciousness that survives without the body and that continues along with its store of karmic seeds from one life to the next.

Vajrayana response

When we study the Buddhist understanding of life, death and the dying process, the *Tibetan Book of the Dead* is one of the most detailed accounts we find. According to the tradition associated with that book, the mind is categorised into two: the pure, pristine, primordial mind that has no beginning and no end (*rigpa*), and the conditioned, conceptual mind which is the mind that is deluded (*sem*). The primordial mind is the nature of the mind itself; it is never stained by our negative thoughts and emotions and always remains pure. The deluded mind is that aspect of mind that does not recognise its own nature and gets lost in its thoughts, emotions and projections.

At the moment of death we naturally revert to our primordial mind and if we recognise this we become instantly enlightened. But unless we have been an advanced meditator in life we will be unable to recognise the nature of mind as such and our delusion will begin all over again. It is that chain of deluded

thoughts and emotions that will produce the next rebirth. So for an instant at death the deluded mind dissolves, and what continues is the primordial mind that is universal and not specific to any individual. However, unless we have learned to control our minds through spiritual practice this moment will not last very long. In the next moment, the primordial mind manifests as mental clarity, which is individual, and if we are not enlightened that clarity exists simultaneously with delusion. In that delusion, our karmic patterns will arise again and sweep us along in a strong current of thoughts and emotions that will be the causal links to the next rebirth.

Graham Price

Figure 9.1 Vajrasattva: the Sambhogakaya buddha embodying the principle of purity and purification who appears to us after death, according to the Tibetan tradition

In the Tibetan tradition, rebirth is not immediate; rather, it occurs after an intermediate period called *bardo*. *Bardo* means 'interval' and here it refers to the interval between one life and the next. This interval varies in length from a few days up to 49 days, depending on karma and the deceased's state of mind, and Buddhists will generally conduct prayer ceremonies for the deceased for the full 49 days. In the *bardo* state the consciousness experiences various visions that present themselves in several phases, and the way we react to these visions (for example, whether they provoke fear in us, or anger, or longing, and so on) is critical in determining our rebirth. It can be seen from this that the purpose of meditation is not only to gain peace and clarity of mind in this life but to strengthen our minds so we are better able to cope in the *bardo* after death. This is because meditation is the only systematic way of developing familiarity with the pure nature of our minds. In this sense, Buddhist practice can literally be seen as a preparation for death.

Where is the evidence?

Millions of Buddhists, Hindus and Jains believe in rebirth or reincarnation, and a Gallup poll in the USA at the turn of the twenty-first century showed that 23% of Americans believe in it too. But where is the proof? How can we decide whether rebirth is valid or not? Indeed, is it possible for rebirth to be scientifically proved? First, we will consider some of the criteria for researching rebirth, and, second, we will look at four types of research currently being carried out on rebirth.

Criteria for researching rebirth

The sceptic's position

Many people in the modern world react to the idea of rebirth incredulously, pointing out that it is impossible for anyone to know what happens after death. Indeed, this is the conclusion most commonly drawn when students are asked to evaluate rebirth: that since we cannot know for sure what happens after death, the theory of rebirth is no less plausible than the Christian theory of heaven and hell, or the materialist theory that death is annihilation. In other words, this approach leads us to a sceptical position: not only do we not know but we can't know. From this standpoint, anything we say about existence after death is mere speculation.

The sceptical view is based on two key assumptions:

1 That for any statement to be valid it must be based on empirical and verifiable evidence, and the absence of such evidence renders the statement either untrue or inconclusive.

2 That scriptural authority is not an accepted source of authority, and for it to become acceptable its statements must be corroborated by science, reasoning and empirical evidence.

We cannot enter into a discussion about these principles here, but the interesting point is that the after-life is a topic that does not fit comfortably with either of these assumptions. Even if we were to accept the first assumption as a truth criterion that applies in general, how can it be valid to require verifiable evidence of what happens after death? Aren't after-death states by definition beyond the limitations of scientific investigation? What sort of events would we be looking for as forms of evidence? How could such experiments be conducted?

The second assumption depends on the first insofar as reason is given primacy over 'faith' with respect to truth claims. This means that we would not believe what the scriptures tell us simply because it is Jesus, or a prophet, or the Buddha, who said so; there is no notion of spiritual authority. But it could be argued against the sceptics that life after death is one topic that lies specifically within the domain of religion rather than that of reason and science, because after-death states are a dimension that is beyond normal avenues of human knowledge. However, this argument itself assumes that religion is a valid field of knowledge in its own right, and that is what the sceptic questions.

Another theoretical difficulty for research into this area is the belief that what continues is a soul or spirit defined as independent from matter. This could be the case with Christian belief in an after-life, for example. The problem is that science cannot prove that something spiritual such as a soul continues after

death, because this spiritual essence is beyond the bounds of the physical world (by definition) and therefore beyond experimentation. Faced with this, the scientists would have to say they didn't know and were unable to find out.

Rebirth proved by logical reasoning

Some Buddhists consider that rebirth is validated by logical reasoning. The argument is as follows: everything in the universe is produced by causes, and those causes must be related to their effects according to the law that like produces like. Physical phenomena are produced by physical causes, so our body is produced by a sperm and egg, together with associated physical conditions such as food, drink, temperature and so on. Likewise our mind is produced by mental causes, specifically the previous moments of our past consciousness. Buddhist philosophers do not accept that the mind is reducible to matter, or that the mind can be produced by matter. Mind is not the by-product of a complex nervous system, for example. Our mind can only have been produced by a previous moment of the same continuum of consciousness.

Most scientists believe that thoughts are caused by chemical changes in the brain, and these in turn create physiological changes in the body; but their working assumption is that mind depends on the body or brain. No research has been carried out on the basis of the opposite assumption, that pure thought can give rise to chemical changes in the brain. If one can accept the body/mind model of Buddhism, where mind is a principle in its own right, then rebirth becomes logically probable.

Buddhists redefine the debate

Buddhist scholars take the debate further and redefine its parameters. The US scholar Robert Thurman writes:

> The inner science of Buddhism is based on a thorough and comprehensive knowledge of reality, on an already assessed, depth understanding of self and environment, that is to say, on the complete enlightenment of the Buddha.
>
> Robert Thurman, *Inner Revolution*

Buddhism is an 'inner science', a science of the 'inner world', a science of the mind. The Buddha and the Buddhist masters who have followed him have come to their conclusions about the mind and about life and death after meticulous study and exploration. The knowledge gained through complete enlightenment is this: a complete and thorough knowledge of the mind and the universe. The source of the Buddhist teachings on death and rebirth is the enlightened mind itself. The Tibetan master Sogyal Rinpoche explains:

(This) answer may seem initially difficult to understand for many readers, because the notion of the mind the West now has is an extremely narrow one. Despite the major breakthroughs of recent years, especially in mind/body science and transpersonal psychology, the great majority of scientists continue to reduce the mind to no more than physical processes in the brain, which goes against the testimony of thousands of years of experience of mystics and meditators of all religions.

Sogyal Rinpoche, *The Tibetan Book of Living and Dying*

Enlightenment and the possibility for a human being to become a buddha mean that Buddhism redefines the boundaries of what it is possible for humans to know. The Buddhist teachings on rebirth, and on the cycle of life and death, are based on insight and knowledge gained through enlightened meditation states and mystical states, and this knowledge is accessible to anyone engaging in the appropriate religious practices. One can argue that this knowledge is valid because it is replicable; anyone engaging in such meditations will have the same knowledge as the Buddha had. Indeed, this is exactly what the tradition claims: that subsequent meditators and mystics shared the same insights as the Buddha. Buddhists believe in the authority of mystical knowledge that is replicable and verifiable against another's experience, and that does not contradict reason. This is the basis of the theory of rebirth.

Types of research on rebirth

Children's testimony about past lives

The most respected researcher of children's testimonies about their past lives is Dr Ian Stevenson, who worked in the Division of Personality Studies at the University of Virginia in the USA. He documented hundreds of cases of young children who claimed to have memories of past lives, including names, locations, the specific way they died in their previous life, and intimate details about people they could not possibly have known in any other way. His methods were scientific, and it is hard to ignore the large amount of data he collected.

One case concerned a 5-year-old Indian boy named Parmod Sharma, who remembered specific details about a man named Parmanand and street directions in Parmanand's city. He visited the factory Parmanand owned and, despite being only five, gave directions for repairing complicated machinery.

Some sceptics are critical of this type of research because most cases occur in countries with a belief in reincarnation, so children might be predisposed to make up stories involving past lives. Nevertheless, there are documented cases of past-life memories of children, in the USA and Europe as well, in families with no belief in past lives. And we still need to explain the many accurate details in these children's accounts.

Birthmark matches

Several researchers have studied birthmarks as a possible source of evidence of past life connections. The size and location of a child's birthmark have been found in many cases to correspond to injuries sustained 'in a past life'. Where this evidence is strong, medical records including X-rays have confirmed the location and type of injury sustained. In the case of a Sri Lankan girl who remembered being hit and killed by a bus, the birthmark on her chest corresponded to the drawing of the injuries in the medical records of the deceased.

It has been argued that it is statistically improbable that such birthmarks are coincidences, given the precision of location and patterns. Birthmarks are convincing because they do not depend on any cultural beliefs in the family or on a child's imagination: they have an objective value. Nevertheless, sceptics maintain that such birthmarks are just a matter of chance.

Adult regression therapy

Some believe that memories that surface during hypnotherapy may offer evidence of a person's past life. Under hypnosis, adults have recounted details about past lives in other historical periods: as a foot soldier in the Middle Ages, or a middle eastern warrior, or a European peasant and so on. In one famous case, an American woman from Colorado remembered her life as a nineteenth-century woman from Cork in Ireland, and under hypnosis she spoke in an Irish dialect, sang Irish songs and remembered kissing the Blarney stone.

Some psychiatrists find the level of detail in these accounts persuasive, while critics claim that most of these so-called memories are merely wishful thinking. This type of evidence has not been researched as rigorously as children's memories and birthmarks, and because the past lives in question have usually taken place in the distant past the statements made under hypnosis cannot be verified as accurate. The evidential value of adult regression is therefore thin.

Near-death experiences

Near-death experiences (NDEs) are the most convincing type of evidence that there is some type of survival after death, particularly for those who have had the experience. An NDE occurs when a person has almost died and is later medically resuscitated. Such experiences occur relatively frequently these days after road accidents and complex medical interventions. In a US survey in Connecticut in 1993, as many as 70% of people who had had an NDE subsequently believed in reincarnation, even though many had no previous religious beliefs at all.

Experiences included floating out of the body, travelling down a tunnel and emerging in a world of light, meeting a radiant figure of light, and meeting people who were dead. Dr Kenneth Ring, a pioneer in this research field, was told by one of his subjects:

> My whole life went before me of things I have done and haven't done, but not just of this one lifetime, but of all the lifetimes. I know for a fact there is reincarnation. This is an absolute. I was shown all those lives and how I had overcome some of the things I had done in other lives. There was still some things to be corrected.
>
> Reported by A. Wells in the *Journal of Near-Death Studies* (1993)

Raymond Moody, another NDE researcher, reports another testimony:

> Now, my entire life through, I am thoroughly convinced that there is life after death, without a shadow of a doubt, and I am not afraid to die. I am not. Some people I have known are so afraid, so scared. I always smile to myself when I hear people doubt there is an afterlife, or say, 'When you're dead, you're gone'. I think to myself, 'They really don't know'.
>
> Raymond Moody, *Life After Life*

Many subjects say that the main purpose underlying rebirth is learning, or enlightenment. For example:

> We progress at our own rate to reach the light. If you do things that take you away from the light, then you are perpetuating your time here.
>
> Reported by A. Wells in the *Journal of Near-Death Studies* (1993)

Such descriptions mean that NDEs can be classified as a religious experience, and in particular as a noetic experience, that is, an experience giving certainty and new knowledge. The new knowledge derived from NDEs specifically concerns subjective certainty about rebirth.

Although the subjects' accounts might be considered persuasive, most scientific attempts at validation are inconclusive. For example, scientists have tried to demonstrate that there is *something* that leaves the body and that explains out-of-body experiences, but the problem is the impossibility of measuring the non-physical. Some critics claim that NDEs are an instance of dreaming, or a hallucination caused by lack of oxygen to the brain. But Dr Michael Sabom has been successful in carefully documenting reports from patients who suffered cardiac arrest and who accurately observed readings on medical machines which were out of their line of vision, thereby pointing to the possibility of visualisation far removed from the body. This research is verifiable and potentially reproducible; certain readings, for instance, can be timed and shown to have occurred when the patient was brain dead. So,

although there is no scientific consensus on the status of NDEs at present, their religious significance cannot be discounted.

Conclusion

Rebirth is an important part of the Buddhist view of the world and accounts for the different realms and types of existence in the universe (see Chapter 11). It plays a key role in the presentation of Buddhist ethics. Buddhists of different traditions put forward a number of rational and logical explanations for rebirth, covering topics such as the nature of what continues after death, the events that take place between one life and another, and the philosophical reasons justifying rebirth, based on the nature of the mind.

Some people consider that scientific research into related areas such as near-death experiences (NDEs) and past-life memories may strengthen the Buddhist case for rebirth, but others remain sceptical. Understanding rebirth may well be similar to understanding no-self (*anatta*) in the sense that logical explanations alone are usually not enough to convince us of such unfamiliar truths. Religious experience appears to be the main factor that brings complete personal conviction about rebirth: such experiences may take the form of NDEs, past-life memories or meditation experiences.

Questions

1 'Karma and rebirth are not acceptable ideas in a modern scientifically based world view.' How far do you agree with this statement?
2 Compare the Buddhist view of life after death with one or more Western views.
3 Analyse the philosophical concepts associated with belief in life after death in Buddhism, and evaluate the strengths and weaknesses of the belief.
4 Can you be a Buddhist without believing in rebirth?

Chapter 10

Karma and the causes of suffering

If you want to know your past life, look into your present condition; if you want to know your future life, look at your present actions.

Padmasambhava

The causes of suffering

It was in the second watch of the night as he was meditating under the bodhi tree, we learn, that the Buddha fully realised the laws that determine why each one of us has the life situation we have, and how the process of rebirth occurs. He developed a detailed and elaborate explanation of the law of karma on the basis of this insight.

Fundamentally, everyone wants to be happy, and Buddhism sees nothing wrong with that. On the contrary, it is quite natural that not only human beings but also animals have a strong wish to be happy. But if we are all looking for happiness, why is it that we suffer instead? This is the question addressed by the second Noble Truth, which is the truth of the causes of suffering. In that teaching the Buddha explains that our problem comes from the fact that we do not understand what happiness really is. We go for small happinesses — fleeting pleasures, momentary gratification — and so never find the lasting happiness that we seek deep down.

The Buddhist approach to this topic is quite different from the way most of us are brought up to think, whether we follow a religion or not. In Buddhism, the root causes of all our suffering are said to be not in anything or anyone else that is external to us, but in our own minds. These causes are called the Three Poisons of craving, aggression and delusion. They distort our understanding of true happiness and our ability to go about searching for happiness in an effective way. They cause us to act selfishly for our own benefit, but unfortunately this selfishness backfires. As the Dalai Lama puts it, if we want to be happy we

should at least be 'wisely selfish', and realise that happiness comes from altruism — being compassionate and kind. Since we are all connected with each other, it is impossible to be happy if we are surrounded by others who are suffering. The Indian poet Shantideva wrote:

> All the joy the world contains
> Has come through wishing happiness for others.
> All the misery the world contains
> Has come through wanting pleasure for oneself.

Shantideva, Bodhicharyavatara 8.129

The point of the Buddhist path is to train people's minds so they are less self-ish and more compassionate. At the moment our untrained minds are dominated by the Three Poisons, which influence our motivation to act, and as a result our actions will be unskilful. Bad or unskilful actions will produce suffering, either immediately or in the long term, and either for oneself only or for others as well. Good or skilful actions bring spiritual benefit both to oneself and to others and are rooted in a state of mind that is free from the Three Poisons.

Three Poisons ⟶ intentions ⟶ unskilful actions ⟶ suffering

Craving

The Pali word *tanha* means 'thirst', but is usually translated as 'craving'. The suggestion is that deep within our minds there is a strong greed or craving that manifests as an unquenchable thirst, and this is the main factor behind our suffering. The Buddha identifies three types of craving:

- the craving for objects of sense desire
- the craving for existence
- the craving for non-existence

We are all familiar with **craving for sense objects**: certain things give us pleasure, and our attachment to the experience of pleasure means we are never satisfied with just one experience but are constantly looking for more. Examples of sense objects are chocolate, alcohol, drugs, music and sex. The problem here is that all sense objects are unreliable sources of pleasure (or of happiness defined as pleasure) because the experience doesn't last and needs to be repeated endlessly. In fact, desire for sense objects tends to increase the more we indulge it, so we are never satisfied and look for more and more intense experiences. The sense objects themselves are unreliable — they can be taken away from us and are subject to change. It is a tragic irony that craving for sense objects leads to suffering, because by following a craving we imagine it will bring us the reverse — pleasure and contentment.

Craving for existence refers to the desire to be someone. Some of us want to be a particular kind of person with a particular image or a particular profession. Some people crave to be famous; in the far east especially, many people crave immortality. We therefore do things to bring about our goal, but even if we succeed we find that it is not what we imagined. Once you are famous, for example, you find you have a new set of problems you didn't have before — the attention of the press, fanatical admirers, people who want your money, and so on. Even if we become the person we crave to be, it will not last for ever; we will grow old, things will move on and what we have achieved may become meaningless.

Craving for non-existence means the opposite: wanting to be a nobody. We may experience this when we are depressed. As the saying goes, we wish we were dead; we wish we had never been born; we wish that we could somehow disappear so we would not have to interact with the world; we close up and hide in our shell. At an extreme, we may even consider committing suicide because we think that death is annihilation. It is clear that if we act upon our craving for non-existence it will probably produce harmful actions that will make us suffer far more.

Aggression

The poison of aggression or hatred includes types of emotion such as anger, jealousy, thirst for revenge and so on. Aggression can manifest as either 'hot' or 'cold': hot aggression could take the form of physically assaulting someone, while cold aggression might mean ignoring them. It is generally accepted in our society that aggressive actions do lead to suffering and tragedy. If we act on anger we will automatically set out to harm the other person either verbally or physically, and the effects of this will rebound on us in the form of retaliation, or police arrest, or feelings of guilt. Recent medical research has found that anger and aggression have a harmful effect on our health, increasing our blood pressure, for example.

The fundamental mistake we make by being aggressive is that we are putting the blame for our situation on someone else. Buddhism teaches that, instead of of putting blame on things outside ourselves, we should look inside ourselves. It's as though we think that aggression will relieve us of our pain; somehow, if we can lay the blame at someone else's door, our suffering will go away. From a Buddhist point of view, this is faulty logic.

Delusion or ignorance

The Pali word for delusion is *moha*, which means virtually the same as ignorance, *avijja* (Sanskrit *avidya*), and this refers specifically to not knowing how things really are. We do not know the true nature of things, and on top of

this we construct ideas of what we *think* the true nature of things is; when we start believing in our own ideas this is called delusion.

Ignorance is the root of the other two poisons of craving and aggression. For example, it is because we don't know what true happiness is that we follow our cravings. We don't understand what the true causes of suffering are and we become aggressive to others. But the key element of our delusion from the Buddhist point of view is the belief in the existence of a permanent self. It is because we believe that we exist as an unchanging individual that we defend ourselves through aggression or seek to gratify ourselves through pleasure. All Three Poisons working together produce self-centred thinking and selfish actions. When we are motivated by craving and aggression we only care about how *we* feel and don't stop to ask ourselves about the effects of our behaviour on others. This, then, is the mechanism that leads to suffering. When craving, aggression or ignorance produce the motivation to act, the result of our actions rebounds on us like a boomerang, and cause us pain and suffering.

Karma and the law of karma

The Indian word *karma* is now in the Oxford English Dictionary, which defines it as '(in Buddhism and Hinduism) the sum of a person's actions in one of his or her successive existences, thought to decide his or her fate for the next'. This is generally what Westerners understand by karma; that it is about the moral consequences of our actions, and that it determines our future. Although this is correct, it is imprecise.

This chapter examines the understanding of karma that is specific to Buddhism. The Pali word *kamma* and the Sanskrit word *karma* both mean 'action' or 'doing'. (We will use the Sanskrit word in this chapter because that is the term that has current usage in English.) In the Buddhist theory of karma, the word is given a more specific meaning and refers only to 'volitional action' or 'intentional action', in other words an action that is deliberately willed. This means that Buddhists distinguish between actions that are carried out with no clear intention — like getting out of bed, brushing your teeth, walking down the street and so forth — and actions that are motivated by the wish to achieve a particular goal. Only the latter kind, volitional actions, carry a moral consequence; other actions are morally neutral.

Many of us use the word 'karma' quite loosely to refer not just to actions but to the results of our actions. If someone is in a difficult situation, a friend might turn to him and say, 'It must be your karma.' But in Buddhism karma does not technically refer to the effect of our actions, which is known as the 'fruit' (*phala*) or 'result' of our karma.

In addition to using the word karma for volitional action, Buddhism speaks of 'the law of karma', and indeed it is the law of karma that this chapter is really about. We can define this as follows:

> The law of karma is the moral law of cause and effect related to intentional action.

There are a number of points to note in this definition. First, we are dealing with the *moral* nature of action and the moral consequences of action, not all consequences. For example, if I throw your favourite cup on the floor, the physical consequence of my action is that it breaks into pieces, but the moral consequence is something quite different. It might be that I acted out of anger or revenge, that I was deliberately trying to upset you. If so, according to Buddhism, the karmic result will come according to these intentions. You might fly into a rage and hit me, for example.

A second point to note is that the law of karma is a law of causation, a law that says that certain types of causes (actions) will bring about certain types of effects (karmic consequences). Here we are talking specifically about the laws of causation that govern moral actions, not about causation in general. Theravada philosophers identify five laws governing causation, called the five *niyamas* or 'natural laws'.

1 Physical laws operate in the natural environment, for example those that govern the weather, the way plants grow, or gravity.

2 Genetic laws govern heredity — 'as the seed, so the fruit'.

3 Laws govern the workings of the mind, the process of perception and knowledge, and the way we react to things.

4 Moral laws govern intentional actions (the law of karma).

5 The general law governs the relationship and interdependence of all things, and determines how everything arises, exists and then ceases.

The five *niyamas* make it clear that we cannot ascribe everything that happens to the law of karma in a simplistic way. Several different types of law can operate together in any given situation. So, for instance, if we go out in winter without a coat and catch a chill, we could explain this by reference to physical laws about the effect of temperatures on our bodies; we could explain it in terms of genetic laws, because we happen to have inherited from our mother a chronic weakness of the chest; and we could also ascribe it to our own mindlessness, acting thoughtlessly without taking care of ourselves, which means we acted out of ignorance.

Volitional actions are classified as good and bad, and the general rule is that good actions produce good results and bad actions produce bad results. The big question is: what do Buddhists consider a 'good' action and what do they consider a 'bad' action?

What makes an action good or bad?

There are two factors that determine whether an action is good or bad. The first is the intention behind the action, and the second is the type of result it produces. Intention is always the main factor in the Buddhist theory of karma, since even the result produced depends on intention. The Buddha said:

> It is will (*cetana*), O monks, that I call karma; having willed, one acts through body, speech and mind.

For example, we need to distinguish between the act of killing and the intention to kill. If you kill someone even by accident this is not considered a good action, but the moral consequences of the action are not the same as if you had deliberately set out to murder the person. A traditional example of this is the story about cutting a pumpkin. One day you are in the kitchen with your mother and you are making pumpkin pie. Pumpkins can be enormous things, so you are using a large knife to cut yours into segments. Unfortunately, your knife slips while your mother happens to be standing close by and the knife goes into her stomach and kills her. What is the karmic consequence of such a tragedy? The basic principle is that you will not be subjected to the karmic result of the act of killing because it was not your intention to kill; you will nevertheless suffer from the karmic result of a mindless action because you failed to take care and control your movement.

A modern example that can affect us all is a car accident. You approach a crossroads; it's foggy and you can't see very clearly. On top of this you are tired and not concentrating. Suddenly, out of the blue it seems, you find yourself in a collision and discover that you have killed the driver of the other car.

If the law of karma is about intentions, what makes intentions good or bad? The Buddhist answer is that it depends on whether, and to what extent, a person's intention is governed by one or more of the Three Poisons of craving, aggression and ignorance. The more one's mind is subject to these, the more morally harmful one's actions will be, and similarly the less one's mind is governed by these poisons, and the more one cultivates their opposites of generosity, kindness and wisdom, the more one will be able to act in a way that is beneficial for others as well as oneself. From this we can see just how important meditation is for ethical behaviour, because meditation is a way of taming our negative emotions and clearing our minds, which in turn leads to more ethical action.

When we consider an action's effects, a good action is called *kusala*, meaning 'skilful' or 'wholesome', while a harmful action is called *akusala*, meaning 'unskilful' or 'unwholesome'. Skilful actions uplift the mental state of the doer,

others involved, or both. Unskilful actions, on the other hand, go against intuitive wisdom, cause distress and are detrimental to the actor's spiritual progress. Generally speaking, the harm caused by unskilful actions refers to spiritual harm rather than physical harm.

One of the implications of the Buddhist approach to moral action is that actions are never black or white, they are different shades of grey. We all have some negative emotions and some positive emotions, so neither our motivations nor our actions will ever be absolutely good or absolutely bad. Goodness and badness are relative to our minds and to our situations. The law of karma functions in accordance with all these various factors and is not some rigid law of fate.

This ties in, of course, with the fact that Buddhism does not accept the existence of God or the Devil, personifying absolute good and evil respectively. Buddhists do not believe in the ontological existence of moral absolutes, in other words, they do not believe that these have a real and independent existence as entities. This is why Buddhists do not use the term 'evil' at all because it has a connotation of being absolutely and irredeemably bad. The goodness and badness of people is a function of their craving and aggression, their misunderstanding of how things work and of who they really are, and the conditioning that has shaped their lives. Nobody is intrinsically evil. If all these factors can be changed and eventually eliminated, we can attain nirvana and be free from karma altogether, both from the effects of previous actions and from producing more karmic results for the future.

How the law of karma works

Some Buddhist philosophers, such as the Indian scholar Vasubandhu, argue that both intention and action have karmic effects. They say that each one of the three parts of an action, the intention, action and result, has the power to produce its own associated karmic effects. The most powerful karma will be generated if we have the intention to do something, if we do it, and if we achieve the result we wanted. However, the karmic consequences of an action, whether good or bad, will be less powerful if only two or three of these factors come into play.

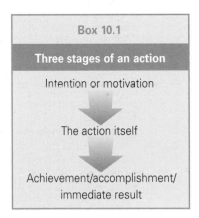

Box 10.1

Three stages of an action

Intention or motivation

The action itself

Achievement/accomplishment/
immediate result

Imagine the case of someone who wants to burgle your house. Scenario 1 is that the person intends to steal, is experienced and skilled in doing so, and manages to break in and take your things, then succeeds in running off

without being caught. He or she feels really pleased at having pulled it off. This would produce the maximum karmic effect for an act of stealing. In scenario 2, the person intends to steal from you but something goes wrong. They can't manage to break the window or get through the door, so the mission is aborted and they go home disappointed and empty-handed. In this case they produce the karmic results of the intention to steal, and also the results of being disappointed that they didn't manage to steal, but they have not produced the karmic effect of stealing itself. In scenario 3, the person intends to steal from you and succeeds in doing so, but back home, looking at all the things he or she has stolen, feels a strong sense of guilt and regret. In this case, he or she does not have the karmic effect produced by satisfaction in accomplishing the action.

What form do karmic effects take?

Buddhists claim that karmic results affect us either mentally, physically or both. In the case of a bad action, for instance, the effects might be as follows:

- Mentally, we might experience certain life situations as painful and difficult and full of suffering. This could explain why some people find situations such as poverty, illness or rejection hard to take, while other people don't have the same reaction.
- We might develop bad mental habits and tendencies. For example, if we succeed in stealing once, it is easier to steal a second time, and this can lead us to develop a propensity to steal.
- Physically we might experience our external environment as difficult, or our body might be prone to illness.

We can relate these points to the fourth aggregate (*khandha*) of personality, mental formations, which, as explained in Chapter 8, includes karma. The principle of this fourth aggregate is that the karmic consequences of our actions shape our character and mindset and so indirectly become causes of future karmic actions in an endless chain of cause and effect. Karmic effects colour the way we experience the world as well as the way we relate to ourselves.

According to the Buddhist scriptures, certain actions cause particular karmic effects. For example meanness leads to being poor, injuring others leads to frequent or chronic illness, and anger leads to being ugly. On the positive side, patience leads to being attractive, generosity leads to prosperity, and saving lives leads to having a long life. In general there are four types of karmic effect.

1 **The fully ripened effect** or maximum effect of an action. For example, an action motivated by hatred will cause rebirth in the hells.

2 **The effect similar to the cause.** For example, if we are often criticised, belittled or lied to by others, this is the result of lying in the past. If we have

spoken harsh words in the past, everything that is said to us seems offensive or insulting, and whatever we say provokes an argument.

3 **The conditioning effect** acts on our environment. For example stealing may cause rebirth in areas stricken by famine.

4 **The proliferation effect** refers to the way that whatever action we did before we will tend to repeat again and again. It will become a habit.

Buddhist texts contain many examples of karmic effects. For instance, once there was a beggar who was lying in the gateway of a royal palace thinking, 'I wish that the king would have his head cut off and I could take his place!' This thought went round and round in his head all night long. Towards morning he fell asleep and while he was sleeping the king drove out in his carriage. One of the wheels rolled over the beggar's neck and cut off his head. This story illustrates an effect similar to the cause.

What is the time frame for karmic results?

The time that elapses between an action and its karmic effects can vary considerably. A karmic result might be immediate, or it might come in the medium term or in the long term. Karmic effects can come either in this present life or in the next life or in later future lives. For this reason it is almost impossible for us to know what the precise karmic effects of our actions will be; if they occur much later on when the original action is forgotten, we shall not know how to make the link back to their cause.

Sceptics might argue that this seriously weakens the Buddhist theory of karma, because we don't have any clear proof that actions produce moral consequences at all. But such an absence of clear proof does not in itself disprove the theory of karma. The Buddha uses analogies to make this point: 'Bad karma is like freshly squeezed milk…it takes time to sour.'

The idea that karmic effects do not necessarily follow on immediately from the actions that produce them creates a philosophical problem: how can we account for the causal link between two distant events? How can we explain the connection between an action carried out in, say, 1990 and its moral consequence, which does not happen until 2020? The reason this is problematic is because in Buddhist logic, as we saw in Chapter 8, a cause must *immediately* precede its effect; a cause occurs in the very moment preceding the existence of its effect in a long chain of causal moments. So how do Buddhists solve this question?

Their solution is to explain that the immediate karmic consequence of an action is to plant a 'karmic seed' (*bija*) or imprint in the mind of the actor. This imprint can either ripen very quickly and bear its fruit soon afterwards, or it can lie dormant for an indeterminate period of time until circumstances create the

right opportunity for it to ripen and bear its effects. These karmic imprints are present in the mind as a continuous chain of moments and, crucially, they are carried by the subtle consciousness after death from one life to the next. This accounts for the way karmic results can occur many lifetimes after the event.

Reward and punishment, fairness and justice

The law of karma is seen as a natural law inherent in the nature of things, just like physical laws, genetic laws and so on. Karma is not operated by God or any other supreme being, because for Buddhists natural laws do not require any supernatural intervention in order to function. Most of us accept that the law of gravity operates as a natural part of the physical world and that, for example, God doesn't have to intervene every time an apple falls to the ground. Karma is just the same; good actions produce good results and bad actions produce bad results naturally, without any outside intervention.

This means that the results of karma are not described by Buddhists as forms of 'reward' or 'punishment', because the idea of reward and punishment depends on a belief in a supreme power sitting in judgement on us and sharing out good and bad experiences in accordance with that judgement. In Buddhism, there is nobody to judge us, there is nobody to decide our future. We determine our future by the way we act and the way we think. We have nobody to blame but ourselves for any unfortunate karmic results that we may suffer. The first verse of the *Dhammapada* expresses this clearly.

> Our life is shaped by our mind; we become what we think. Suffering follows an evil thought as the wheels of a cart follow the oxen that draw it. Our life is shaped by our mind; we become what we think. Joy follows a pure thought like a shadow that never leaves.

Dhammapada 1–2

Many people react against the Buddhist understanding of karma because they feel it is unfair and unjust. A few years ago, Glen Hoddle, the former England football manager, let slip to the press his belief that physical disability might be the result of negative actions in a past life. This idea was considered politically unacceptable and was strongly rejected in the media. Why? Because most people feel it is unfair to blame disabled people for their condition; they assume that, whatever their predicament, disabled people are innocent victims of life and cannot be held responsible for their situation. This is, of course, very different from the Buddhist approach, which teaches that each one of us is largely responsible for our life situation. The five *niyamas* are a way of saying that no situation can be explained solely in terms of physical or genetic factors

— which presumably is the way that disability would be explained by general consensus — and that there might also be moral factors at work.

For a Buddhist, whenever karmic results catch up with someone, this cannot be seen as unfair or unjust. The results of karma appear because of certain laws and none of us can change those laws. When an apple falls to the ground because of gravity and is bruised, do we consider it unfair that the apple gets bruised? No; that's just how it is. Likewise, if I suffer because I have harmed someone deliberately, that is just how it is. There is nobody we can complain to. The Dharma is there to point out the actions we should avoid so that we don't have to suffer. At the same time, the Buddhist response to another person's suffering is not a gloating 'they deserved it', but a compassionate 'unfortunately this is the result of a harmful action'.

It is important to understand that karma is considered a universal law that applies to every human being, whether or not they are Buddhist. Karmic results do not depend on which religion we follow, or on whether we follow a religion at all. Nor do karmic results depend on whether or not we believe in the law of karma. Karma works whether we believe in it or not, according to our motivations, and anybody of any faith can have good intentions or bad intentions. From a Buddhist point of view, all the world religions encourage their followers to cultivate virtuous behaviour. If one does a good deed as a Christian or a Muslim, the karmic effect will be no different from an identical motivation and deed on the part of a Buddhist.

Fate and freedom

The other common misunderstanding about karma, which is part of its Oxford English Dictionary definition, is that the law of karma is basically a law of fate. This is not the case in Buddhism. The idea of fate implies determinism; the belief that the future is determined by the past in a rigid way that allows for no changes, exceptions or freedom. In a theistic religion the idea of fate might also refer to a decision that God takes about your future, and which you are powerless to influence. As we saw in Chapter 2, the Buddha rejected fatalism because it allows for no individual freedom and therefore undermines the very existence of morality. The law of karma is never presented as deterministic.

It is true that a particular karmic action will inevitably produce its associated karmic consequence if left unchecked, but the crucial point is that there are ways we can intervene and change the course of our future. As Buddhist masters put it, 'the future is in our hands'. We can divide the methods used into three groups:

1 **Methods to purify past harmful actions before their effects fully ripen.** Buddhism offers a number of ways to purify our past karma, and each Buddhist tradition lays special emphasis on one or another of these ways. The practice of meditation and mindfulness helps us to become aware of our thoughts and mental habits, and in that process they can dissolve. The practice of loving kindness and compassion enables us to transform judgemental, aggressive or jealous thoughts into wholesome ones. The practice of confession (usually to peers) is a way of coming to terms with past misdeeds. Regret and the resolve not to act in a harmful way again are also considered important for purifying karma. Finally, Vajrayana Buddhism employs visualisation and mantra as a powerful practice of healing and transforming negativity.

2 **Methods to create a wholesome future by changing our behaviour now and acting ethically.** Ethical conduct outlined in the Eightfold Path and the *Bodhisattva* Path provides the guidelines for moral behaviour. By following these guidelines, one accumulates virtue or 'merit' (*puñña*), that is, the positive energy that will give rise to favourable circumstances in the future. Sometimes Buddhists engage in deliberate acts of charity or kindness (generously giving to monks, for instance, or freeing animals being sent for slaughter) and these acts serve as an antidote to negative actions committed in the past.

3 **Prayers when a loved one dies that are especially directed at purifying his or her karma.** The moment of death is critical for a Buddhist, because it is at that juncture that one's rebirth is determined by one's past karma. Buddhist rites for the dead involve transferring any merit one may have accumulated to the deceased person to enable a more favourable rebirth. When a parent dies, some Buddhists will do a short retreat or go on pilgrimage as a deliberate way of accumulating merit that is then directed to the deceased through prayer.

There are striking examples in the scriptures of individuals of doubtful moral character who regret their bad actions and change completely. One such story is that of Angulimala, the mass murderer converted by the Buddha (Chapter 1); another is the conversion of Emperor Ashoka (Chapter 3). These stories illustrate that we are not necessarily a slave to our past; we can change our future if we wish to do so strongly enough. They show that nobody should ever be judged on their actions alone, because each of us has the ability to change.

> One who previously made bad karma but who reforms and creates good karma brightens the world like the moon appearing from behind a cloud.
>
> *Dhammapada* 173

10

This discussion implies that if Buddhism seeks to defend the possibility of moral action, it must believe in some form of freedom. However, it is difficult to say that Buddhism accepts free will in the sense that this is understood in Western ethics. If we take free will to mean an inherent (God-given) freedom of the mind to make moral judgements, then Buddhism does not accept this because it considers the mind to be conditioned. Just like everything else in the world, my mind is produced by causes and conditions, and in particular is conditioned by society, education, life experience, past karma and so forth, as well as the functioning of my body. I would be deluding myself if I imagined that I was really free to make all the choices that present themselves to me in life. From a Buddhist point of view mental freedom is certainly possible, but it is difficult to achieve. Walpola Rahula puts it this way:

> Mind is only a faculty or organ like the eye or the ear. It can be controlled and developed like any other faculty.
>
> Walpola Rahula, *What the Buddha Taught*

This is arguably the key to understanding the entire theory of karma. If the mind functions just like any other sense organ, and is dependent on numerous factors to exist and to operate, then it is justified to say that the intentions it produces are subject to natural laws just as other senses are subject to natural laws. And surely it is because many other philosophies and religions consider mind (or spirit) to be an ontological principle radically opposed to matter, and irreducible to matter, that they address morality quite differently. Such non-Buddhist views might hold, for example, that laws of causation apply only to matter and that the mind, being of a radically different nature, is not subject to them; this is one definition of freedom. On the other hand, non-Buddhist materialist views might hold that there is no such thing as mind, defined as a different entity from matter, and that mental freedom and morality are impossible to explain. Furthermore, the ontologies of other religions and some other philosophies allow for God-given moral values which human beings simply need to know and follow; what is good and bad is already laid down for us. This, too, is quite different from Buddhism, where no absolute values exist as such in a metaphysical dimension.

In Buddhism, freedom of mind only comes when we are free from the Three Poisons; that is what 'liberation' means. Until then our thoughts and emotions operate primarily at the mercy of the Three Poisons. Freedom from them is the point of attaining nirvana or enlightenment, and liberating ourselves from suffering and the causes of suffering. Until we have reached nirvana, freedom is only ever relative and occasional; different people have different degrees of freedom according to the extent to which they are able to tame their minds.

Within the human world, moral freedom is not absolute but relative. Only a buddha is totally free.

Is karma a matter of faith?

The Buddhist theory of karma is hard to accept because it lays such tremendous responsibility on our own shoulders. It is up to us to work on ourselves, transform our minds and improve our behaviour so that we create favourable conditions for ourselves and others and so that ultimately we become free of the cycle of suffering altogether. The Buddha is not like a catapult that can miraculously propel us to a heavenly realm or to enlightenment; we have to do the hard work ourselves.

Buddhism is doubly hard to accept if we consider that we might be suffering today from the results of an action in a past life which we are not aware of. Whether or not this is the case, Buddhism encourages an attitude of acceptance and patience in the face of difficulties, not in a weak or passive way but in a constructive way, because the manner in which we react to each situation will itself generate new karmic consequences and we might as well do our best to ensure they are good ones. For example, if I blame you for the trouble I am in and then decide to take it out on you, whether or not you played a part in the situation, my negative reaction will only bring about more suffering for me in the future. The Buddhist approach is therefore not sympathetic to a 'compensation culture'. Buddhists take the long-term view.

If we find the law of karma hard to swallow we will want to have some evidence for it. Why should we believe in karma? What proof is there for karma? Surely everyone gets away with bad actions some of the time. There are many nasty people who seem to have quite a comfortable life and who might even be popular; it does not seem that *they* are suffering from the consequences of their actions. And, similarly, there are many good and kind people who have a hard time, have accidents, become ill and seem to be innocent victims of circumstance. So we can argue that life situations tend to disprove the theory of karma rather than the reverse.

Buddhists would have to accept these arguments and their only justification for the theory of karma would be that the consequences of actions occur over time, and sometimes over several lifetimes. So although your nasty neighbour seems to be successful now, from a Buddhist point of view he or she is bound to suffer for those bad actions some time in the future. The problem with this logic, of course, is that none of us knows what our future will be and therefore we have no evidence that this is true. As we get older, however, we can perhaps look back on life and see that people's fortunes do change. Rich people can end

up poor, poor people can become rich, presidents can be deposed and cast out as beggars. The Buddha said:

> A fool is happy until his mischief turns against him.
> And a good man may suffer until his goodness flowers.
>
> *Dhammapada* 119

The Buddha only understood the law of karma immediately before he attained full enlightenment. He acknowledged that only an enlightened buddha fully understands how karma works. So, although theoretically we can all grasp the law of karma, in practice this is only possible when we reach enlightenment, and until then karma is, at least partly, a matter of faith.

Buddhists would argue that karma is acceptable not just as a matter of faith but also on the basis of logical reasoning. Isn't it reasonable to explain certain situations with reference to karma, especially when they involve the suffering of apparently innocent and good-hearted people? Such situations are impossible to explain rationally in any other way; religious explanations defer to the will of God, which cannot be fathomed by human beings, so this is not a reasoned response. It could therefore be argued that karma is the best explanation of suffering that we have. Furthermore, we do sometimes experience the moral consequences of our actions for ourselves — when we feel bad or guilty about something we have done, for example, our peace of mind is taken away. So, even within the limits of our present life, it is possible to validate the general idea of karmic consequences through experience.

Summary of main points

- 'Karma' means 'action', and the law of karma is the law of cause and effect which applies to intentional actions.
- Good actions produce happiness and bad actions produce suffering for the person doing the action.
- Bad or harmful actions are motivated by craving, aggression or ignorance. They are selfish or self-centred actions.
- Good actions arise from generosity, kindness and wisdom, and benefit all concerned.
- In Buddhism, the intention is more important in determining a karmic result than the action itself.
- Karmic results may take place at any time in the future and even in future lives.
- The law of karma means that each human being is responsible for his or her own situation; there is no God who judges us — karma is a natural law.

• Freedom to make moral choices is relative and depends on the degree to which we can free our minds from craving, aggression and ignorance.

Questions

1 Explain the relationship between karma and rebirth (see also Chapter 9).

2 Explain what Buddhists believe about karma.

3 'Buddhists believe that each person is responsible for his or her own suffering, so there is no need to take pity on the less fortunate.' Do you agree with this claim?

4 'The belief in karma and rebirth means that for Buddhists evil and suffering do not present a philosophical problem.' Discuss.

Chapter 11

Samsara and nirvana

Religions always point to the relationship of the mortal, or the conditioned, with the unconditioned. That is, if you strip any religion down to its very basic essence, you will find that it is pointing to where the mortal — the conditioned and time-bound — ceases. In that cessation is the realization and the understanding of the unconditioned.

Ajahn Sumedho, *The Mind and the Way*

The Buddhist world view

Buddhists see the world differently from the way we do in the modern West. The world we consider to be real is the world of our sense experience — what we can touch, hear, smell, taste and see either directly or through the use of scientific instruments such as telescopes or microscopes. If we can't perceive something in such a way, we conclude that it doesn't exist. It must simply stem from the imagination, from hallucination or from delusion.

The world view of all Indian religions is vaster than this because it is not centred on human beings and what human beings know or don't know. It presents us with a picture of an infinite cosmos with countless world systems, each containing many different forms of life. This means that for Buddhists the world is not limited to the type of beings we are familiar with, such as other human beings and animals, but also contains forms of life that we cannot perceive with our normal senses. Buddhists believe that some types of being exist without a physical body, for example.

Buddhists do not merely describe this immense universe and all its inhabitants, they also explain why different beings are born in a particular realm and have particular characteristics. This explanation is possible because of a correlation between our mental state and the world we live in. Rupert Gethin calls

this 'the principle of the equivalence of cosmology and psychology'. The universe is a map not just of different realms of existence but also of every type of possible experience. It is karma and rebirth that enable this to function, so that each being is reborn into a particular situation according to his or her karma and its corresponding mental disposition.

The Buddhist world-view recognises two distinct types of existence called samsara and nirvana. Samsara refers to 'the cycle of conditioned existence', also called 'the round of rebirth', where all beings are subject to birth and death and where life is characterised by suffering (*dukkha*). Nirvana is the opposite of this: it is an existence where suffering is completely eliminated and which is characterised by peace. For Buddhists, there are enlightened beings in the world who are not subject to conditioned existence — buddhas and advanced *bodhisattvas*, for example.

When the Buddha taught the first Noble Truth (*dukkha*), he was making people aware of the nature of samsara, and of the way that suffering pervades our life. When the Buddha taught the third Noble Truth (cessation), he explained that this suffering can be brought to an end and that true peace and happiness are possible. In fact, the whole purpose of Buddhism is to free us from samsara and enable us to attain nirvana. This is what Buddhism is all about: a buddha is, by definition, someone who has gone beyond the cycle of life and death and who is free from suffering.

This last point is crucial in understanding the way Buddhists have developed their world view. It is only because the Buddha became enlightened and was free of samsara that he was able to comprehend it fully. When we are immersed in samsara we are unable to see it for what it is because we ourselves are part of the problem. It is only when we are outside the cycle of life and death that we have sufficient perspective to be able to see samsara as a whole.

The Buddhist framework of samsara and nirvana arises directly from the enlightened understanding of the Buddha, and cannot be fathomed completely by the ordinary human mind. The cosmos as a whole is beyond the limitations of human understanding; if we don't know certain things about it, this could be because we *can't* know them as long as we are limited by our senses and our defiled human mind. Buddhists, therefore, would not say that if we can't perceive something it doesn't exist; instead, they might say that the limitations of our minds prevent us from being able to say for certain whether it exists or not. The only way out of this impasse is to transform our minds and deepen our understanding.

In this chapter we examine how samsara and nirvana are described in the Buddhist scriptures, and how they are understood in relation to each other. First, we will look at the basic Buddhist understanding that is common to all Buddhist

traditions, and, second, we will examine the points on which Mahayana Buddhists have a different view.

Samsara

The image that is often used to describe samsara is that of an ocean: many Buddhist scriptures and prayers talk about 'the ocean of samsara', or 'the ocean of suffering'. The process of freeing ourselves from this is often called 'crossing the ocean of existence', which means crossing over from the near shore (of samsara), which is fraught with dangers of all kinds, and reaching the far shore (of nirvana), which is safe and free from danger.

The Sanskrit word samsara literally means 'wandering on', which conveys the idea of a process that is long and aimless. We 'wander' endlessly from life to life, and from rebirth to rebirth, trying to find a permanent home where we can feel at ease and secure and experience lasting happiness. However, because we are all bound to die sooner or later, whatever kind of existence we have will not bring us the security we are looking for, and we will then be reborn somewhere else.

We can also relate samsara to the quality of experience we have when we feel that life is pointless. Sometimes we just see our life as a routine, we might feel like cogs in a wheel or trapped on an endless treadmill. We think that life is meaningless, that all our efforts are like running on the same spot, getting nowhere. Somehow we want to break out of our situation, out of our own personality even, yet we don't know how. At such times we experience the nature of samsaric existence and have a taste of the third type of suffering presented in the first Noble Truth, the suffering of conditioned existence.

The Buddha taught that as long as we remain in samsara our search for happiness is futile because we have not understood why we suffer and what happiness depends upon. In the second Noble Truth he explained that the factors that produce suffering are mental defilements like ignorance, craving and aggression, while the factors that bring about happiness are the opposites of these, that is, positive emotions based on love and compassion that lead to virtuous actions. Rather than looking for happiness in external life situations, we should look at our own minds and transform our harmful tendencies.

The six realms of rebirth

There are people who do not understand suffering. They do not know where it comes from, where it totally ceases, or how to get to where it totally ceases. So without a chance to free the mind or achieve liberation through knowledge, they cannot bring suffering to an end. They can only go on and on, being born and getting old.

The Buddha, *Sutta Nipata*

Although many people in the West do not reject the general idea of rebirth out of hand, some find it more difficult to accept the Buddhist theory that there are six different realms of existence into which beings are reborn, and that according to our karma we can be reborn into any one of them at any given time. This is hard to accept because it means that we will not necessarily 'come back' as a human being; we might be reborn as a cow, or a slug, or a god, or even, in very unfortunate circumstances, as a being in the hells. This is not a pleasant thought, nor is it something we can readily imagine.

The six realms of conditioned existence are the realms of:

- the gods
- the demi-gods
- human beings
- animals
- hungry ghosts
- the hells

Each realm has unique characteristics (see Table 11.1), and our rebirth there results from particularly strong karmic actions. Anger and aggression, for example, are the main cause of rebirth in the hell realm, while desire is said to be the main cause of being born a human being.

The **god realms** are heavenly realms characterised by all things pleasant, beautiful and satisfying. In the **realm of the demi-gods** or *asuras*, beings are prone to conflict and fighting; they are never satisfied and always want what the gods have. The **human realm** is the world that we experience as human beings. The dominant karmic cause of being reborn in this realm is desire. In the **realm of animals**, beings live in constant fear of their lives. Some are subject to the suffering of being used as draught animals by human beings. In the **realm of hungry ghosts** or *pretas*, the hungry ghosts are never satisfied, but when they try to eat they have difficulty swallowing their food on account of their tiny throats. When their food does reach their stomachs it produces a burning sensation and turns to vomit. The **hell realms** are where suffering is at its most intense and relentless. There are several types of hells, some characterised by extreme heat, others by extreme cold. Beings here suffer many different types of physical, emotional and mental torture and never have a moment of respite. However, beings in the hells will eventually be reborn elsewhere in the samsaric cycle when their bad karma is exhausted.

How are the six realms to be understood? There are two different approaches in the scriptures.

1 The realms are understood as different places. We could imagine that the six realms can be found on different planets, in different solar systems and different universes. They might be different dimensions of being, so that the beings in certain realms might not have tangible bodies and, even if they were present on earth, we would not see them.

2 The six realms are understood as states of mind, and therefore as psychological worlds. A human being could live in any one of these psychological realms and might go through several realms in the course of a lifetime. The gods might correspond to people who have everything to make them happy and who live in a 'perfect' bubble; hungry ghosts might be people who are never satisfied, who have a strong sense of lack and, at an extreme, those suffering from famine or malnutrition. Some people's lives seem to be a series of 'nightmares' entailing intense physical and emotional pain, and these people will say that 'life is hell'.

Table 11.1 The six realms of conditioned existence

Realm	Characteristics	Dominant karmic cause
Gods	Beautiful palaces and gardens, music, silks, perfumes and beautiful goddesses; the gods are absorbed in bliss, have very long lives but suffer tremendously when their life comes to an end.	Pride
Demi-gods or *asuras*	Constantly wage war on the gods. The tree of long life has its roots in this realm but its branches and fruit are in the god realm; the demi-gods constantly fight to obtain the fruit they think should be theirs. It's a losing battle.	Jealousy, envy
Humans	Eight forms of misery: birth, illness, old age, death, separation from loved ones, meeting those we don't like, not having what we covet, fear of losing our possessions. Despite this, the human realm is the most fortunate of all realms because wisdom and compassion can be developed and enlightenment is possible.	Desire
Animals	Four categories: with many legs (insects), four legs (mammals), two legs (apes and birds) and no legs (fish and snakes). Most animals live in the ocean. Animals suffer from hunger and thirst, heat and cold, human abuse and hunting, destruction of their habitat and being eaten by carnivores.	Ignorance, delusion
Hungry ghosts or pretas	Some pretas have long thin necks and swollen bellies and are unable to swallow their food; some breathe, excrete and urinate streams of fire. Food and water turn to pus and vomit. They live in a barren landscape and suffer constantly from hunger, thirst, heat, cold and seeing mirages.	Greed, insatiable craving, miserliness
Hells	There are eight hot hells, eight cold hells, and two auxiliary hells. They are said to be located deep inside the earth. Beings are tortured by extreme heat or cold, by fire, molten iron or by having their bodies sawn, crushed, impaled or devoured.	Aggression, anger, hatred

Seeing the six realms as psychological states rather than physical places does not make them any less real. The Buddhist understanding is that our mental states cause us to see any given situation in particular ways and that they therefore determine how we experience life. As the *Dhammapada* says, 'Our life is shaped by our mind; we become what we think.' Buddhism does not claim that our minds create our physical world, but, rather, that they create the world of our experience. Whatever our experience is, it will feel completely real to us.

If the six realms can be mental states, it is easier to understand how we are reborn into one of them according to our thoughts and actions in previous lives. The link between one life and the next is a mental one, so it is logical to say that when we are reborn our particular psychological outlook is produced from mental tendencies in previous lives. This is how Buddhists understand the functioning of the Wheel of Life.

Life in some realms is said to be extraordinarily long — for instance, one day in certain god realms is equivalent to 50 human years. We are not speaking of some objective measure of time, but rather of how long things feel subjectively; the more intense our experiences, the longer they seem to last. None of these six realms is eternal, and beings transmigrate according to their karma until such time as they free themselves from karma altogether. Even the gods are still trapped within the cycle of life and death. Contrary to the heaven and hell of Jewish, Christian and Muslim belief, the heavens and hells understood by Buddhism are not eternal.

It is important not to confuse the gods living in the god realm with the idea of God in monotheism. Buddhism accepts the existence of many gods but not the one creator God. The gods are beings who have practised advanced meditation in previous lives and have considerable mental power; some can influence circumstances in the human world. But the gods have not transcended life and death, cause and effect, and the law of karma; when the karma for life in the god realm is exhausted they are reborn into one of the other six realms.

The Wheel of Life

Buddhists depict samsara as a large wheel called the Wheel of Life (see Figure 11.1) This is entirely symbolic and brings together all the different factors that define and characterise the cycle of conditioned existence.

- **The hub of the wheel.** At the centre of the wheel are three animals representing the Three Poisons. The pig symbolises ignorance; the cock symbolises craving; and the snake symbolises aggression. These lie at the heart of the mechanism that makes the cycle of rebirth go round. It is the Three Poisons that perpetuate our existence in samsara.

Figure 11.1 The Wheel of Life

Buddhism

- **The first circle.** The first circle shows various ghost-like beings feeling their way towards their next rebirth. The idea is that, depending on our past karma, we will find our way to an appropriate rebirth. The beings in this circle are in the *bardo* state between one life and the next in accordance with the views of Tibetan Buddhism (see Chapter 9).
- **The second and widest circle: the six realms of samsara.** This circle depicts the six realms into which beings in samsara may be reborn. There are three higher realms (gods, humans, demi-gods), in which suffering is less intense, and three lower realms (hells, animals, hungry ghosts), where suffering is intense and a major hindrance to spiritual progress.
- **The outer rim of the wheel.** Around the rim of the wheel we find the Twelve Nidanas, known as the Twelve Links, or the Twelve Links of Dependent Arising. These are a pictorial way of presenting the chain of causes and effects through which samsara is continually recreated (see Table 11.2). They can be interpreted in two ways:
  - as the chain of causes which links one life to the next. In this case the first two links relate to the past life; links 3–9 relate to the present life; and links 10–12 relate to the future life
  - as the chain of causes which operates in every moment of our life, linking our intentions, our actions and their results

The Twelve Nidanas can either be shown as a circle or as a list, but the important point is that they operate as an endless cycle, with the twelfth link leading

Table 11.2 The Twelve Links of Dependent Arising

Each link leads to the next

Link (Nidana)	Symbol in Wheel of Life
1 **Ignorance** (of the nature of life as analysed in the Four Noble Truths)	Blind man
2 **Karma-formations** (impulses or tendencies resulting from actions or thoughts)	Potter
3 **Consciousness** (which continues from one life to the next)	Monkey in a tree
4 **Name and form** (the five skandhas including the consciousness of the present life)	Boat and four passengers
5 **The six senses** (sight, hearing, touch, smell, taste and mind)	House with six openings
6 **Contact** (with the objects of the senses)	Man and woman embracing
7 **Feeling** (pleasant, unpleasant or neutral)	Man with arrow in his eye
8 **Craving** (for experience, for life or for oblivion)	Man takes drink from woman
9 **Grasping** (at life, sense pleasures, etc.)	Man picking fruit
10 **Becoming** (process of creating situations and then living them)	Pregnant woman
11 **Rebirth**	Childbirth
12 **Suffering, decay and death**	Corpse

to the first one so that the cycle starts all over again. There is no first cause in this cycle: the first link (ignorance) is not seen as the first cause, which sets the wheel in motion, because ignorance itself is produced from causes. It is therefore clearer to depict the links in a circle.

The Twelve Nidanas illustrate the vicious cycle of samsara, where nothing happens by random chance but everything comes about from one or several causes. In practice, this means that when our existence is entirely determined by these causes we have little or no freedom. For example, our choices will be determined by karmic tendencies, cravings and so on, and will not be made freely. So can we ever break out of the circle? Yes; there are two weak links in the chain, namely craving and ignorance. By tackling one or both of these (through cultivating discipline and meditation, for example), we will weaken these links still further and help to break the chain. The effect of long-term spiritual practice is to break this chain down completely.

- **Yama, the lord of death.** The whole Wheel of Life sits in the arms of a monster called Yama, who symbolises death. This illustrates the fact that all the beings who exist within the wheel are subject to death.

How does the Wheel of Life work in practice? The process it depicts means that any being can be reborn in any one of the six realms, depending on karma. This means that we will not necessarily be reborn as human beings next time.

Of all these six realms the human realm is considered the most fortunate because it is the one in which one can attain enlightenment. It is even more fortunate than the god realm, because we generally have just the right amount of suffering not to be overwhelmed by it, and just enough to be motivated to want to find a way out. The gods have little or no obvious suffering and can easily be trapped within their experience of bliss, feeling completely content and impervious to the sufferings of others. This is why Buddhism strongly encourages us not to waste our lives in meaningless activity but to make every effort to progress spiritually, because human birth is our best opportunity to do so.

Nirvana

What is nirvana? 'The extinction of craving, the extinction of hatred, the extinction of delusion', said the Buddha's disciple Shariputra.

Samyutta Nikaya, IV.252

Nirvana (*nibbana* in Pali) means 'blowing out, extinguishing', and here it refers to the extinguishing of the fires of craving, hatred and delusion that rage inside us. These are, of course, the fundamental causes of suffering, which implies that as soon as they have been extinguished we automatically cease to suffer. If the

causes of suffering do not exist then suffering cannot be produced. It follows that nirvana is taken to mean the end of suffering, or the cessation (*nirodha*) of suffering.

The logic of this process means that as soon as the causes of suffering have been extinguished, our actions no longer create karmic consequences. Karmic results depend primarily on motivation, and once the Three Poisons have been eliminated from our minds, our motivations are free from both good and bad thoughts. This situation in turn means that we will not be bringing about a karmic rebirth after death, and this is why nirvana is said to be freedom from rebirth. Once we have attained nirvana we are free of the cycle of birth and death, and we are no longer bound to be reborn within samsara.

It is important to remember that nirvana is not a 'thing'; it is not something that we can get if we follow the Buddhist path; neither is nirvana a place, like a heaven, where we will go as a result of or as a reward for practising Buddhism. Nirvana is a realisation, a way of seeing things. As soon as we understand deeply the nature of things according to the Four Noble Truths, in that moment we have attained nirvana.

What is nirvana like?

Nirvana is generally used as a synonym for enlightenment, and the question most people ask is: 'What is the experience of nirvana like?' The only possible reply is that it cannot be put into words. Nirvana is beyond words, because words cannot convey the true nature even of ordinary things, let alone what enlightenment is. Imagine trying to describe in words the taste of a tomato to someone who has never seen or tasted a tomato; or trying to describe to a child what the experience of true love is like. Language is inadequate at communicating the quality of experience, and likewise it is considered misleading as a means of expressing ultimate truth.

As a result, nirvana is described in two ways. It is sometimes described positively in the form of metaphors, but more often it is described in terms of what it is not. This second way is similar to the *via negativa* in Christian and Sufi mysticism. The Buddhist scriptures use a number of classical images for nirvana, and the list below is taken from *The Questions of King Milinda*.

Positive images of nirvana

- Like cool water that relieves fever, nirvana relieves the fever of the passions.
- Like medicine that puts an end to illness, nirvana puts an end to all sufferings.
- Like an unshakeable mountain peak, nirvana is unshakeable.
- Like the wind that you cannot actually see, nirvana is there but you cannot point to it.

Negative expressions of nirvana

- It is not something that is produced, nor is it unproduced.
- It is not past, or future, or present.
- It cannot be perceived by the senses.
- It is unborn, deathless and unconditioned.
- It is extinction or absence of craving, hatred and ignorance.
- It is freedom from suffering/absence of suffering.
- It is freedom from rebirth.

Some non-Buddhists have interpreted the negative expressions of nirvana as meaning that nirvana is a negative state, a state of 'nothingness', blankness or self-annihilation. This is a misunderstanding. Nirvana is freedom from suffering, from the causes of suffering and from rebirth, and nobody would say that freedom was negative. Nirvana is also beyond time and space, and beyond human perception; this is not intended to convey a negative state but rather to inspire us with the idea of a transcendent state. Other people are horrified at the idea that we would no longer have any passions or emotions, and imagine that enlightenment would turn us all into boring, lifeless vegetables. This hardly seems an attractive religious goal. But the experience of nirvana is associated in the scriptures with joy, happiness, serenity, gentleness, compassion, kindness, tolerance and understanding. These are said to be the qualities of someone who has attained nirvana.

The experience of nirvana

- **Nirvana can be experienced in life.** Buddhism is quite different from most other religions in that its religious goal can be experienced in life and not only after death. The life of the Buddha is an example of this.
- **Nirvana and *parinirvana*.** When nirvana is experienced in life it is called 'nirvana with remainder' because we still have our body, which is something of a limitation. When it is experienced at death it is called *parinirvana* or complete nirvana, 'nirvana without remainder' because then we are also free of the body, and so rebirth, or the reconstituting of the five aggregates, will not occur.
- **Nirvana and pain.** After nirvana has been attained in life, the person appears to think and function much the same as everyone else, but the difference is that his or her mind is quite different. For example, the body can still become ill or injured and can still feel pain, but the pain will not affect the mental state.
- **The *arhat*.** Whoever attains nirvana is called an *arhat*, meaning one who has conquered his or her mind and the 'enemy' of the Three Poisons. This is the goal of Theravada Buddhism.

Nirvana cannot be produced

Although in one sense nirvana is seen as the result of many years or many lifetimes of virtuous effort, in another sense nirvana is not the result of anything. If it were the result of something this would mean that it was produced by something and that it was conditioned and therefore impermanent. But nirvana is permanent in the sense that it is beyond time. The truth of nirvana is always there, whether we realise it or not. Buddhists have to tread carefully between saying that nirvana is unconditioned, on the one hand, and that one attains enlightenment by following the Buddhist path, on the other hand.

Are these two statements contradictory? Possibly not, because nirvana does not automatically occur as the result of any particular action. There is no guarantee that if you meditate for *x* hours or behave virtuously for *x* years, you will automatically attain nirvana. It is more elusive than this and cannot be brought about through this type of approach. Like all mystical states, it is beyond our control. *The Questions of King Milinda* illustrates this point with an image. It says that a path does not cause a mountain, it just leads there.

The Mahayana understanding of samsara and nirvana

The Mahayana master Nagarjuna, who lived in India in the second century CE, famously made the startling statement that samsara is no different from nirvana. What could he mean? Does this not contradict all the Buddha's teachings on the subject? Was he not inventing a renegade belief of his own? Nagarjuna wrote:

> There is no distinction whatever between nirvana and samsara. The limit of nirvana is the limit of samsara. There is not the slightest difference between the two.
>
> Nagarjuna, *Mula Madhyamika Karika*

Mahayana Buddhists understand samsara and nirvana within the framework of the Two Truths, that is, ultimate truth and relative truth. According to Madhyamaka philosophy, the ultimate truth of all things is that they are empty of inherent existence, which means that they do not exist independently, permanently or as a single entity. Nagarjuna believed that some scholars of the Nikaya schools treated nirvana as though it were an exception to this rule: they regarded it as a permanent state, something that was unproduced and that existed independently of anything else, and as a result they treated it as an ultimate reality that actually exists. Nagarjuna argued that this is a serious mistake for a Buddhist to make, and that there should be no exceptions whatsoever to the principle that the ultimate nature of everything is emptiness (*shunyata*).

It follows from this that both samsara and nirvana are ultimately empty in nature. Since they both have the same nature, one can therefore say that they are the same as each other in ultimate truth. On the relative level, of course, they are very different and indeed are defined in relation to each other as opposites. So Nagarjuna's statement must be seen as referring specifically to the ultimate state of things, as distinct from the way they appear to us conventionally.

The other major difference between the Mahayana and Nikaya views of this topic is that nirvana is not the ultimate goal of Mahayana Buddhism. As we saw in Chapter 4, Mahayana distinguishes nirvana from complete buddhahood and the individual then considers nirvana to be a worthwhile but provisional goal. Mahayana Buddhists believe that the experience of nirvana eventually comes to an end with a fortunate rebirth and the individual then continues on the path to full buddhahood.

Finally, the doctrine of buddha nature or *tathagatagarbha* explains why Mahayana emphasises that nirvana is not something that we lack and that we are trying to attain, but is something that is there all the time and that we realise once we have purified our ignorance and confusion. In other words, what we need to do is get rid of our ignorance, rather than acquire a new wisdom that we lack. The buddha nature is with us always; we simply have to realise it. Mahayana carries a sense that enlightenment is immanent and fundamentally accessible.

Questions

1 Explain the terms *anatta* and *nibbana* (nirvana).
2 '*Nibbana* is not a worthwhile goal, as it promises nothing but emptiness.' Discuss.
3 Outline the understanding of *nibbana* found in Theravada Buddhism, and assess the claim that *nibbana* cannot be defined with any degree of accuracy.
4 Describe the relation between nirvana and the Eightfold Path.
5 Outline Nagarjuna's teaching on samsara and nirvana, and assess the view that Nagarjuna's teachings are a radical departure from the traditional teachings of the Buddha.

Chapter 12

Buddhist ethics

With gentleness overcome anger. With generosity overcome meanness.

With truth overcome deceit.

Speak the truth; give whatever you can; never be angry.

Dhammapada 223

The principles of Buddhist ethics

The fourth Noble Truth, the Noble Eightfold Path, sets out the main characteristics of the Buddhist way of life. The Buddha presented this path as the
middle way, a way of life that does not fall into extreme views or extremes of
behaviour but cultivates balance and moderation. Buddhist ethics are not based
on the pursuit of sensual or other pleasures (hedonism and utilitarianism), nor
do they encourage extremes of deprivation, poverty or self-sacrifice (as does
asceticism). The various moral guidelines in Buddhism should be taken responsibly but with a light touch.

Ethics is about how we behave and how we act in everyday life. An ethical
system, whether or not it is based on a religion, offers a basic set of moral values
and then sets out the types of action that are encouraged and the types of action
that are discouraged. Walpola Rahula emphasises that the key values underlying
all ethical conduct in Buddhism are love and compassion.

> Ethical conduct (*shila*) is built on the vast conception of universal love and
> compassion for all living beings, on which the Buddha's teaching is based. It is regret-
> table that many scholars forget this great ideal of the Buddha's teaching, and indulge
> in only dry philosophical and metaphysical divagations when they talk and write
> about Buddhism. The Buddha gave his teaching 'for the good of the many, for the
> happiness of the many, out of compassion for the world'.
>
> Walpola Rahula, *What the Buddha Taught*

In Chapter 10 we saw which types of action are thought of as good and which
are considered bad: the main criterion is related to intention, and the determining factor is whether we are acting out of selfish desire and craving, out of

anger or hatred, or out of mindlessness or ignorance. Any actions that are motivated in this way will in the end cause suffering to ourselves and to others. On the other hand, if our actions are motivated by love and compassion they will bring well-being and happiness to ourselves and to others.

In Buddhism, ethical behaviour depends ultimately on the mind and not on the body. Yet the Buddha gave specific advice about which actions are generally harmful and should be avoided. On the basis of this advice, Buddhism has developed various types of ethical guidance that Buddhists do their best to follow. It is important to add, however, that Buddhist ethical rules are never dogmatic or rigid. It is accepted that everyone will do their best and there is a general atmosphere of moral tolerance. The ethical disciplines of Buddhism can be divided into the guidelines for lay people and the guidelines for monastics (monks and nuns).

Lay morality

When you become a Buddhist you begin by taking the Three Refuges, refuge in the Buddha, Dharma and Sangha. The main commitment is to refrain from harming others and to adopt the approach of non-violence (*ahimsa*). Non-violence is another of the fundamental principles of Buddhist ethics.

> In this world hate never yet dispelled hate. Only love dispels hate.
>
> *Dhammapada 5*

Lay people can also take one or several of the Five Precepts, which are five basic vows that underpin the Buddhist way of life. The Five Precepts are:
- I undertake to refrain from killing.
- I undertake to refrain from taking what is not freely given.
- I undertake to refrain from misusing sexuality.
- I undertake to refrain from harmful speech.
- I undertake to refrain from taking intoxicants.

These are reasonably self-explanatory, but there are one or two differences between the Buddhist understanding of the precepts and, say, any corresponding commandments in the Bible. In Buddhism, killing refers not only to human beings but also to animals, even insects. 'Taking what is not freely given' means stealing in any of its forms, not just stealing possessions but, for example, wasting your employer's time. Misusing sexuality is generally interpreted as using sexual relationships in a way that causes harm to someone else, so it is very broad and can include adultery, incest, rape, paedophilia and so on. False or harmful speech includes lying, slander, harsh words and idle gossip. Intoxicants are discouraged because they cloud our minds and impair our

judgement, and, as a result, we might perform actions that we will later regret. Such intoxicants include alcohol and non-medical drugs. Some modern teachers also include tobacco, which is considered harmful to both body and mind.

As well as giving guidelines on what not to do, Buddhism encourages positive attitudes and actions. Love and compassion for all beings, generosity, tolerance, patience and contentment are all cultivated by Buddhists. In his advice to a young man called Sigala, recorded in the Pali Canon, the Buddha explained how this positive approach can be applied in daily life within the framework of Six Relationships.

1 **Take care of your family.** Respect, listen to and support your parents and look after them when they are old. Look after your children, see they are well educated, find appropriate work and marry well.

2 **Take care of your marriage.** Be loving and faithful to your partner and work hard at your side of the partnership. Husbands and wives should be fair to each other, trust each other and not squander joint money. They should also enjoy themselves together, and the Buddha even suggests that a husband should buy his wife presents and jewellery.

3 **Keep good company** and choose the right friends. Keep away from those who will have a bad influence on you. Be kind to your friends, keep promises and help them in times of trouble.

4 **Develop good relationships between teachers and students.** Respect your teachers, appreciate their help, be polite to them and work hard. Teachers should respect their pupils and give them the best education possible.

5 **Develop good relationships between employers and employees**, or workers and management. Employers should take care of their workers, give them decent wages and fair work conditions. Employees should respect their employers, work hard and not waste time. Both should work harmoniously together and not complain about each other, but praise each other.

6 **Develop a supportive and harmonious relationship with the monastic Sangha.** Earn money in a wholesome way so you can offer material goods to help them.

The Buddha's advice was practical, and he often gave the reasons behind his guidance so that people would be convinced. We all know that, if someone tells us not to do something, that is not usually enough to stop us from doing it; we need reasons. So, for example, he said that drinking alcohol is bad because it wastes money, leads to quarrels, makes you ill, gives you a bad reputation, leads you to do immoral things you will later regret, and weakens the brain. As for gambling, he said it is bad because, if you lose, you lose money; if you win, you make enemies, nobody trusts you, friends despise you and nobody will want to be married to you.

> Set your heart on doing good. Do it over and over again and you will be filled with joy.
>
> *Dhammapada* 118

In the Noble Eightfold Path, ethical conduct includes three factors which overlap with the Five Precepts and Six Relationships:

1 **Right action** encourages honourable and honest conduct. In particular, we should not kill, steal, misuse sexuality or take intoxicants, and we should not engage in activities considered dishonest, such as gambling.

2 **Right speech** means refraining from:
- telling lies
- backbiting and slander, and any talk that brings about disunity, disharmony or hatred between people
- harsh, rude, impolite words, or speech that is malicious and deliberately sets out to hurt someone
- idle gossip, or useless chatter which wastes time and misuses the power of speech

3 **Right livelihood** means choosing a profession or a job that does not harm others and does not oblige us to break any of the Five Precepts. The types of job to avoid include trading in weapons or drugs, selling alcohol, killing animals (e.g. working in a slaughterhouse or as a fisherman), being a lawyer, a politician or a journalist if this involves lying.

Lay morality rests on the principle that lay people aim to minimise their bad actions and maximise their good actions so that they have a better rebirth. Most lay people do not expect to attain enlightenment in this life, mainly because they are so busy with worldly things. Their goal is to gain a better rebirth and morality is indispensable for this. In summary, a lay Buddhist who follows the precepts and guidelines will be a responsible citizen, a responsible family member, and will try to be kind, respectful and appreciative of everyone he or she relates to. Buddhists will lead a life of moderation and try to cultivate generosity, tolerance and a non-violent attitude. Buddhist moral conduct aims to bring about harmony and happiness both for the individual and for society. If everyone lived like this maybe society would be more harmonious and peaceful.

Monastic morality

In traditional Buddhist societies, Buddhists have the option to become monastics. If they decide to take this step, they follow a strict lifestyle. Like lay people, monastics take the Three Refuges and all the Five Precepts, but as soon as they ordain as a novice they take an additional five precepts:

- to abstain from food after midday
- to abstain from a luxurious bed (i.e. high off the floor — a sign of wealth)
- to abstain from entertainment (music, dancing, shows, television)
- to abstain from personal adornments (i.e. jewellery, perfume)
- not to touch gold or silver (i.e. money)

Buddhist monastics do not eat after midday, although they can drink. One reason given for this is that over-eating or eating before going to sleep makes the mind sleepy and is not conducive to meditation. They take no alcohol at all. They should avoid places of entertainment, partly because these are a waste of precious time and partly because they can lead to sexual temptation. Instead of the sexual misconduct precept (of the first Five Precepts) monastics take a vow to refrain from any type of sexual activity.

As we can see from the list above, some of the monastic rules are culture-bound — in other words they relate to the social conditions of ancient India and might be difficult to follow today. For example, in the Buddha's day money was not common and communities traded by barter. As a result, a small number of the monastic rules have been adapted in some countries to apply to modern conditions.

A fully ordained monk in the Theravada tradition takes 227 precepts which are found in the Vinaya. Some of these relate to the practicalities of everyday life in a community: taking care of sick monks, wearing soft shoes, not preaching to a woman alone. Others relate to genuinely moral actions. The rules are recited once a fortnight by the whole community at a ceremony called the Uposatha. If any monastic has infringed a rule, he or she is expected to confess publicly to the community or in some cases to one other monk. The senior monks give punishments according to rules that are laid down, but only in serious cases can a monk be expelled from the monastic order and asked to disrobe and become a lay person again. There are four actions that lead to expulsion: sexual intercourse, serious theft, murder (or encouraging someone to commit suicide) and making false claims about having supernatural powers. Less serious actions lead to temporary expulsion, while for even lesser offences monks forfeit certain rights.

In Buddhism there is no equivalent to the excommunication possible in Christianity, where certain actions lead to the culprit's being forced out of the religion altogether. A monk is only expelled from the monastic order, not from being a Buddhist practitioner, and he could continue following his religion as a householder or lay man (*upasaka*).

Women probably had inferior social and religious status in the wider society of the Buddha's day, and the Buddha took a radical step in accepting women as monastics at all. Nuns have more rules than monks, however, and some of

the additional rules for women emphasise the fact that all monks, however young and new, have higher status than a nun. For example, in a joint assembly nuns should always take a lower seat than even the youngest monk. The nuns' rules may have been the only acceptable way of dealing with the social beliefs at the time the rules were made, but they remain the same today. Nevertheless, many monastic communities have significantly improved conditions for nuns over recent years.

In general, Buddhist monastics do their best to follow all their precepts and rules strictly, not only for their own spiritual training but also because they have a duty to provide an example to the wider community. If discipline becomes lax, lay people will no longer respect monastics and may withhold their material support, so the system has built-in safeguards against moral laziness or corruption.

Mahayana ethics

The principles of Mahayana ethics are basically the same as for Theravada and other schools of Nikaya Buddhism. The key difference is *bodhichitta*: the realisation of ultimate wisdom and limitless compassion which gives rise to the altruistic path of the *bodhisattva*. Ultimate wisdom means the realisation of emptiness (*shunyata*), and the limitless compassion of the *bodhisattva* is the wish to bring all beings to enlightenment and the commitment to do everything possible to ensure this happens. It is because all actions are motivated by *bodhichitta* that they are completely selfless and are therefore called 'transcendental actions' or 'perfected actions' (*paramitas*).

Ethical actions in Mahayana are those that are free of any notion of someone who is acting and someone else who is benefiting, and a virtuous action linking the two. Ethical actions transcend this subject/object thinking altogether; they arise from the pure motivation that is possible only when we have realised no-self (*anatta*).

From the Mahayana point of view, it is the motivation of *bodhichitta* that demarcates an action as ethical. The six *paramitas* of generosity, moral discipline, patience, diligence, meditation and wisdom are all expressions of *bodhichitta* in action.

Skilful means (*upaya*)

Characteristic of Mahayana ethics is the use of skilful means or *upaya*, which depends upon the ability of the *bodhisattva* always to know the right action to take in order to help beings towards liberation in any given circumstance. Skilful means is only possible when it is based on both compassion and wisdom, not

only on the wish to help but on the wisdom to know how best to help. We might say that *bodhichitta* is what is meant by skilful means in Mahayana, that any action motivated by *bodhichitta* will naturally be of spiritual benefit to others. In practice, skilful means can only be used by more advanced *bodhisattvas* with powerful *bodhichitta*.

The most important implication of the idea of skilful means for Buddhist ethics is that the *bodhisattva* is free to perform *any* action that will achieve the goal of liberating others. The morality of an action is determined by its ultimate outcome and not by the nature of the action itself. This means that the *bodhisattva* is not constrained by the ethical guidelines of Buddhism that were described above. Even actions that in any other circumstance would be considered harmful — such as lying, stealing and killing — could be used as

---

Box 12.1

The story of the burning house

The traditional story about the burning house illustrates skilful means. It comes from the Lotus Sutra. See *The Buddhist Scriptures*, translated by E. Conze, pages 203–206.

There once lived an old man who was weak in health and strength but quite rich and well-to-do. He had a large house, but the house was old and in a state of disrepair, with a thatched roof and only one door. One day a fire suddenly broke out inside the house and the building began to burn from all sides. The old man managed to get out but then realised that his young sons were still inside playing with their toys. He was beside himself with fear. He knew that they were too young to understand what fire is and what danger they were in, and that was why they continued to play unawares.

So the old man cried out to his sons: 'Come here, my boys, come out of the house! It is burning fiercely. If you don't come out soon you will all be burned.' But the children took no notice of him; they were neither alarmed nor terrified and carried on playing. Next the old man thought of a plan to lure them out, and he called to them to come out quickly because he had lots of beautiful new toys for them — in

particular bullock carts, goat carts and deer carts. When they heard their father's words all the children rushed out of the house to see their toys. As soon as he was assured they were safe and sound, the father took them down to the village and bought them the best toys money could buy — ox carts!

What should we learn from this story? Was the old man wrong to lie to his boys and tell them he had lots of toys for them when this was not the case? The Buddha says in the sutra that he was not wrong, because he had tried conventional means and they didn't work, and this was the only way he could save their lives.

The story is seen as symbolic. The burning house represents samsara, the fire represents the fire of the passions or mental poisons, the only door out of the house is the Buddhist path to liberation. The children's unawareness in the face of danger represents our ignorance of the causes of suffering. The old man is like the Buddha, who inspires us to renounce samsara and certain death. The three carts he offered represent the three '*yanas*' or vehicles of Buddhism, while the ox carts represent buddhahood itself

skilful means in a particular situation, provided they were motivated by *bodhichitta*. Buddhist teachers caution that the circumstances that might require someone to go against conventional morality and apply skilful means are rare. Conventional methods should always be tried first. Nevertheless, the principle of skilful means explains why Mahayana Buddhism tends to be more flexible than Theravada in adapting traditional guidelines to modern situations.

A contemporary example can be used to illustrate skilful means. Suppose an advanced *bodhisattva* with tremendous compassion and wisdom had been alive in Hitler's day and could have foreseen that Hitler would cause great suffering and death to many people. It is conceivable that such a *bodhisattva* might have applied skilful means in order to prevent Hitler from doing this — thereby saving millions of people from suffering and saving Hitler from the bad karmic consequences of his own actions. We could imagine that the skilful means might involve killing Hitler, which in any other situation would be a harmful thing to do but in this case could be seen as a moral action according to Mahayana ethics. Such pre-emptive action, though, is only moral if it is genuinely motivated by the highest and most selfless compassion and wisdom, totally free of any hint of self-interest or aggression.

Both the Theravada and the Mahayana models of ethics place ethical conduct firmly within the framework of a graduated spiritual path. However, some Mahayana schools place little emphasis on the gradual approach and express ethics differently. Two of these schools are Zen Buddhism and Pure Land Buddhism.

Ethics in Zen Buddhism

Dogen (1200–53) established the Soto school of Zen in Japan, which emphasised a strict and simple life of monastic discipline. After many centuries, during which Buddhist monasteries had become rather prosperous and comfortable, Dogen advocated a monastic life of poverty and simplicity whose focus was on spiritual practice and the effort to be of benefit to others. This was seen as part of a return to the true Buddhism taught by the Buddha in ancient India.

Soto Zen sees both *zazen* meditation and ethics as ways to make manifest one's inherent buddha nature. If people already have the buddha nature (*tathagata-garbha*), why do they need to exert themselves to attain buddhahood? Ethical conduct and meditation are not methods to attain enlightenment, but are themselves enlightenment; they are ways of expressing the buddha nature that is inherent in us.

The Rinzai school of Zen, founded in Japan by Eisai (1141–1215), combines the principles of skilful means (*upaya*) and buddha nature (*tathagatagarbha*) to

create a distinctively dramatic form of Buddhism. Buddhist masters enforce discipline and communicate the Dharma by means of eccentric methods such as shouting and beating. These constitute skilful means since it is believed that peaceful meditation alone is not powerful enough to bring such defiled beings as ourselves to enlightenment. Students sometimes have to follow a tough discipline and extreme physical conditions as part of their training. The methods used in Rinzai are aimed at bringing about sudden glimpses of enlightenment (*satori*), which are possible because the buddha nature is always present within.

Ethics in True Pure Land Buddhism

Shinran (1173–1263), the founder of the school of True Pure Land, also known as Shin Buddhism, was extremely sceptical about the Buddhist teachings on ethical conduct. He felt that human beings are helplessly full of passion and depravity and are ignorant of what is truly good and evil. Even in the case of those who try to follow a path of virtue, ethical action only becomes a source of pride and self-righteousness and a cause for loss of faith in Amida Buddha. The only way to make spiritual progress is to put one's total reliance on the power and blessing of Amida Buddha.

Shinran criticised the Buddhist attitude of trying to earn merit by following moral guidelines. He said 'even a good man will be received in Buddha's land, how much more a bad man' — emphasising the mercy of Amida Buddha. By relying on Amida Buddha we remain humble in the thought that we ourselves do not have the power to effect the personal transformation necessary to attain enlightenment.

In Shin Buddhism, there is no monastic celibacy. A small number of married clergy perform certain rituals and ceremonies, but there are no traditional monastic ethics based on the Vinaya. Discipline in Pure Land Buddhism is the mental discipline of remembering the presence of Amida Buddha throughout one's everyday life. Although this sounds quite simple, it is not, because maintaining genuine devotion to Amida all day and every day requires tremendous mental effort and diligence.

Applied ethics in Buddhism

To illustrate how a Buddhist might approach some of the ethical problems of today, we will look at the examples of abortion, vegetarianism and cloning. It is important to remember that Buddhist ethics vary in emphasis from one tradition to another, so there is no single 'Buddhist' approach to any of these questions. All we can do is outline possible approaches.

Abortion

- A foetus is considered to be a living being in the sense that it is endowed with both a body and a mind. The karmic consequences of killing another human therefore apply to abortion.
- Motivation is important. If I abort my unborn baby for selfish reasons — the timing is inconvenient, I don't want to give up my career, I think I don't have the right circumstances to bring up a child and so on — then this is an unethical act.
- There may be mitigating circumstances, such as when the mother's life is threatened by her pregnancy. This is a difficult case, since choosing abortion is tantamount to saying that the mother's life is more important than the life of the child. In Buddhism all lives are equally precious. If an abortion is carried out reluctantly for medical reasons, there are purification practices in Buddhism to counteract its negative karmic effects.

Vegetarianism

There are many different views on vegetarianism, which make it the subject of lively debate within Buddhism.

- Buddhists consider that the karmic effects of eating meat and fish are quite different from the effects of slaughtering animals and fish for market. It is easy to eat a hamburger, but how easy would you find it to slit the throat of a cow?
- Nevertheless, eating meat and fish is a way of participating in the chain of activities that cause animals to be killed for food, so there is some karmic responsibility involved.
- Many Buddhists believe that vegetarianism is the only option if they are to be true to the principles of not killing and non-violence.
- The Pure Land school in Japan does not consider ethical action as important as devotional practice to Amida Buddha, so it rapidly became very popular with fishermen. The Japanese eat a lot of fish because the geography of their country supports little agriculture.
- Theravadins are generally not vegetarians, and Tibetans live in a climate where vegetarianism is impractical.
- Some Buddhists argue that modern methods used to raise farm animals and slaughter them are so insensitive that they cause tremendous suffering to the animals as well as producing unhealthy meat. They argue that vegetarianism is the only option.
- Other Buddhists point out that vegetarianism is not really a solution because of the enormous number of insects killed through the use of pesticides on vegetable crops.

- The Dalai Lama has said he supports vegetarianism but occasionally eats meat on the advice of his doctors.

Cloning

There are two types of genetic cloning.

1 **Therapeutic cloning** is intended to produce an embryo that can be used to generate stem cells for medical purposes. Such embryos are not allowed to develop beyond 14 days, which is the point at which scientists believe the ability to feel pain is formed.

2 **Reproductive cloning** is intended to produce a foetus that will grow into an individual animal or human.

How would a Buddhist decide whether or not cloning is a moral activity?

- Buddhists do not have problems with the idea that we are 'playing God' by creating life, since they do not believe in a creator God. Cloning and other genetic engineering techniques are therefore not sacrilegious in the way they might be to followers of other faiths.
- Motivation would be the determining factor. For example, in the case of reproductive cloning, if one chose to clone a child to satisfy one's own desire to have a child, that would be unethical, whereas, if one chose cloning as a way of bearing children without passing on hereditary diseases such as cystic fibrosis, then one could be acting out of compassion and the action would be ethical.
- In the case of therapeutic cloning, the question for Buddhists is whether an embryo can be considered a person or animal even for the first 14 days of its life. Technically, this would depend on whether a consciousness has joined with the embryo or not. Traditionally, Buddhists consider that the consciousness joins the embryo at fertilisation, but some contemporary teachers have said that the point in time when this occurs varies from case to case and is difficult to determine. Some Buddhist masters say that it is possible that in the first few days an embryo is not a complete being with body and mind and that therefore this form of cloning may be ethical. If this were not the case, however, Buddhists would not wish to sacrifice the life of a foetus to aid the medical treatment of someone else, since all lives are equally precious.

Classifying the Buddhist ethical system

Buddhist ethics can be considered an instance of virtue ethics, centred on the idea that the basis of morality is the development of good character traits or virtues, which, in Aristotle's system for example, include intelligence, wisdom

and the ability to discern between good and bad. Acting ethically is not merely a question of 'What should I do?' but more importantly a question of 'How should I be?' The Buddha did not place the emphasis on the idea of doing one's duty, but rather on becoming a kind, compassionate and wise person and then acting accordingly.

Peter Harvey has argued that the Mahayana idea of skilful means (*upaya*) is similar to Christian situation ethics because it allows ethical principles to be overridden in certain situations in the name of wisdom and *bodhichitta*. Situation ethics was developed by Joseph Fletcher in 1966 in his book of that name, and has become a prevalent view within the Protestant churches. Fletcher claims it offers a middle way between the extremes of legalism or divine command theory on the one hand, for which there can be no exceptions to the rule, and antinomianism on the other hand where there is no foundation at all with which we can evaluate our morality.

Situation ethics does not propose rules, but rather suggests a guiding principle to decision making — that principle is love. Acting morally means acting in the most loving way in any given situation. This principle can be applied, for example, to the case of abortion where all the circumstances would be taken into account before a moral decision was made. Rather like the approach of *upaya* in Mahayana, situation ethics does not ignore or reject traditional values but is not bound by them. Both systems may therefore allow the act of 'compassionate killing'. There is a story in the suttas of how, in one of his past lives, the Buddha killed a robber to stop him from killing a number of *bodhisattvas*, and thus prevented the robber from suffering in the hells for aeons. The difference, though, is that in Buddhism only a very advanced *bodhisattva* is permitted to break with the traditional values, while situation ethics can be applied by anyone with a loving heart.

Another possible way of classifying Buddhist ethics in Western terms is by relating it to 'soft determinism'. Soft determinists tread a middle path between the hard determinism of philosophers such as Hobbes, Hume and John Stuart Mill, who assert that the law of cause and effect is universal and for whom, therefore, moral freedom is not really possible, and libertarians who hold that uncaused, unconditional choices can be made and that free will exists. Immanuel Kant, for example, believed that free will was essential for morality. To resolve this debate, A. J. Ayer advocates a type of soft determinism which accepts that everything has a cause, but which defines particular actions as free volitions. An action is considered to be a free volition provided that: (a) if you had had the volition not to do the action, you would not have done it and (b) nobody compelled you to do it. For Ayer, we have responsibility for our volitional actions.

In order to explain the difference between phenomena that are caused and free volitions, some soft determinists distinguish between the internal and external causes of an action, for example between its circumstantial and psychological causes. It can be argued that, while the external causes are determined, the psychological causes are not always so. This is similar to the Buddhist view which states that physical objects and circumstances are always determined through causes and conditions, that some mental decisions are determined both by physical and physiological causes and by psychological ones, and that certain mental thoughts or decisions are free to the extent that one has conquered one's own mind.

Summary of main points

- In Theravada, ethical action must always be motivated by *ahimsa*, the wish not to cause harm.
- In Theravada, ethical conduct on the Noble Eightfold Path involves right action, right speech and right livelihood.
- For lay Buddhists, the main ethical guidelines are: generosity (*dana*), the Five Precepts and the Six Relationships.
- For Theravada monks, the main ethical guidelines are the 227 precepts of a monk.
- In Mahayana, ethical action must always be motivated by *bodhichitta*, the wish to attain enlightenment for the benefit of others.
- Ethical behaviour on the *bodhisattva* path consists of the six *paramitas* or transcendental actions.
- In Mahayana, advanced *bodhisattvas* are permitted to use skilful means (*upaya*) in exceptional circumstances to override traditional values, by applying their great wisdom and compassion for the spiritual benefit of others.

Questions

1 'Actions themselves are neither good nor bad.' Evaluate this claim in the context of Buddhist ethics.
2 Explain what Buddhists mean by 'right action'.
3 'Buddhism is simply an ethical philosophy.' Discuss.
4 How useful is the concept of the middle way in helping Buddhists know how to act?
5 Buddhism is often associated with the principle of non-violence. Examine and assess the Buddhist arguments for this position.
6 What are the main features of Buddhist ethics for the laity? Compare these with the moral precepts of Theravada monks.

7 How did Buddhist values differ from those prevailing in Indian society between the time of the Buddha and Ashoka (see also Chapter 2)?

8 How important is the Noble Eightfold Path as a means to enlightenment?

Chapter 13

Society and the Buddhist way of life

Always remember, Dhamma is not an escape. It is an art of living: living in peace and harmony with oneself and also with all others.

S. N. Goenka, *Words of Dhamma*

Buddhism in Sri Lanka and Thailand

As it spread across Asia, Buddhism adapted to each new society, especially on the level of social customs. As a result, the social aspects of the Buddhist religion are culturally specific, and each cultural area needs to be studied in its own right. Here we will focus only on Sri Lanka and Thailand, where the basic way of life of the Buddhist community is still very close to the way it would have been in India in the Buddha's day.

The main feature of Buddhist society in these countries is that it can be divided into two distinct groups of people: lay people or householders who have families, jobs and property; and monastics, mainly monks, who give up the householder life to live in a monastic community.

There are three widespread misunderstandings of this situation.

- First, not all Buddhists are monks. Many Westerners imagine that to be a Buddhist means becoming a monk or nun, but this is not the case. It is a matter of personal choice.
- Second, monastics do not live completely isolated from the community, in seclusion behind the monastery walls. There is no Buddhist equivalent to the cloistered monasteries and nunneries found in Roman Catholicism and orthodox Christianity. Monks interact with lay people.
- Third, monks to not spend the whole day in meditation. This is often the image we have of Buddhist monks. They do have meditation sessions, but much of the day is taken up with practical duties around the monastery,

advising lay people who come for help, performing rituals and working as teachers. Young monks spend most of the day doing their studies. Only those in forest monasteries spend their days in meditation.

Becoming a monastic

In the Theravada countries of south and southeast asia, a child can be admitted to a monastery (*vihara*) around the age of seven. At that age he would become a novice (*samanera*) and receive a good education. Only around the age of 21 does he need to decide whether he wishes to commit himself to being ordained as a monk (*bhikkhu*) for the rest of his life. He is free to leave the monastery at that point, if he wishes, and can become a householder. However, he could choose to take the 227 precepts of a fully ordained monk, and most novices decide to do this.

The ordination ceremony follows instructions laid down in the time of the Buddha. First the candidate's hair and beard are shaved off completely as a symbol of impermanence and of abandoning attachment to worldly values and any idea that we are physically attractive to the opposite sex. Then he is bathed in water as a symbol of purification, and prepares the objects that are required for monastic life: an alms bowl, robe, sandals and umbrella (also used as a sun shade). These are the monk's only possessions and are usually donated by his family. If the ordination is to full monkhood, the candidate is questioned on his knowledge of the Dharma.

Figure 13.1
A Theravada monk in Thailand offers a candle

The ordination ceremony normally requires the presence of ten monks of good standing and takes place within the monastery grounds. The candidate wears the white robes of a lay man and carries his yellow robes as he approaches and kneels in front of the presiding monk. He asks permission to wear the yellow robe and become ordained. The presiding monk ties the sash of the robe around his neck and the candidate then puts on the robe while chanting. He asks forgiveness for any faults he might have committed, and asks to take the Three Refuges and ten precepts of a novice, or 227 precepts of a *bhikkhu* (see Chapter 12).

When a Buddhist becomes a monk or nun, the intention is generally to remain so throughout life, especially in Sri Lanka. However, if circumstances later change and they decide to give it up, they are free to do so without any shame. They go through a simple ceremony and hand back their robes. In Thailand, it is customary for every adult male to spend a few months of his life as a monk in a monastery. This is done especially after a bereavement, when it is socially accepted that someone might wish to retreat as a monk for a few months before returning to family and job.

Monasteries are run democratically. Respect is shown for seniority, so those who have been monks the longest are the most respected. Many decisions are taken by the community as a whole, following the rule that 'silence means consent'.

The typical day of a monk might look like this:
- early rising
- two meals, breakfast and lunch
- periods both morning and evening for communal chanting
- periods for meditation
- periods for study
- periods for services to lay people
- free time

The situation for nuns in southeast Asia is unfortunate since the ordination line in Theravada died out in the eleventh century. Because ordination ceremonies require the presence of at least five ordained monks and a number of nuns, when Buddhism has been under pressure this requirement has proved difficult to meet and so ordination has been impossible. Once the ordination line of a particular tradition has been broken, it has gone for ever. Nevertheless, there are women who shave their heads and wear robes and keep the precepts of novice nuns. They are technically called lay sisters (*upasikas*) and have lower status than monks. They find it harder to get economic support, and some have to do their own shopping and cooking. This situation is being reviewed in the light of modern social changes. In recent years, the ordination of nuns has been revived in Sri Lanka and Thailand by ordained nuns from the Chinese and Korean tradition where the line had not died out.

The relationship between monastics and the lay community

Monasteries, or *viharas*, are of three main kinds. There are large monasteries in the big cities, where there is considerable interaction between the monks and the local community. There are small monasteries in villages, which play a similar role but on a smaller scale and with fewer resources; and there is a 'forest tradition' of monks living in isolated areas in the forest away from society. The relationship between monastics and lay people varies according to each type of monastery. In the case of forest monks, their role within the community is negligible.

In general, the relationship between monastics and lay people in Theravada countries is one of mutual benefit and mutual dependence. Each group plays a specific role in the life of the religion, and both groups are necessary for Buddhism to survive. This relationship has probably changed very little since the first centuries after the Buddha.

The special role played by monastics is to uphold the traditions and practices of the Buddhist religion to the practical benefit of the community. First, they play an educational role. In centuries past, long before Europe introduced secular schooling, monasteries provided the only source of education and literacy in the community, just as Christian monasteries did in Europe. Now they offer an alternative educational route alongside secular schools.

Monasteries continue to play an important role in educating all children in the basics of Buddhism. For example, Sri Lanka, influenced by colonialism and Christian missionaries, has introduced 'Sunday school' classes in Buddhism for children.

The second role of the monks, which is considered important by the community, is conducting funerals and supporting the bereaved. Death is perhaps the most important moment in a Buddhist's life. Since Buddhists believe in rebirth, death marks the gateway to another life. The way we live and the way we die, and the genuine prayers of loved ones, affect the type of rebirth that we may have. For these reasons monks are greatly appreciated for easing the passage to a better rebirth. They receive alms on behalf of the dead so that merit can be transferred to them.

In modern times there are many examples of monks in Sri Lanka and Thailand assisting in the economic and social development of their villages. After a monastic education, which naturally means they can read and write, they are in a privileged position to help poor local communities to better themselves. They can fill in forms to apply for grants and help with the administration of development projects for the benefit of all. Some

Figure 13.2 Bodhi tree in Sri Lanka decked with prayer flags

monks have championed environmental projects, applying Buddhist values of non-violence and non-harming to the development process.

The lay community, for its part, supports the monastic community with material gifts. Above all it provides food, clothing, medicines and shelter. Monks are forbidden by the Vinaya to have any possessions other than the basic necessities, so the lay community's generosity is not abused. By providing the economic basis for monasticism, lay people ensure that those who wish to can engage full-time in this way of life. The Vinaya forbids monks to earn money and to engage in agriculture, so if monks are to follow these rules they are materially dependent on others for their survival. People from the local community support their monastery by volunteering to clean, cook, do the gardening, go shopping and carry out building maintenance. Generally speaking, the monks do not have to engage in routine tasks and can focus on their specific duties.

Both lay people and monastics come together to celebrate festival days. It is at those times that they can all be seen to belong to one community. The most important festival celebrates the Buddha's birth, enlightenment and passing away on the full moon day in May; this is called Vesakha or Wesak. In addition, each Buddhist country has its own national festivals.

The monastic year is marked by the *vassa* or rainy season retreat, a 3-month period during which all monks restrict their movements and remain as much as possible within the monastery boundary. During that time they intensify their chanting, meditation and Dharma study. Throughout southeast Asia many lay people are temporarily ordained for this period. For a month after the end of the retreat, Kathina ceremonies take place, when the whole lay community goes to the monastery bearing food, flowers, new robes and other gifts, and everyone joins together to eat, drink and exchange news.

This system relies on a shared belief that the pursuit of religious and spiritual goals is worthwhile and even supreme. It has continued uninterrupted in southeast Asia since Buddhism was first introduced there.

Other regions of Asia have been more troubled. Over the past 100 years the dominance of materialist views and communism has challenged this system to breaking point. If one dismisses the value of religion, then one may well look upon Buddhist monks as 'social parasites', on the grounds that they make no economic contribution to society. In country after country across Asia, Communist regimes have tried to eradicate the Buddhist religion by destroying the monasteries and either killing the monks or forcing them to disrobe and become householders. This struggle has taken place in China, Cambodia, North Korea, Tibet and Mongolia. After decades of suppression, there are signs in the twenty-first century of a Buddhist revival in all these countries.

Questions

1 Describe the main features of life as a Buddhist monk in a Theravada monastery.

2 Explain the relationship between a monastery and its lay community, and assess the claim that dependence on the lay community weakens the traditional role of a Buddhist monk.

3 Assess the claim that monastic Buddhism is too remote from lay people to have any impact on them.

4 'The Sangha puts more into the Buddhist community than it takes out.' Discuss.

Chapter 14

Meditation in Theravada

It is better to conquer yourself than to win a thousand battles.

Dhammapada 103

The purpose of meditation in Buddhism

Meditation is the main method used in Buddhism to transform people's minds from their present state of confusion, distraction and emotional entanglement to a state of peace and clarity. The Buddha himself discovered the special value of meditation — he gave up all his other religious practices in the forest in favour of meditating under the bodhi tree, and it was through meditation that he finally gained enlightenment. The importance of meditation in Buddhism is therefore based on the Buddha's personal experience of its benefits.

How should we meditate? And what happens when we do? These days meditation is taught widely in the West by many different groups, some religious and others not, but the word 'meditation' is not always taken to mean the same thing. For some, meditation is about sitting in a particular posture; for others, it is about changing one's mood through guided practices of the imagination — feeling good as you imagine lying on a tropical beach with the sun shining down on you, for example. Some people meditate by closing their eyes and cutting themselves off from their environment. Many people think of meditation as a way of escaping from life, a way of de-stressing, or a way of entering some mysterious state of trance or learning how to levitate. This is not what Buddhists mean by meditation, so we need to define its precise meaning in Buddhism.

The purpose of meditation in Buddhism is to purify the mind, put a complete end to suffering and its causes and lead people to enlightenment. Meditation has a spiritual purpose, not a worldly purpose. Even though it is true that

meditation can help people relax and feel less stressed, these are considered secondary benefits and are not the main point. The Sanskrit and Pali term for meditation is *bhavana*, which means 'cultivation' or 'development', that is, mental cultivation or development, a way of training the mind. Meditation aims at freeing the mind from greed and craving, anger, ill-will, laziness, anxiety, doubts and hesitation, and cultivating positive qualities such as concentration, awareness, intelligence, willpower, diligence, confidence, joy and tranquillity.

Ultimately, meditation aims to cut through thoughts and emotions to access the very nature of our minds, through which we attain the highest wisdom, compassion and peace.

> Examining the nature of the mind, you can observe that in its natural state it has no preoccupations. It's like a flag on the end of a pole or like a leaf on a tree. By itself, it remains still; if it flutters, that is because of the wind, an external force. In its natural state, the mind is the same, without attraction or aversion, without ascribing characteristics to things or finding fault with people. It is independent, existing in a state of purity that is clear, radiant and stainless. In its natural state the mind is peaceful, without happiness or suffering. This is the true state of the mind.
>
> Ajahn Chah, *Being Dharma*

Buddhist meditation is not a way of escaping from life or avoiding responsibilities; rather, it aims to give buddhists the strength and confidence to face responsibilities and to live life well. The paradox is that, even though its main purpose is a long-term one, meditation brings tangible benefits in the short term, too.

It is important to note that meditation was practised in India before the Buddha and that he learned it from *shramana* teachers in the forest. Nevertheless, certain meditation methods were developed by the Buddha and are unique to Buddhism. There are two main types of meditation in Buddhism: *samatha* and *vipassana*. *Samatha* probably existed before the Buddha and is still practised by Hindus today, whereas *vipassana* was developed by the Buddha himself and is a method practised specifically by Buddhists.

Whatever form of meditation one does, it is usually practised in formal sessions, that is, timed sessions that have a clear beginning and end. The first thing to do is to create a pleasant environment: make sure the room is clean, tidy and well aired; create an area of the room where you are comfortable and place something inspiring such as a flower, a candle or a favourite picture as an object of focus; make sure you will not be disturbed. You can sit either cross-legged on a cushion on the floor, in full lotus posture if possible, or otherwise on a chair. The most important point about the physical posture is to keep your back straight. Make sure you are comfortable, and breathe normally.

Most Buddhists in the West try to meditate at least once a day. It is not usual for lay Buddhists to go to temples or monasteries to meditate; instead, they practise at home where they create a special corner for the purpose. Beginners are generally advised to meditate for only short periods at a time, say 5 or 10 minutes, because regularity is considered more important than lengthy sessions. Traditionally in Asia only monks and nuns meditate regularly, but as Buddhism has spread to Western countries this pattern has changed, because most Buddhists here are lay people. However, lay people in Asia do engage in chanting, and this has a definite meditative quality, arousing joy, calm, concentration and mindfulness, for example.

Samatha meditation

Samatha meditation develops mental concentration and focus and brings about peace of mind. The word means 'calm abiding' and so *samatha* is sometimes called 'tranquillity meditation'; it allows all our busy thoughts to settle of their own accord until we are able to rest peacefully and at ease with ourselves.

The first step in *samatha* meditation is the cultivation of 'mindfulness', by which is meant awareness of ourselves and our state of mind. There are four main types of mindfulness to practice: mindfulness of body, of feelings and sensations, of mind and of mental states. We simply focus on one of these for a short while and become aware of it and of how it feels. Focusing the mind like this calms both the mind and the body and is a useful preliminary to other *samatha* practices.

One of the first methods taught to beginners is often breathing meditation, which can be part of the mindfulness of body. The idea is to rest the mind solely on the breath and not let it get carried away by distracting thoughts and emotions. We can either just notice the breath going in and out; or count the breaths from one to ten, on the out breath, several times over; or focus on the sensation of the air moving in and out of the nostrils. As soon as we notice that we are daydreaming, that our mind has wandered off and we are thinking about something else entirely, we simply bring our focus back to the breathing and begin again.

We can replace the breath with other objects of focus: a candle flame, a flower, a picture, or a statue of the Buddha, for example. The object simply acts as a support for our concentration. Gradually our thoughts slow down, we become less distracted and more centred. Imagine leaving a glass of muddy water on a table; if you don't stir the water, the mud will gradually settle to the bottom quite naturally and the water will become clear. *Samatha* is like this: the thoughts and emotions slowly settle and the mind naturally becomes clear and undisturbed.

Samatha meditation can be pursued to reach much higher states of consciousness; this occurs in four stages or *jhanas* (Sanskrit *dhyanas*).

- The first *jhana* brings detachment, clarity, concentration.
- In the second *jhana* one rests in stillness, rapture and joy.
- The third *jhana* brings a more rarefied joy.
- The fourth *jhana* is a state of clear, calm consciousness, totally peaceful and undisturbed.

Samatha can lead on to various mystical states, such as the 'Sphere of Nothingness' and the 'Sphere of Neither Perception nor Non-perception'. However, the Buddha was not satisfied with these states because he found that they do not lead to liberation from samsara. This is why *samatha* is always taught together with *vipassana*.

The meditations on love

> Just as a mother would protect her only child at the risk of her own life, even so, let him cultivate a boundless heart towards all beings.
>
> The Buddha, *Metta Sutta*

You might think that merely focusing on an object is a dry and abstract type of meditation, but there are many other methods, and one of the most popular is the *brahma viharas* or 'divine abidings'. There are four types: meditation on loving kindness, on compassion, on joy and on equanimity. The point of these practices is to help develop the capacity to love others. We do want to love other people and be kind to them, but all too often our love is blocked in some way and we don't know how to love fully. Maybe we are afraid of getting hurt; maybe we have been traumatised by a past experience of failure or abuse. The meditations on love aim to help us to re-connect with the love deep inside us and to have confidence in ourselves, so that we are then better able to love others. These practices aim to enable us to pass from virtuous aspirations to the reality of action, and to extend our love genuinely, equally and impartially to all beings, without prejudice or boundaries of any kind.

- **Loving kindness** or *metta* is the genuine wish that everyone should be happy. The meditation begins with remembering the feeling of having been loved. This love does not necessarily have to have come from your parents or partner; you might have felt most love from your grandparents or even a pet, for example. Whatever your experience of the love and kindness of others, however small, you remember that and recognise that you are lovable and worthy of love. Once this is well established, you extend that loving feeling progressively, in ever increasing circles, first to those who are dear to you, then to people you feel neutral or indifferent towards, and finally to those you

have problems with. Finally, your love embraces all beings in the universe. With each phase of the practice you repeat the following phrase to yourself: 'May I/you be happy, may I/you be well.'

- **Compassion** or *karuna* is the genuine wish to free all beings from suffering. The meditation focuses on individuals or groups with specific types of suffering, and generates the resolution that you will do everything in your power to help them.
- **Joy** or *mudita* is sincere rejoicing at the happiness of others. It counteracts jealousy. The meditation involves thinking of the happiness of particular individuals and generating sympathetic joy, beginning with situations that come easily and culminating in those you find difficult.
- **Equanimity** or *upekkha* means the loving of all beings equally. This counteracts prejudice and discrimination, likes and dislikes. We extend our love to family and friends, and then systematically extend our love in exactly the same way to others we usually have less sympathy for. Equanimity also includes developing even-mindedness throughout the ups and downs of life. There is no virtue in being dragged down or depressed by the misfortunes of others or ourselves.

Each one of these meditations develops positive qualities in us which act as an antidote to particular negative emotions.

- Loving kindness is the antidote to aggression.
- Compassion is the antidote to cruelty.
- Joy is the antidote to envy and jealousy.
- Equanimity is the antidote to prejudice and resentment.

The meditations on love or 'divine abidings' are said to develop the mental qualities of the higher gods, the *brahmas*, and are also known as immeasurable as they give us a 'big heart'. They are considered important for Buddhist practice because Buddhism in general lays so much emphasis on having a kind, loving and compassionate attitude. As the Buddha says in *Dhammapada* 254: 'The way is not in the sky; the way is in the heart'.

Other subjects of meditation

The fifth century CE Theravadin scholar Buddhaghosa recommends many other subjects for contemplation and especially Ten Recollections: the qualities of the Buddha, the qualities of the Dharma, the qualities of the Sangha, virtue, generosity, faith, death, the human body, breathing and peace.

Buddhaghosa recommends that certain topics are particularly suitable for different types of people. For example, meditation on death or on the human body (focusing on what the body is composed of — organs, waste matter and so on) may be appropriate for extrovert people who are attached to material things and worldly pleasures, but would be quite unsuitable for anyone who was sad and depressed. Cheerful people with strong faith should meditate on the many qualities of the Buddha, the Dharma or the Sangha. Those who are aggressive and full of hatred should meditate on the four *brahma viharas* or aspects of love.

Vipassana meditation

Vipassana is often translated as 'insight meditation' as it aims to develop insight into the very nature of things, ultimately leading to wisdom and realisation of the ultimate truth of nirvana. *Vipassana* uses our intelligence and our powers of observation and analysis to bring us to a deeper level of understanding. Usually *samatha* is practised first, as the basis for *vipassana*; this is because one needs to be mindful and focused in order to analyse a topic for any length of time without getting distracted.

The topics that a Buddhist might choose to take as the focus for *vipassana* meditation are almost limitless, but in general the main topics are related to the Four Noble Truths.

It is possible to contemplate any life situations that we wish to understand more deeply and come to terms with. *Vipassana* cultivates a type of understanding that is neither based on the senses nor on ordinary consciousness but on what we might call the intuitive mind. In particular, meditators train their minds to see the impermanence, suffering quality and non-inherent existence of each object of meditation.

The point of *vipassana* meditation is that understanding of the Dharma does not remain theoretical but becomes personal and related to experience. In this way, Buddhists develop personal conviction about the truths of the Dharma and believe in them not simply because they have been taught to do so. It is also a way of developing an understanding of life that is in accord with the Dharma.

Because it is important to adapt meditation practice to our state of mind, Buddhism emphasises the importance of practising under the guidance of an experienced meditation teacher. Learning from books is unsatisfactory because we need advice and guidance when questions or difficulties arise.

Benefits of meditation

Meditation eliminates the Three Poisons of craving, aggression and ignorance. In particular, *samatha* eliminates craving and aggression, while *vipassana* eliminates ignorance, but in practice these two methods work together. In addition to eliminating negative emotions, meditation develops positive

emotions — for example the *brahma viharas* develop love, compassion, joy and equanimity.

Mental qualities

Each type of meditation acts as an antidote to negative emotions or attitudes and helps to develop the positive counterpart. Sustained meditation practice carried out correctly over many years brings about the corresponding qualities and virtues: peace of mind, kindness, love and compassion, joy and impartiality, freedom from doubts and hesitation, clarity and insightfulness. You may wonder how one can tell whether one is meditating correctly or not. Buddhist masters often say that the main sign of successful practice is an increase in love and compassion.

'Magical' powers

Advanced *Samatha* meditation is said to develop supernatural powers such as clairvoyance, clairaudience, the knowledge of others' thoughts and the recollection of former lives. However, Buddhists underplay the importance of such powers, and monks are forbidden to boast of their powers to others or even to display their powers in public. Such powers are not considered essential for gaining nirvana; on the contrary, they can become a distraction on the spiritual path because one might become quite attached to them and proud of them. They are perhaps spoken of in a symbolic way, but Buddhists do believe they are possible to achieve in reality.

A recent example of the type of extraordinary power that meditation can bring was the tragic burning of the Buddhist monk Thich Quang Doc during the Vietnam War. On 11 June 1963 he drove to a busy road junction in Saigon, sat in the road and poured petrol on himself to draw the world's attention to the inhumanity of the war. Watched by a horrified crowd of passers-by and reporters, he lit a match and over the course of a few moments burned to death. As he burned he continued to sit in a meditation posture and did not move a muscle or utter a sound. His silence and composure were haunting. This event was shown on television around the world and it became a turning point after which Vietnam protests became widespread in the USA. This was not a suicide from desperation but out of self-sacrifice.

Social benefits

Meditation practice has been introduced in prisons to remarkable effect. The first experiments occurred in Indian gaols, where the Burmese teacher Goenka has taught 10-day meditation retreats open to prisoners of all religions. The first 3 days focus on *samatha* and the last 7 days on *vipassana*. Meditation has helped

many inmates come to terms with the crimes they have committed, ask forgiveness of their victims, and has given them the strength to change and begin a new life. This has obvious social benefits. Similarly, meditation has been introduced on a voluntary basis in prisons in the USA and the UK with positive effects. It is acknowledged as a more effective method for bringing about a change of heart in criminals than a penitentiary system that lacks compassion and understanding.

Summary of main points

- *Samatha* meditation means 'calm abiding'. It helps to calm the mind, counteracts distraction and brings about mental focus and peace of mind.
- *Vipassana* meditation is 'insight meditation'. It uses the intelligence in a focused way to contemplate different topics as well as life situations. It develops mental clarity and understanding.
- The *brahma viharas* are meditations on love, compassion, joy and equanimity.
- In Buddhism, meditation plays a crucial role on the path to enlightenment by eliminating the Three Poisons.

Questions

1 Explain the aims and methods of meditation in Theravada.
2 Discuss the importance of meditation for the achievement of *nibbana*.
3 Describe how Buddhists practise *samatha* meditation and explain its spiritual benefits.
4 Do you agree that Buddhists practise meditation simply to escape from the problems of life?

Chapter 15

Meditation in Mahayana and Vajrayana

Overview

Meditation is just as important in Mahayana and Vajrayana Buddhism as it is in Theravada. It plays a similar role on the path to enlightenment. The two main methods of *shamatha* and *vipasyana* (the Sanskrit equivalents of *samatha* and *vipassana*) are also practised in Mahayana Buddhism. So what is the difference between meditation in Theravada and meditation in Mahayana and Vajrayana Buddhism? There are three main factors:

- *tathagatagarbha*
- skilful means (*upaya*)
- the master–disciple relationship

The first difference is the principle of *tathagatagarbha* or buddha nature (see Chapter 4). According to this principle, every being has the potential for buddhahood or enlightenment within, so the spiritual path is simply a way of re-discovering it, uncovering it and bringing it to fulfilment. As a result of this perspective, meditation in Mahayana and Vajrayana has two characteristics:

- Meditation is described not as a method to acquire qualities one does not already have, but rather as the way of revealing and realising the qualities one has deep within.
- Because buddhahood is within us all the time, it is theoretically possible to realise this at any time. Enlightenment is immanent and could be attained right now, suddenly and immediately, just as it could be attained gradually through a life-long process of religious practice.

In Mahayana and Vajrayana there are two ways of attaining enlightenment, the sudden way and the gradual way, and different meditation methods are used in each. In the light of this we can better understand the following description of meditation by the Tibetan master Sogyal Rinpoche.

> The purpose of meditation is to awaken in us the sky-like nature of mind, and to introduce us to that which we really are, our unchanging pure awareness, which underlies the whole of life and death.
>
> In the stillness and silence of meditation, we glimpse and return to that deep inner nature that we have so long ago lost sight of amid the busyness and distraction of our minds. Isn't it extraordinary that our minds cannot stay still for longer than a few moments without grasping after distraction; they are so restless and preoccupied. According to some authorities, up to 13% of people in the United States suffer from some kind of mental disorder. What does that say about the way we live?
>
> We are fragmented into so many different aspects. We don't know who we really are, or what aspects of ourselves we should identify with or believe in. So many contradictory voices, dictates, and feelings fight for control over our inner lives that we find ourselves scattered everywhere, in all directions, leaving nobody at home.
>
> Meditation, then, is bringing the mind home.
>
> Sogyal Rinpoche, *The Tibetan Book of Living and Dying*

The purpose of meditation is to awaken our buddha nature and it follows that any method that has this effect is considered a valid skilful means. Skilful means (*upaya*) is the second key principle of meditation in both these vehicles. This is the reason why so many different meditational methods are used in Mahayana and Vajrayana in addition to the *shamatha* and *vipasyana* methods described in Chapter 14.

Each method is effective for a particular state of mind, a particular mental tendency or a particular situation. These methods include visualisations, reciting mantras or *nembutsu*, and meditating on *koans* (riddles), for example. We will look briefly at the methods used in the Zen and Pure Land traditions in particular.

The other characteristic of meditation in Mahayana and Vajrayana generally, though less in Pure Land, is that the teacher plays a different role in the student's development on the path. The teacher or master has a one-to-one relationship with each student and gives advice on meditation according to individual needs. The teacher is seen as being able to transmit his or her understanding to the student wordlessly, with the aid of various techniques that communicate the ultimate truth of things directly, without concepts, from mind to mind. It is considered that this special transmission of spiritual understanding from master

to disciple lies at the very heart of Mahayana and Vajrayana traditions and ensures that the power and authenticity of the Buddhist teaching is continued from one generation to the next.

Meditation in Zen Buddhism

The term Ch'an (Chinese) or Zen (Japanese) means 'meditation'. It is derived from the Sanskrit word *dhyana*. This in itself reflects the importance given to meditation in Zen Buddhism. Zen is founded on the direct grasp of reality that is passed down from master to student and does not rely on study of the scriptures. One Chinese master described Zen teaching as follows:

> a direct transmission of awakened consciousness outside tradition and outside scripture; not founded on words; directly pointing to the human heart; seeing into one's own nature and realising buddhahood.
>
> Cited in H. Dumoulin, *A History of Zen Buddhism*

Meditation is accorded more importance than the study of Buddhist scriptures in Zen. Since the ultimate truth is beyond words, it cannot be conveyed in ordinary language. Intellectual study is often considered to be a hindrance rather than a help in understanding what is non-conceptual. If the scriptures are studied at all, preference is given to the Lankavatara Sutra, the Heart Sutra and the Diamond Sutra, but the extent to which study is encouraged varies from teacher to teacher. In the Rinzai tradition, students read episodes from the lives of past masters and students in that tradition and use these as subjects for meditation.

These words emphasise the importance of the mind-to-mind transmission of the ultimate truth from master to disciple. The teacher uses methods that point directly to the student's heart so that he or she can realise his or her own nature there and then. This is the skilful, effective and rapid way of attaining buddhahood according to Zen. The experience that is sought in Zen is that of perfect wisdom or *prajñaparamita*, the realisation of *shunyata* or the empty nature of all things as described in Madhyamaka, or again the realisation of the non-dual nature of things spoken of in Chittamatra. Fully realising this is seeing the world as it really is, and this is enlightenment.

Meditation in Rinzai Zen

The Rinzai tradition emphasises the sudden approach to enlightenment. The sudden, instantaneous insight into enlightenment is called *wu* in Chinese and *satori* in Japanese. *Satori* has been likened to the shattering of a block of ice and as a classic mystical experience of great unity, great peace, a feeling of really

knowing the truth, of having transcended time and space, and experiencing a higher state of consciousness that is impossible to put into words. Many of the methods used in Rinzai aim to bring about *satori* and produce a sense of shock or surprise in the student which awakens him or her from the sleep of ignorance. The purpose of Rinzai has been described as bringing about 'a revolution in the seat of consciousness', entailing a total shift from confusion to enlightenment. The methods used are eccentric and dramatic, such as shouting, beating and hurling insults. It is believed that gentler methods will not be powerful enough to jolt us out of the deep-seated torpor of ignorance that clouds our minds, and that defilements and negative habits are so strong in this day and age that only dramatic methods will work. These methods are seen as examples of skilful means applied by the Zen master to an individual student.

The other method used in Rinzai is meditation on *kung-an* (Chinese) or *koans* (Japanese), which are riddles, and on *mondos*, which take the form of questions and answers. Here are some examples of *koans*.

> What is the sound of one hand clapping?
> If you meet the Buddha on the road, kill him.
> Why did Bodhidharma come from the West?

Examples of *mondos* include:

> What is the Buddha? Three pounds of flax.
> Is there buddha nature in a dog? Emptiness.

One can attempt some form of explanation for *koans* and *mondos*, but the main point is that they cannot be understood with the rational mind. As students struggle to understand them their minds get exhausted, and in that exhaustion the intellect gives up and an intuitive insight dawns. We could say that all these methods in Rinzai have the effect of purging the mind so that the student breaks through from the ordinary mind to the wisdom mind (*prajña*) and the buddha nature.

Meditation in Soto Zen

Soto Zen emphasises the gradual approach to enlightenment and brings about a progressive understanding of the truth, primarily through intensive daily practise of meditation.

Sitting meditation is called *zazen*. The sitting posture is important, with legs crossed in lotus position, the back straight and the hands resting one upon the other in the lap. *Zazen* is practised with the eyes open because the material world of the senses is not rejected. Soto monks will often sit in a simple meditation hall in rows with their backs to each other, staring at the blank wall. They

practise concentration on their breathing and observation of thoughts, similar to the methods of *shamatha* and *vipasyana*.

The aim is simply to sit mindfully. Meditation is not seen as a method of reaching a goal, but as the goal itself. Meditation is the expression of buddha nature. There is a cartoon that illustrates this: an older monk and a younger monk are meditating together and the younger one says, 'Well, I've been doing this for 5 years now. What's next?' The older monk replies, 'What do you mean "What's next"? This is it!'

Soto students practise meditation in long sessions, and, to prevent anyone from falling asleep, the master may patrol the meditation hall and strike anyone who is drowsy on the shoulder with a stick. Sitting meditation alternates with walking meditation (*kin hin*), when students will walk slowly in a circle round the room or courtyard, maintaining mindfulness of every bodily movement and sensation as well as every thought in the mind.

Meditation and the martial arts

Bodhidharma founded Shao-lin monastery in southern China, and it has since become famous as the home of kung fu. It is said that, while he was in a 9-year retreat, Bodhidharma felt the need to practise some form of physical exercise and developed martial arts as a way of expressing meditation in action. Originally, martial arts were practised only by those who had eliminated selfish desires and aggression through meditation practice, and served as a non-violent form of defence without weapons and completely free from anger, jealousy, greed or any other negative motivation.

Figure 15.1
The famous
Shao-lin temple,
China

World Religions Photo Library/B. Smith

The integration of martial arts into Zen practice proved attractive to Japanese warriors following the Rinzai school between the thirteenth and seventeenth centuries. Unfortunately, the practice became decadent, to the extent that groups of monks were hired as mercenary armies by rival warlords and the Buddhist values on which martial arts were originally based were forgotten.

The expression of meditation in everyday life

The purpose of meditation is to develop a state of mind beyond thought, the state of 'no thought' where there is no separation between subject and object. Once this state has been attained, it extends beyond meditation sessions and continues throughout the day and night. This pure concentration means that one is completely present and mindful in whatever one is doing, hence the Zen saying: 'When I eat, I eat; when I sleep, I sleep.' Zen Buddhists in Japan, too, developed a number of formal ways of expressing the peaceful and harmonious qualities of meditation in life. These formal expressions include calligraphy, painting and drawing, archery, the tea ceremony, gardening and flower arranging (*ikebana*).

One of the pioneers of Japanese Zen was Eisai (1141–1215), who popularised the drinking of tea, arguing that it would be better for warriors than alcohol. Zen monks found it helpfully refreshing. 'Whenever one is in poor spirits, one should drink tea,' said Eisai. During the civil unrest in Japan in the fourteenth and fifteenth centuries, Soto Zen monasteries developed the tea ceremony, a ritual lasting several hours and performed in complete silence, involving the preparation of a large pot of tea by the Zen priest. The atmosphere of the ceremony is one of total peace and calm; every movement and gesture is graceful, mindful and harmonious; and all those who look on remain in meditation throughout.

Both gardening and flower arranging are ways of taking natural elements such as landscape, trees, plants, flowers, stones and water, and combining them in such a way that a sense of balance and harmony is created. The spirit of these activities was influenced by Taoism and its closeness to nature. The result is a garden or a flower arrangement that naturally inspires meditation and is conducive to meditation practice.

Meditation in Pure Land Buddhism

Pure Land Buddhism is based on devotion to Buddha Amitabha (Sanskrit) or Amida Buddha (Japanese) — see Chapter 16. The Pure Land tradition emphasises devotional and meditational practices over scriptural study, thus

making it accessible to ordinary people leading busy lives. In both China and Japan Pure Land became the religion of the masses.

Pure Land began in China in the fourth to fifth centuries CE. By the seventh century CE five main practices were taught:

- reciting the name of Amida Buddha
- reciting the Mahayana sutras
- meditating on the wonders of the Pure Land, the heaven of Sukhavati
- paying respect to statues of Buddha Amitabha
- singing Buddha Amitabha's praises

These five practices were not continued for very long, however, and the path in Pure Land Buddhism gradually became limited to *nien fo* or reciting the name of Amida Buddha. When Pure Land was introduced into Japan in the ninth century, the recitation of Amida's name and singing his praises were practised by the Tendai sect alongside their own forms of practice. But when Pure Land was established as a separate school in Japan by Honen (1133–1212), who founded Pure Land, and Shinran (1173–1262), who founded True Pure Land (also known as Shin Buddhism), the recitation of the name of Amida Buddha became virtually the sole practice.

Figure 15.2 Amitabha

Pure Land Buddhism emphasises devotion, and reciting the name of Amida Buddha is the main vehicle for expressing that devotion. It is called the *nembutsu* and in Japanese is *Namu Amida Butsu*, meaning 'I bow to Amida Buddha'. The *nembutsu* is recited over and over again throughout the day, and can be recited while one is carrying out one's daily activities. It is a way of keeping the presence of Amida Buddha in mind at all times and continually asking for his protection and help.

Some scholars claim that the *nembutsu* is a meditation method and not only a devotional practice. At the outset, followers acknowledge the darkness of their ignorance and with the *nembutsu* call out to Amida Buddha to transform them with his immeasurable light. Taitetsu Unno writes that constant recitation of the *nembutsu* asks us to become authentically real as human beings by awakening us to the boundless compassion that sustains us, which is embodied by Amida Buddha. Philosophically speaking, Unno says that the *nembutsu* is 'the self-articulation of fundamental reality', and by reciting it we transcend our ordinary ways of thinking and come to understand reality as it is.

At the core of nembutsu experience is a noetic element that enables us to see things as they are, so that we are no longer fooled or agitated by delusions.

Taitetsu Unno, *River of Fire, River of Water*

Through this practice one can come to embody the *dharmakaya*, the ultimate reality that is beyond words, and one's whole being becomes vibrant with the boundless compassion of Amida Buddha. It is an experiential process that requires great self-discipline and mental focus, just as meditation does in other Buddhist traditions.

There are two differences between *nembutsu* practice and meditation in other traditions. First, the benefits of *nembutsu* recitation are not seen to depend only on the follower's own efforts but more especially on the blessings of Amida Buddha, which infuse the bodies and minds of devotees. In other words, this practice combines meditation and devotion together, and is not only an own-powered practice but an other-powered practice. Second, the *nembutsu* does not have to be recited only in formal sessions, sitting in a particular posture, but can be called out at any time and during periods of daily activity. This makes *nembutsu* practice flexible and easily adapted to busy working lives.

The Pure Land school of Honen allows devotion to buddhas and *bodhisattvas* other than Amida Buddha, but Shin Buddhism discourages this. Shin Buddhism considers that the merit gained from virtuous activity is not powerful enough in this degenerate age to be of any real help on the path to enlightenment, so devotion is the only practice that is effective. Pure Land Buddhism teaches that rebirth in *sukhavati* speeds up one's path to enlightenment and that after a certain time one is reborn again to continue this path. However, Shin Buddhism teaches that rebirth in *sukhavati* is the final goal, the equivalent to nirvana or buddhahood, rather than a step on the way there. This may sound far removed from the original teaching given by the Buddha in ancient India, but it is seen as a form of skilful means (*upaya*) appropriate for an age in which confusion and negativity are rampant and people no longer have the time to spend many years in scriptural study or formal meditation.

The importance of devotion in Pure Land Buddhism indicates that this practice is closer to Vajrayana than to Mahayana. Indeed, *nembutsu* recitation plays the same role as the recitation of mantras in Vajrayana.

Meditation in Tibetan Buddhism

Tibetan Buddhism incorporates both Mahayana and Vajrayana forms of Buddhism. Devotion plays an important role on the path as it does in Pure Land, but it is directed not only to the buddhas and *bodhisattvas* but also to the

lama or spiritual master who guides the student and who transmits the highest wisdom directly to him or her.

All schools of Tibetan Buddhism teach that we have buddha nature (*tathagatagarbha*) and that meditation and other practices are all ways of uncovering this buddha nature and allowing it to reach its full potential. Generally speaking, Tibetan Buddhism teaches the gradual approach to meditation and to enlightenment, through *shamatha* and *vipasyana*, but the Dzogchen tradition taught by the Nyingma school — the oldest Buddhist school of Tibet — also teaches the direct approach. The direct approach requires devotion to a lama, which enables the lama to transmit his wisdom mind directly to the student, either silently through gestures or in words. This is called 'the transmission of the nature of mind' and it can happen very subtly in apparently quite normal situations. Devotion is important because, unless the mind of the student is completely open, he or she will not be able to recognise and realise what is being transmitted. The highest meditation is simply resting in, and abiding by, this recognition of the nature of mind. The twentieth-century master Dudjom Rinpoche describes it like this:

> No words can describe it
> No example can point to it
> Samsara does not make it worse
> Nirvana does not make it better
> It has never been born
> It has never ceased
> It has never been liberated
> It has never been deluded
> It has never existed
> It has never been nonexistent
> It has no limits at all
> It does not fall into any kind of category.

A number of meditational methods are characteristic of Tibetan Buddhism, in particular the use of mantras and visualisations.

Mantras are sacred words of power, almost always in Sanskrit, the recitation of which has a deeply transformative effect on the practitioner. Each buddha and *bodhisattva* has his or her own mantra, so the mantra is like a name that invokes the being one is praying to and causes the mind of the practitioner to 'tune in' to his or her presence, qualities and power. Buddhas and *bodhisattvas* are not seen simply as external beings, but as reflections of the qualities of one's own mind. Mantra recitation is a method of awakening the corresponding qualities in one's own mind so that ultimately one's mind and that of the buddhas become one and the same. This is the meaning of yoga in Vajrayana Buddhism: the merging

or union of one's mind with the enlightened mind of the buddhas or the lama. Guru yoga lies at the heart of Tibetan Buddhism, and underlines the importance given to devotion as a method for attaining enlightenment.

The musical quality of chanting mantras is said to have a significant healing effect and calms the emotions in a similar way to the effects of certain musical chords. Mantra practice is sometimes used as a preliminary to *shamatha* or *vipasyana* practice, because it helps the mind become relaxed and peaceful quite quickly and effortlessly, making further meditation much easier.

Mantras are recited over and over again either within formal meditation sessions or informally, in everyday life. Most Tibetan lay people would recite mantras quietly to themselves all day long as they went about their work, especially the mantra of Chenresig, the *bodhisattva* of compassion, which is *Om mane padme hum*. It is traditional to print mantras onto cloths and hoist them as prayer flags, in the belief that the wind will carry the blessings of the mantra far and wide.

Mantras are usually combined with visualisation of the buddha or deity concerned. A detailed description is given of the being to be visualised, often depicted in Sambhogakaya form (see Chapter 4), and the practice entails focusing mentally on the image until one can see it effortlessly in the mind's eye. Visualisation practice is therefore a form of *shamatha* concentration.

To help practitioners develop their ability to visualise, there are paintings or *thangkas* depicting these beings in full and inspiring detail. It is always emphasised that visualisation is not simply a way of developing the imagination or of fabricating images that have no relation to reality, nor is it a way of whitewashing ordinary life by superimposing a perfect reality that is only wishful thinking. Visualisation is understood as a method for developing the ability to perceive the Sambhogakaya dimension of reality, a way of expanding our minds to be in touch with dimensions of being that are unknown to the ordinary human mind.

Benefits of meditation

Tibetan Buddhists have been particularly active in exploring the physiological and mental effects of meditation from a scientific point of view. Lamas have volunteered for experiments in Harvard, Wisconsin and New York universities. There is now documented evidence of a wide range of physical benefits arising from meditation. Some findings provide measurable evidence for emotional benefits, too.

- The journal *Stroke* published a study of 60 African-Americans with artherosclerosis or hardening of the arteries, who practised meditation for 6–9 months. The meditators showed a marked decrease in the thickness of

their artery walls, while non-meditators showed an increase. Meditation brought about a potential 11% decrease in the risk of heart attack and an 8–15% decrease in the risk of stroke.

- Researchers at Harvard Medical School have monitored the brain activity of meditators. They have found meditation activates the sections of the brain in charge of the autonomic nervous system, which governs bodily functions we cannot normally control, such as digestion and blood pressure. This may explain why meditation helps to ward off stress-related conditions such as heart disease, digestive problems and infertility.

- The journal *New Scientist* reported brain-scanning experiments on experienced Buddhist meditators in the University of Wisconsin, USA. Both during meditation and afterwards the meditators showed persistent activity in the left prefrontal lobes, which are associated with positive emotions and good moods.

- Research at New York University suggests that Buddhist mindfulness practice might tame the amygdala, a subcortical area of the brain involved in relatively automatic emotional and behavioural responses. This would explain why meditators in the experiment did not become as flustered, shocked or surprised as ordinary people by unpredictable sounds, even those as loud as gunshots, and did not become as angry.

Paul Ekman of University of California San Francisco Medical School concluded, 'The most reasonable hypothesis is that there is something about conscientious Buddhist practice that results in the kind of happiness we all seek.' The *New Scientist* wrote, 'Scientists have evidence to show that Buddhists really are happier and calmer than other people.'

Questions

1 'Many different methods but only one aim'. Is this a fair assessment of Buddhist meditation?
2 Explain the distinctive features of Zen meditation.
3 To what extent is Zen meditation completely different from *samatha* and *vipassana*?
4 'The main goal of the various forms of Buddhist meditation is to learn more about yourself.' Explain and assess this view.
5 Explain why devotion in Pure Land is completely different from devotion in any other tradition.

Chapter 16

Brief history of Zen and Pure Land

Ch'an/Zen

Ch'an (Chinese) or Zen (Japanese) claims to be a special line of transmission of the Buddhist teachings that began with the historical Buddha Shakyamuni. According to the traditional account of its origins, the Buddha was once surrounded by several disciples and at one point he silently held up a flower and turned it in his hand. Only one disciple, Kasyapa, understood the message in this gesture, and he smiled in recognition. As a result, the 'special transmission' of which Zen speaks is a silent one, in which the truth of the Dharma is conveyed primarily in gestures and actions. It claims to bring a direct, intuitive grasp of reality which is personally transmitted 'from mind to mind' by a master to his disciple.

The Zen tradition asserts that this transmission was passed on from generation to generation in ancient India as an alternative, and in parallel, to the scriptural tradition. However, there are no records of this, and scholars have no evidence to show that this was recognised as a distinct tradition in India. It is therefore unclear whether Ch'an as a tradition began in India or in China.

Bodhidharma

What we do know is that in 520 CE the Indian master Bodhidharma travelled to China and reportedly founded the line of Ch'an masters there. Bodhidharma was a colourful character, and there are many legends about his life. It is said that as part of his training he meditated for 9 years facing a wall until his legs fell off, and he cut off his eyelids to keep himself from dozing in meditation. He is said to have insulted the Chinese emperor by telling him that good deeds, such as sponsoring monasteries and the copying of scriptures, would earn him no merit at all; the Ch'an tradition does not place as much value on scriptural study as it does on meditation practice. Bodhidharma is recognised as the

founder of the famous Shao-lin temple in southern China, the home of kung fu (this is the temple in which Bruce Lee trained before he made the film *Enter the Dragon*). It is said that Bodhidharma developed the martial arts during a long period of retreat as a means of maintaining physical health and strength.

Modern scholars accept that Bodhidharma is likely to have been a historical figure, but some put the date of his arrival in China a little earlier, at around 480 CE. Although Bodhidharma discouraged intensive study of the scriptures, he did have a special connection with the Lankavatara Sutra, which is still the main scripture of this tradition. This Mahayana Sutra teaches the emptiness (*shunyata*) teachings of the Second Turning of the Dharma Wheel as well as the teachings of the Third Turning on buddha nature (*tathagatagarbha*).

The patriarchs

After Bodhidharma there were six generations of 'patriarchs', the name given to the most prominent Ch'an master in each period. The fifth patriarch was Hung jen (601–675), who decided to run a poetry competition to choose his successor. The most learned chief monk, Shen hsiu, who was expected to win this title, wrote the following poem:

> The body is the bodhi tree
> The mind is like a clear mirror
> At all times we must strive to polish it
> And must not let the dust collect.

This verse was a conventional Buddhist expression of the need to purify the mind of the ignorance that prevents us from seeing clearly. But an illiterate servant named Hui neng, who worked in the monastery kitchen, was also moved to enter the competition and his poem read:

> The bodhi tree is originally not a tree
> The mirror has no stand
> Buddha nature is always clean and pure
> Where is there room for dust?
>
> The mind is the bodhi tree
> The body is the mirror stand
> The mirror is originally clean and pure
> Where can it be stained by dust?

S. Bercholz and S. Kohn, Entering the Stream

These poems express a deeper level of understanding, because from the enlightened point of view the buddha nature is unchanging, always pure and can never be stained. The 'dust' of karma and ignorance is an illusion, and when

we become enlightened we realise that it was never really there. Hui neng was chosen as the sixth patriarch, which was an important step in the history of Ch'an, because he was illiterate. His success vividly demonstrated that scriptural study in itself does not bring true depth of spiritual understanding.

Soto and Rinzai

Ch'an survived the persecution of Buddhism in China in 845 CE because it did not depend on large monasteries or vast libraries of scriptures. Its teachings did not require elaborate institutions that needed wealth to support them, and so it escaped political suppression. During the course of the ninth and tenth centuries, Ch'an split into several different schools, the two main ones being Lin chi and Ts'ao tung, which later became the Soto and Rinzai schools of Japanese Zen. These two schools remained separate in Japan, but merged in China under the Ming dynasty (1368–1644). Ch'an continued as a live Buddhist tradition in China until the Communist revolution in 1949 and continues to flourish in Taiwan and South Korea.

Ch'an meditation practices were introduced into Japan as early as the seventh century via Korea, but it was not until the twelfth century that Zen became popular in Japan. The master who established Zen was Eisai (1141–1215), a Japanese monk in the Tendai tradition, who travelled to China to further his studies and later brought back the Lin chi (Rinzai) tradition to his homeland. Rinzai attracted Japan's educated warrior and political classes because of the way it cultivates toughness, the martial arts and intellectual riddles called *koans*. But the Tendai monk Dogen (1200–1253) was not satisfied with the Rinzai teachings and decided to go to China himself in search of something more meaningful. He brought back to Japan the Tsao tung (Soto) tradition, which emphasises quiet meditation and a simple life of poverty and peace, uninvolved in worldly intrigue. It is often said that the character of Soto Zen attracted the farmer and peasant classes.

Dogen is widely regarded as a remarkable Buddhist saint. He studied the sutras of Nikaya and Mahayana Buddhism, but felt that study becomes a distraction if it is not done to support meditation. He chose to follow the example of the Buddha and led a simple life of poverty, entirely dedicated to benefiting others. It was Dogen who taught the importance of *zazen* or sitting meditation, which now characterises the Soto school.

Both Soto and Rinzai schools of Zen continue in Japan to this day. There have been troubled periods in Japanese history during which Rinzai monasteries became involved in political rivalries, but the character and teachings of both schools have weathered these difficulties. Several Japanese masters introduced Zen to North America in the twentieth century, where it is becoming well established.

Pure Land

A Mahayana sutra of Indian origin tells the story of a monk named Dharmakara, who vowed in the presence of a buddha who lived aeons ago that when he attained enlightenment he would create a perfect paradise out of compassion for the suffering of beings. One of his vows was that beings would only have to think of him and he would lead them to this paradise after death. His vows are expressed in a poem by Tz'u min:

> That Buddha in his bodhisattva stage made the universal vow:
> 'When beings hear my Name and think on me, I will come and welcome them.
> Not discriminating at all between the poor and the rich and well born,
> Not discriminating between the inferior and highly gifted;
> Not choosing the learned and those who uphold pure precepts,
> Not rejecting those who break precepts and whose evil karma is profound,
> Solely making beings turn about and abundantly say the Name
> I can make bits of rubble change into gold.'
>
> Cited in Unno, *River of Fire, River of Water*

Dharmakara gained enlightenment and at that point he became known as Buddha Amitabha (Sanskrit) or Amida Buddha (Japanese), meaning 'the Buddha of infinite light'. He created a perfect heaven called Sukhavati or 'the land of bliss or happiness'. The Pure Land tradition of Buddhism is one that is based on devotion to Buddha Amitabha, and one of the goals of the tradition is to achieve rebirth in his pure land of Sukhavati.

The founder of the Pure Land tradition is said to be the Chinese master Hui Yuan (fourth century CE), but the school's founder and first patriarch is Tan lu'an (sixth century CE), who was inspired by a vision of Buddha Amitabha. He taught that meditating on Amitabha and reciting his name are an unfailing path to liberation for all but the very worst sinners. Then Tao cho (562–645) added to this doctrine the principle that it is the only method that is suitable for this morally decadent age when the Three Poisons are extremely strong. Traditional methods, including scriptural study, will not work with beings as defiled as we are now, nor do our lives allow us the time to pursue religion as our only focus. In such circumstances, devotion is the only method that is powerful enough to bring about liberation.

Pure Land became extremely popular in China, especially with the masses who could not pursue philosophical studies. It also attracted people with morally questionable livelihoods such as fishing, which according to the classic Eightfold Path is to be seriously discouraged because it involves killing fish.

Pure Land teaches that genuine devotion is more effective than virtuous action

as a means to attain Sukhavati. Pure Land remained the most popular form of Buddhism in China until the twentieth century, and it is estimated that in the 1930s almost 70% of Chinese Buddhists followed Pure Land Buddhism.

In Japan, the recitation of Amida Buddha's name, the *nembutsu*, was integrated into existing Buddhist meditation and study in the ninth century, but Pure Land only became a distinct school in the thirteenth century. The founder of the Pure Land school, Jodoshu, is considered to be Honen (1133–1212), a scholar-monk who taught that Buddhist institutions had become corrupt and the only way to salvation was devotion to Amida Buddha. He believed that the long programmes of scriptural study in the Tendai school were too difficult for most and taught 'the easy path' of devotion. The Tendai authorities did not appreciate his criticism of what they saw as orthodoxy, and Honen was forced to disrobe and was banished from Kyoto. He simply continued to teach in the country-side. He did not himself found a new school; this was done by his followers. Most of his followers remained celibate monks and led a simple life.

An important disciple of Honen, Shinran, founded the True Pure Land school or Jodo-shinshu, sometimes known as Shin Buddhism. Shinran believed that his was the only correct understanding of Honen's teaching. He criticised the principle of gaining merit through virtuous action, saying that this only leads to pride and self-importance. We are all hopeless sinners and have no power of our own to bring about enlightenment; instead we must rely entirely and whole-heartedly on the power of Amida Buddha to help us. He discouraged practices of devotion and respect to any Buddhist figure other than Amida Buddha.

Shinran had a dream in which he had a vision of the *bodhisattva* of compassion, Kwannon, who advised him to get married. As a result, priests in the True Pure Land school get married and have families and jobs, so there is no monastic tradition in this school. The responsibilities of the priest's role are usually handed down through heredity, from father to son. Shin Buddhism remains a popular form of Buddhism in Japan today.

Questions

1 Examine the ways to liberation taught by Pure Land and Zen Buddhism. Are these teachings opposed to each other?

2 To what extent could it be argued that Pure Land does not follow the main principles of the Buddha's teaching?

Buddhism

Chapter 17

Religious authority

Western philosophy of religion refers to four types of religious authority: tradition, scripture, reason and religious experience. We can apply this model for analysing religious authority in any of the world's religions, and we will find that each religion has specific definitions for each of these areas as well as a unique balance between the different types of authority. For example, Islam considers its scriptures to be more authoritative than reason, while within Christianity some churches emphasise the importance of religious experience and others do not. In this chapter we look at how each type of authority is considered in Buddhism, and at the issues raised by the question of religious authority in contemporary Buddhism.

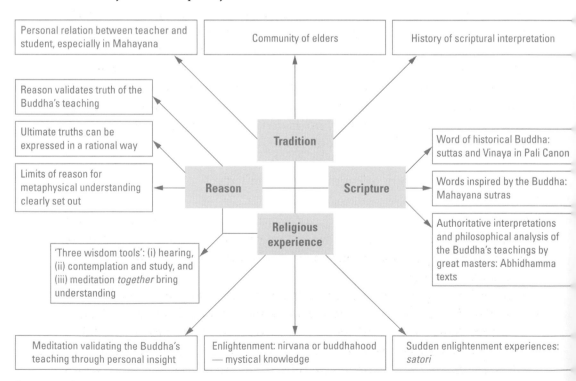

Figure 17.1 Model of authority in Buddhism

While Buddhism accepts all four of these sources of authority, it considers that some sources are more important than others. For example, in Theravada, the commentator Buddhaghosa presents their order of priority as follows:

- scripture
- what is in conformity with scripture
- the commentaries by great scholars
- personal interpretation based on reasoning and religious experience

Scripture is without doubt the most important source of authority, and the other three must be in accord with the scriptures to be authoritative.

In Mahayana this is presented slightly differently, but scripture remains the most important source of authority. Based on Indian Mahayana sources, they are given by Deshung Rinpoche in his *The Three Levels of Spiritual Perception* (2003) as follows:

- scripture
- the commentaries by great scholars
- the spiritual teacher
- religious experience

This is the order in which they are presented in the texts, but in terms of a person's experience it is said that the order is the other way round. First one develops some valid experience, then one appreciates the importance and value of a teacher. Respect for the teacher brings more respect for the commentaries he or she is teaching from, and finally for the original scriptures taught by the Buddha.

Although Buddhism expresses itself differently on the sources of authority that it recognises compared to Western models of thinking, the differences are not critical. We will therefore look at authority in Buddhism according to the four areas identified earlier to make it easier to compare Buddhism with the other faiths examined in philosophy of religion.

Scripture

Chapter 5 gave an overview of the Buddhist scriptures and explained which scriptures are considered authoritative by each tradition and school. Here we summarise the main points concerning the authority of the various collections of Buddhist scriptures.

- The Pali Canon, the scriptures of the Theravada school, comprises three categories of scripture: the Vinaya, the Suttas and the Abhidhamma. The Vinaya and the Suttas are considered authoritative by all traditions of Buddhism because they are believed to contain the words of the historical Buddha.
- The Theravada Abhidhamma is considered authoritative by most Theravadins because it contains philosophical and psychological analysis by scholars who

are accepted as great masters of the tradition. In addition, some believe that the Abhidhamma was originally taught by the Buddha himself when, using his supernatural powers, he visited his deceased mother in the Tushita heaven during the teaching phase of his life. Those who believe in this account accept the authority of the Abhidhamma on the grounds that it is the word of the Buddha.

- The Mahayana sutras are accepted as authoritative only by the followers of Mahayana and Vajrayana Buddhism. These followers believe that the sutras contain words inspired by the Buddha or taught by the Buddha in Sambhogakaya form and that their authority derives from this. Some Mahayana Buddhists believe that the doctrine of these sutras was also taught by the historical Buddha during his lifetime, and recent textual discoveries in Afghanistan may attest to the existence of Mahayana teachings much earlier than first thought by modern scholars.

In Buddhism, the authority of the scriptures is supreme but is relative to the specific scriptures accepted by each tradition. But the whole of Buddhism follows the principle laid down by the Buddha, which is that scripture is never to be accepted blindly on trust but tested against reasoning and religious experience. Buddhists do not follow any of their scriptures dogmatically; instead they systematically set out to validate their truth by applying logical arguments and by examining their meaning in the light of their meditation experience. So in Buddhism, the authority of scripture is intimately connected with the authority of reason and the authority of religious experience.

Tradition

Community of elders

Buddhism has no church or other institution that has the authority to decide what is orthodox or not and what is accepted by the tradition or not. Instead, there are three elements that safeguard tradition: the community of elders, the historical lineage of scriptural interpretation, and the personal relationship between teacher and student, especially in Mahayana and Vajrayana Buddhism.

The 'community of elders' refers to the monastic community and, to some extent, to the community of each monastery rather than of all Buddhist monasteries. As we have seen in previous chapters, the role of the monastics is to uphold religious traditions such as ceremonies, festivals and other rituals. Monks and nuns uphold the traditional values of Buddhism by keeping all their precepts and vows and by being living examples of ethical behaviour. They keep knowledge of the religion alive by studying the scriptures. All these traditions

are accepted as authoritative by the Buddhist community as a whole, because most of them were first established by the Buddha himself and have been continued from one generation to the next since the Buddha's time.

Within each Theravadin monastery, authority is conferred democratically upon the abbot or head of the monastery, who is usually elected (or in Thailand sometimes appointed by Buddhist authorities) on the basis of his knowledge of the scriptures and his length of continuous monastic service. All but the most critical decisions are taken by the body of monks (in practice, either all the monks within a given monastery or an elected group) on the basis of consensus. Both monks and lay people accept the authority of this mechanism because it stems from the time of the Buddha. However, in Tibetan monasteries authority is often less democratic because the head lama of each monastery is considered to have more power and authority than anyone else.

History of scriptural interpretation

Although the scriptures are authoritative in Buddhism, as important as the texts themselves is the way they are interpreted. Each Buddhist school has one or more traditions of scriptural interpretation, which are seen as the only authoritative ways of understanding scripture. In other words, in Buddhism the scriptures are not completely open to individual interpretation, and, because there are ancient traditions that establish the meaning of each text, there is no room for anyone to speculate about their meaning. If anyone chose to reinterpret scripture outside this tradition, his or her views would not be considered authoritative. What is accepted, however, is personal interpretation on the part of those who are acknowledged to be great scholars by elders of the tradition. This has given rise to the numerous commentaries which are accepted as authoritative.

When a monk studies the scriptures, he is taught to interpret them in the way that his own teacher was taught; the 'lineage' of interpretation goes back for generations. In one sense, this is similar to the way we might learn at a university in the West when we learn the approach and the views of our professors. In another sense, it is quite different from this, because in India tradition is prized far beyond individual innovation in all areas of philosophy and religion; the student self-consciously aims to belong to a tradition rather than to create a distinct personal viewpoint. For Buddhists, holding tenaciously to one's personal views is just another form of attachment and needs to be abandoned as are all other forms of craving and attachment. Consistent with the doctrine of *anatta* or no-self, it is tradition that is authoritative in Buddhism and not the individual. As a result, new ideas are presented as reassessments of what earlier texts or traditions 'really meant'.

The teacher–student relationship

In previous chapters we have seen how important the teacher–student relationship is in Zen and in Tibetan Buddhism. This is because the teacher is seen to transmit the mind of enlightenment directly to the student, one-to-one, and it is believed that enlightenment is impossible to achieve without the transformative blessing of the teacher. The tremendous authority wielded by the teacher rests on his or her ability to effect this transmission and keep the lineage alive, so that the truth retains its full power and is not just a dead set of ideas.

The other reason for the lama's authority in Tibetan Buddhism is because he or she is considered to be a living embodiment of all the qualities of the enlightened mind. This is why the lama is an object of refuge, so that Vajrayana Buddhists will say, 'I take refuge in the lama, I take refuge in the Buddha, I take refuge in the Dharma, I take refuge in the Sangha'. The lama is a spiritual guide, like the Buddha; his teachings and advice are the Dharma; and he is a friend on the path fulfilling the role of the Sangha. In spiritual terms, therefore, there is nobody higher or more important than one's own lama.

Both in Zen and in Tibetan Buddhism, the student develops devotion to the teacher, meaning an openness of heart and mind and a surrender of the ego that gets in the way of that openness. The student views the teacher's words and actions as so many skilful means (*upaya*) of expressing the Dharma, and takes them as opportunities for learning and personal development. The teacher is accepted as completely authoritative, representing the Buddha, Dharma and Sangha, and the teacher himself must always abide by the Dharma during this teaching process. The authority of the teacher ultimately rests on his or her own spiritual attainment, including both knowledge and compassion.

Reason

Reason plays a more important role in Buddhism than perhaps in any other of the world's religions. An underlying assumption in Buddhist thought is that the truth — even truths that are ultimate and beyond words — can be pointed to in rational language. In the case of ultimate truths, rational language will be able to convey only an approximation of those truths at best, but the principle remains that nothing can be accepted as true if it is irrational, illogical or somehow goes against valid reasoning. In other words, the truth is always compatible with reason.

How can we account for the prominent role of reason within the Buddhist religion? It is connected with the fact that neither the doctrine nor the scriptures of Buddhism are considered divine in origin; consequently there is nothing intrinsically non-human about them and nothing that is inherently inaccessible

to the human mind. There is therefore no justification within Buddhist thought for arguing that ultimate truths must be mysteries by definition.

The Buddhist understanding of enlightenment is that it is the attainment of freedom from ignorance. This naturally implies that knowledge replaces ignorance and, along with the qualities of compassion or *bodhichitta*, is one of the characteristics of both nirvana and buddhahood. For human beings, knowledge is intimately related to reason, and reason, even for philosophies that acknowledge its limits, is an indispensable tool for gaining at least some degree of knowledge. Buddhism is internally consistent in the way it sets out the limits of reason for knowing metaphysical truths, while at the same time valuing reason as a method for helping us reach the point at which we can transcend reason altogether.

Zen Buddhism, and especially Rinzai Zen, may be exceptions to some of the points made above. The Zen approach tends not to accept the value of rational discourse as a stepping stone for understanding higher, non-conceptual truths. Instead, it employs paradoxes and riddles which, on the face of it at least, are far from logical and rational. This Zen approach to language extends to the Buddhist scriptures: only that which directly expresses the ineffable truth can ultimately be considered authoritative.

Religious experience

Religious experience has enormous authority in Buddhism. It is true to say that the authority of the Buddha himself, both during his life and ever since, is due entirely to his enlightenment experience; without this, Shakyamuni would be a human being like any other, albeit a very wise one. In fact, all the teachings of Buddhism arise from the insights gained during his enlightenment, which means that the authority of the scriptures is validated by the Buddha's religious experience. This has important implications for Buddhism as a whole, because the Buddha was a human being and therefore his experience was not unique but can be shared by any one of us. Lewis Lancaster explains it this way:

> While the followers of the Buddha considered that his words possessed special power, the idea that the teaching arose from insights achieved in a special state of yogic development, a state open and available to all who have the ability and the desire to exert the tremendous effort needed to achieve it, meant that the words based on the experience need not be considered as unique or limited to one person in one time.
>
> Lewis Lancaster, *Buddhist Literature*

Mahayana develops this idea to the full when it teaches that the goal of Buddhism is full buddhahood, and when it accepts that a number of Buddhist

masters since the Buddha's time have reached buddahood in their turn, and so have become authoritative. It also helps to explain the authority accorded to Buddhist teachers in Vajrayana when they have attained very high stages of spiritual realisation.

The authenticity of a person's religious experience is not taken for granted in Buddhism, and there are various ways in which it can be verified. For example, the insights gained would have to accord with scripture; and the nature of the experience would need to be attested by a meditation master with extensive experience and preferably with long-standing knowledge of the person concerned.

Authority in contemporary Buddhism

Some issues concerning authority have surfaced over recent years, as Buddhism begins to take root in Europe and North America. These problems stem mainly from the cultural conflict involved when Buddhist ways of thinking are overlaid by Western ways of thinking. Two examples illustrate these cultural differences clearly.

First, some Westerners — especially academic scholars of Buddhism — find it hard to accept the authority of traditional scriptural interpretation and the idea that there is no individual freedom to read the texts and interpret them as one wishes and as one understands them. They argue that this Buddhist custom was determined by the lack of printed texts in ancient times, which meant that one was unable to gain access to scriptures and read them outside a monastic setting. In those days there were no bookshops or libraries. This question has arisen especially in relation to Tibetan Buddhism where a ritualised approach to textual study still exists today. For example, unless one listens to the oral recitation of a text by a qualified scholar, it is believed that one will not be receptive to the transformative blessing of the text when one studies it.

In response, a Buddhist might argue that the 'liberal' way of interpreting scripture stems specifically from Christian Protestantism, which encouraged personal reading of the scriptures, free of the constraints of the church. It is interesting to explore the arguments of both sides in this debate and to separate out what is historically and culturally specific from what is essential to the integrity of the religion.

Second, some Westerners reject the way that Buddhism has always tended to give more authority to men than to women. The monastic code for nuns enshrines the principle that nuns have a lower status than monks and should bow to them at all times. In all Buddhist countries throughout Asia, there has always been a greater number of monks than nuns. Almost all the Buddhist

masters and scholars revered by the tradition are men, and even today most of the Buddhist teachers of all traditions are men.

While these facts are indisputable, it must be remembered that the superior social status of men has been a universal fact in all areas of the globe for millennia, barring a few short-lived exceptions. It is only in the past 80 years or so that women have actively stood up for equal rights as we understand them today. It should therefore be no surprise that Buddhism, which began many centuries ago, does not teach the social equality of men and women.

However, Buddhism certainly does teach that men and women are spiritual equals; women are just as capable of attaining enlightenment as men. At the time of its introduction in India, this idea was very radical, but it is fair to say that the idea of spiritual equality was not reflected in social equality. Many Buddhist traditions are today adapting to the modern world by accepting women on socially equal terms with men. In this respect, the tradition is evolving with the times.

Question

1 'One of the main characteristics of the late twentieth century was that people were accustomed to challenging authority no matter from where it may have been derived.'

   a Examine some of the sources of authority which Buddhists might have believed to be important.

   b Explain some of the ways religious authority has been challenged in Buddhism and assess how effective these challenges have been.

Chapter 18

Religious experience

Religious experience is vitally important in Buddhism. In the case of the Buddha, his religious experiences became the historical foundation of the whole religion. Everything the Buddha taught was based on the insights he gained through his religious practices. To study this topic we will define what we mean by 'religious experience', identify the various types of religious experience and examine if and how each applies to Buddhism.

Defining religious experience

In Western philosophy of religion, there are two main definitions of religious experience. Some thinkers such as Friedrich Schleiermacher describe religious experiences as feelings. They are affective rather than cognitive experiences. In Buddhism we do find examples where religious experiences are described in terms of feelings; nirvana, for instance, is described as an experience of bliss and peace. Other thinkers such as William Alston define religious experiences as a type of perception and therefore as cognitive experiences. This, too, applies in Buddhism. The description of the enlightenment of the Buddha explains how he perceived certain truths in each of the three watches of the night: he saw his past lives in detail, he understood the karma of all beings and the nature of all things.

However, there are differences in what these terms mean when used in Buddhism. If we apply the idea of 'perception' to the Buddha's enlightenment experience we are stretching its usual meaning because we are not referring to sensory perception but to types of mental perception derived from meditation. Nevertheless, enlightenment is understood as a cognitive experience. When Rudolf Otto speaks of perception in the context of numinous experiences he defines it as 'apprehension of the wholly other', which certainly does not apply in Mahayana Buddhism. The whole point of enlightenment is to realise that the

nature of subject and object is the same; all boundaries between 'I' and 'other' dissolve, indeed the sense of 'I' dissolves completely. Buddhahood is not 'other' and unattainable but, on the contrary, *is* our very being. In Theravada, on the other hand, nirvana is presented as the opposite of samsara and is radically different from our deluded self; in this sense it could justifiably be called 'the wholly other'.

To present the Western range of definitions of religious experience very simply, some emphasise the affective while others emphasise the cognitive — but there are several problems associated with both these models. For example, it can be argued that feelings depend on concepts and are conditioned by them; feelings are culturally bound, so for instance my cultural background may lead me to experience a particular type of feeling as important or as unimportant. In the case of cognitive experiences, the belief systems within our culture and society provide a framework for the way we account for our experiences. The very fact that there is such a diversity of religious experience from one culture to another might imply that this diversity depends more on interpretation than on the experiences themselves.

The Buddhist understanding of the cognition process may resolve these problems. One classic Buddhist presentation of cognition based on the eighth-century Indian scholar Dharmakirti is as follows:

- Cognition depends on direct perception and conceptual inference, in that order.
- Direct perception is of at least three types: the senses, the sense consciousnesses and yogic perception.
- There are six senses: sight, hearing, smell, taste, touch and mind. The sixth of these, mental perception, specifically apprehends thoughts and other mental events.
- Conceptual interpretation occurs on the basis of sense perception and after it. Sense perceptions themselves are non-conceptual and apprehend things as they really are. However, concepts come in extremely quickly, so we can only distinguish these two phases of cognition in advanced meditation. Meditation slows down the process so that the conceptual reflex no longer operates.
- The undeluded mind can perceive reality as it is in yogic perception, that is, as an advanced meditational insight.

The Mahayana understanding of religious experience is that it is a mental cognition of reality as it is, undistorted by language and culture. It is a cognition of the undeluded mind purified through the process of the spiritual path; it is not a mental cognition of the ordinary deluded mind subject to strong emotions and conceptual judgements and limited by language. This framework explains how an apprehension of reality is possible.

In Buddhism such noetic (which means bringing new knowledge or insights) religious experiences are not confined to the attainment of enlightenment itself. If this were so, only buddhas would be able to have religious experiences. In fact, practitioners can have glimpses of reality at any time along the path to enlightenment; instances of this are *vipassana* insights and *satori* in Zen Buddhism. However, glimpses such as these may be transient, and the point of continuing on the path is to stabilise these glimpses until wisdom-perception becomes continuous, both in meditation sessions and during the rest of the day and night. This is enlightenment.

Grounds of knowledge claims

If we accept that religious experience in Buddhism has a cognitive element, we have to ask whether it provides adequate grounds for knowledge claims. Consider the following points.

- In Mahayana, enlightenment and glimpses of enlightenment are a non-dual experience, beyond subject and object, and therefore transcend conceptual conditioning.
- In Theravada, enlightenment and glimpses of enlightenment are not a non-dual experience, but they do transcend concepts.
- They are verifiable experiences, because they can be checked by other meditation masters.
- They can be replicated, because they can be experienced by anyone following the same Buddhist path.
- They do not occur haphazardly, because there are specific methods like meditation for attaining enlightenment.
- Enlightenment is internally consistent with the Buddha's teachings, both in being a state of highest realisation and in the methods used to attain it.
- Enlightenment is absence of ignorance, and absence of ignorance gives religious insight. Enlightenment *means* liberation from ignorance.

Types of religious experience

Many different types of religious experience are identified in Western philosophy of religion, in particular visions, numinous experiences, mystical experiences, conversions and revelations. Most books on this subject address religious experience in purely theistic terms and this may be misleading in the sense that readers may imagine that religious experience therefore does not apply to Buddhism at all. This is not so, but of course we need to redefine each type of experience accordingly.

Visions

The Buddha's experience of Mara could be interpreted as a visionary experience, although it is not described as a vision in the scriptures. If we take the story as symbolic, it can be understood as a series of visions. The experience was also noetic (a source of new knowledge), which is a characteristic of authentic visionary experience. In Mahayana and Vajrayana Buddhism, visions are understood as the apprehension of the Sambhogakaya dimension.

Numinous experiences

Numinous experiences bring both fear and wonder at the overwhelming power of an unknown force. When they are not theistic they are related to nature or places or another human being. It seems that nothing in the Buddha's experience fits this description.

Mystical experiences

This category comes closest to describing enlightenment. Some Christian descriptions of mystical experience are extremely close to Buddhist descriptions of enlightenment: 'He knew that the light was within himself' (Richard Bucke); 'distance and nearness become blurred into one, without and within glide into each other'; and 'his understanding and that of God are now both one' (St John of the Cross). But the phenomenological object of mysticism in Buddhism is not God or a permanent substance or force underlying the existence of all things, but the nature of things which is beyond time and space, and beyond the ideas of both existence and non-existence.

William James identifies four characteristics of mystical experience: ineffability, noetic quality, transience and passivity. Do these apply to mystical experience in Buddhism?

- **Ineffability:** both nirvana and buddhahood are said to be beyond words.
- **Noetic quality:** this certainly applies to all forms of enlightenment, because the goal of Buddhism always combines wisdom and knowledge together with compassion.
- **Transience:** this does not apply to nirvana or buddhahood. It is said that once one has attained enlightenment there is no going back; it is a realisation that is present every minute of the day and night and that continues after death. Transience would apply to glimpses of reality and other insights on the path.
- **Passivity:** in one way this does not apply to Buddhism and in another way it does. The descriptions of the Buddha's enlightenment do not convey the impression he was overwhelmed by his experience; on the contrary, he

emerges in complete control. However, no one can bring about such experiences at will. There is no meditational button we can press to attain instant enlightenment whenever we want it, and in this sense we have no control over it. In some Mahayana traditions such as Pure Land Buddhism, the other-powered nature of religion is strongly emphasised, so there is a significant degree of passivity in religious attainment — all attainment being due entirely to the compassion and blessing of Amida Buddha.

Many of the problems that Western thinkers have with mysticism do not necessarily apply to Buddhism. For example, A. J. Ayer is concerned that indescribability means that one cannot say anything rational about mystical experience. In Buddhism, there is an underlying belief that logical reason is not incompatible with mystical knowledge, even though the two are distinct. Reason can help us explain and understand mystical knowledge.

Ayer also argues that mystical experience yields no knowledge of the external world, only knowledge of the mystic's own mind. Buddhists would counter this in a number of ways: first, some would say that mystical experience occurs when subject and object have dissolved, so the dichotomy between the external world and the mystic's own mind no longer applies. Second, Ayer assumes that without the senses the mind's understanding can only be subjective. Buddhism distinguishes between the confused mind, which is indeed subjective, and the wisdom mind that apprehends things as they actually are. Third, Ayer states that true knowledge must be empirically based, meaning it should be derived from the senses and be verifiable by the senses. Buddhism contends that no cognition involves the senses alone; even sense perception involves the corresponding sensory consciousness. Both the senses and the mind are valid sources of cognition, and the mind can recognise reality without the mediation of the five physical senses. It is clear that the assumptions and perspectives of both sides are different.

The role of mystics and mysticism is important in Buddhism. After all, the Buddha himself was a mystic and the goal of the religion is a mystical experience. Buddhism has no church or overall institutional authority in a position to condemn mystics; instead, mystics have played a mainstream role in the development of many Buddhist traditions. Indeed, mystics like Nagarjuna have actually been the source of new scriptural traditions.

Conversions

William James defines conversion as follows: 'To say a man is "converted" means that religious ideas, previously peripheral in his consciousness, now take a central place, and that religious aims form the habitual centre of his energy.' In other words, a conversion experience changes your life. The example that springs

to mind in Buddhism is the moment when the Buddha decided to leave the palace and follow a religious life. The process of seeing the Four Signs or Sights revealed his natural interest for religious questions and formed what nowadays we might call a time of 'spiritual crisis' when he questioned all his values and his way of life. The result was a radical change in his outlook and a decision to make religious aims the focus of his life. In all these ways, this event in the life of the Buddha is a conversion experience.

The Buddha's life story contains many examples of the way the Buddha's disciples were converted, mostly after meeting with him or speaking with him. The stories of Sunita and Angulimala are instances of this (see Chapter 1). The experiences changed the lives of the disciples, who immediately decided to become monks or nuns. So, although we cannot interpret conversion in a theistic way, we can say that conversion experiences exist in Buddhism.

Revelations

If we define revelation in theistic terms as an active communication from God or other external source, it is not an accepted experience in Buddhism. However, it is possible to redefine revelation in a way that does fit with Buddhist thinking.

In the Buddhist sense, 'revelation' is *parivartina* — turning something over, explaining it, making clear what was previously hidden. The Buddha can be said to reveal the truth of the Dharma insofar as he uncovers what was hidden from our view because of ignorance and other mental defilements. When we listen to Buddhist teachings we may find certain truths resonate with us, and at such moments it is as if we recognise something that had been confused or hidden before, as if a hood has been pulled from our head and we see something clearly. We could call these 'moments of personal revelation or personal insight', which are important on an individual's path.

Religious experience as proof of the religion's tenets

In Buddhism, religious experience is never used to prove the existence of God. In fact, the reverse is the case: it is because no Buddhist masters, including the Buddha himself, have ever found God through their religious insights and experience that God's existence is denied. We could say that this lack of experience of God is used as proof for his non-existence, along with reasoned arguments (see Chapter 20).

Buddhist doctrine is based on both reasoning and meditation experience. Religious experience is not held to be incompatible with reason, and, if any doctrine is unreasonable or logically flawed, Buddhists question it.

The ways in which humanity learns of ultimate truths

The world's religions teach a number of different ways which make it possible for human beings to learn of ultimate truths. These include revelations from God, meditation, prayer, ascetic practices and religious experience. Buddhism certainly teaches that it is possible for us to know ultimate truths, through meditation, prayer and religious experience. The precise balance between these three varies from one Buddhist tradition to another. In some traditions, praying to buddhas and *bodhisattvas* is seen to help us understand the ultimate through the transformational blessing we may receive.

Buddhism rejects asceticism as a source of experience or knowledge of the ultimate, because the Buddha found that its excesses only weaken the body and the mind. However, milder forms of renunciation are seen to be helpful to the spiritual life.

It is a basic principle of Buddhism that things are not the way they appear. Relative truth refers to the way things appear to us conventionally, while ultimate truth refers to the way they truly are. The way things appear is what is perceived by an ignorant and uneducated mind, whereas the way things actually are is apprehended by a trained and undeluded mind. The spiritual path that combines moral discipline, meditation and reasoning is the way to transform the human mind from confusion to enlightenment. The ultimate is therefore intrinsically accessible and comprehensible to human beings, and there are proven methods for attaining knowledge of it.

Summary of main points

- Religious experience in Buddhism has both affective and cognitive elements.
- Religious experience entails seeing reality just as it is. It is knowledge of the ultimate truth.
- Religious experience is either transient (insights, *satori*) or lasting (nirvana, buddhahood).
- Religious experience depends on apprehending reality with the undeluded mind. It is free from sensory perception and from conceptualisation. It follows that religious experience is free from the limitations of culture and language.
- The most advanced types of religious experience are beyond words and ineffable, but reasoning and language can be used after the event to express them, and to give others an approximation which serves to point them in the right direction on their path.
- Religious experiences are verifiable and replicable.

Questions

1 Nirvana or enlightenment was one of the most important religious experiences in the life of the Buddha. Describe the main characteristics of this experience.

2 In which sense can nirvana be classified as a mystical experience?

3 How does nirvana differ from any type of religious experience in a theistic religion? You may choose one particular theistic religion to illustrate your answer.

4 'Key figures in the history of religion often become influential because of their religious experience.' Examine two examples where this could be said to be the case in Buddhism.

5 Explain the relationship between religious experience, faith, religious practice and moral behaviour, and assess the importance of religious experience within Buddhism.

6 Explain and assess the Buddhist understanding of religious experience.

Chapter 19

Significant people

Ashoka

Ashoka was one of the greatest emperors of India. He came to the throne in 268 BCE and died in 239 BCE. For the first time in Indian history (and the only time until the arrival of the British), Ashoka united the whole subcontinent except the extreme south under a single leader. He is famous in Buddhist tradition as one of the most powerful patrons the religion has ever had. He single-handedly ensured that Buddhism grew from being a minority religion in northern India to a world religion.

During his reign, missionaries spread the Dharma far and wide, to the West (Syria, Egypt, Macedonia, central Asia, Kashmir), to the south and southeast (Sri Lanka, Burma and other parts of southeast Asia) and throughout the Indian empire. His reign is extremely important to historians because it offers us the first dated historical records of Buddhism and of Indian history. Finally, Ashoka's conversion to Buddhism led to his applying Buddhist values and ethics to social, economic and political life, with far-reaching consequences. His contribution to the history and development of Buddhism is therefore enormous.

We have detailed information about Ashoka's achievements because archaeologists have discovered 32 of the edicts that he had carved into rock faces or pillars throughout India. These edicts are inscriptions ranging from records of historical events, to imperial proclamations, to decrees exhorting his people to behave morally and live together in harmony. One of these edicts (Rock Edict XII) tells us that Ashoka initiated a climate of religious tolerance in India, and we know separately that he supported the institutions of all religions, not only of Buddhism.

> One should not honour only one's own religion and condemn the religions of others, but one should honour others' religions for this or that reason. So doing, one helps one's own religion to grow and renders service to the religions of others too. In acting otherwise one digs the grave of one's own religion and also does harm to other

religions. Whosoever honours his own religion and condemns other religions, does so indeed through devotion to his own religion, thinking, 'I will glorify my own religion'. But on the contrary, in so doing he injures his own religion more gravely. So concord is good. Let all listen, and be willing to listen to the doctrines professed by others.

Cited in J. Bloch, *Les Inscriptions d'Asoka*

The ethical advice given on the edicts never claims to be Buddhist, and this is why some modern scholars like A. L. Basham argue that Ashoka's ideas were not Buddhist at all. According to Buddhist tradition, however, the values encouraged by Ashoka were inspired by and based upon Buddhism, but since Buddhist values have a universal truth there is no need to couch them in sectarian terms, especially for a man in Ashoka's position, trying to unite his country. For example, Ashoka exhorts his subjects to behave responsibly, to obey parents and superiors, to help the poor and the sick, to be fair to servants and employees, and to be generous to holy men. These values are not unique to Buddhism or to Indian culture and are followed throughout the world even today, but in the Indian context we can see that Ashoka could well have learned them from Buddhism. Ashoka wanted his subjects to develop personal moral qualities so he advised them to be truthful and honest, merciful, and not too concerned with material possessions. In particular, he asked people to refrain from killing or harming any living being. We know that Ashoka banned animal sacrifices in his capital (they were still carried out at that time by the Vedic-influenced Hindu religion) and that he also banned hunting, which even in India was 'the sport of kings' and of the aristocracy. It is possible that Ashoka also banned the death penalty. This last set of policies, at least, appears to bear the hallmark of Buddhist thinking, because, although similar non-violent values are taught in Jainism, there is no indication that Ashoka was a Jain.

Many of these ideas may seem quite ordinary to us today, but that is mainly because early Christianity played a similar role in applying compassionate religious values to social and political life in Europe. In Ashoka's day, however, these ideas were totally revolutionary, since the model of kingship was hierarchical, and the leader's role was mainly a military one of protecting his people and his territory from outside enemies and destabilising influences. Kings, after all, belonged to the *kshatriya* class of warriors. Ashoka, however, radically changed the very notion of kingship and extended the role to one of protecting his people morally, through kindness and social justice, and actively directing resources to meet the everyday needs of a peaceful civil society. This was completely new — a form of socialism before its time — and is an example of what is today called 'engaged Buddhism' (see Chapter 21).

Ashoka initiated many social projects throughout the Indian empire. He set up medical and veterinary centres, constructed wells and reservoirs, planted trees for fruit and shade, and provided welfare services and temporary financial support for ex-prisoners. He established the first rest-houses for travellers (especially needed once pilgrimages became a regular feature of life). Under Ashoka officials were encouraged to look after old people and orphans, and to ensure equal judicial standards throughout the empire, and torture was banned.

One of the principal ethical values upheld by Ashoka was *ahimsa* or non-violence, and we have already seen how he applied this to both humans and animals. In time it seems that the entire royal household was asked to become vegetarian. Non-food animals such as birds and fish were protected. Gentleness, sexual morality and contentment were recommended. In modern jargon we could say that Ashoka tried to create a 'compassionate society', and historically this is the first instance of any large-scale attempt to apply Buddhist values on the level of society as a whole. Ashoka's experiment provides a good blueprint for what Buddhism in action can mean, especially in the context of the laity, and is still considered a model of its kind.

In addition to these activities Ashoka offered a great deal of support specifically to Buddhists. Some of his rock edicts, for example, commemorated events in the history of Buddhism, a notable example being the rock pillar in Lumbini, indicating that Lumbini was the Buddha's birthplace. Without such evidence we would have little or no proof of this fact. Ashoka had many Buddhist stupas built throughout India, which became places of pilgrimage; instead of going hunting, he would go on pilgrimages. He donated state resources towards the building of Buddhist monasteries and the upkeep of the monks, thus allowing the religion to establish itself firmly in new parts of India.

In the long run, there were some disadvantages in Buddhism becoming an established religion. In particular, the religious commitment of those wishing to become monks gradually became weaker. With extensive state patronage, monastic life became secure, comfortable and potentially appealing to the less fortunate, who sometimes might have become involved for material rather than religious reasons.

After Ashoka, the dynasty declined and India split up again into several kingdoms, but Buddhism continued to be supported by kings and other wealthy patrons for centuries. It is often claimed that the long-term impact of Ashoka's missions to spread Buddhism outside India effectively secured the survival of the religion until today, because in India it disappeared in the twelfth century.

The Dalai Lama

The Dalai Lama is the current political and religious leader of the Tibetan people. He is today considered a significant person in the development of Buddhism because of the role he has played in helping establish Buddhism in the modern world. This has not been simply a question of transplanting ancient cultural traditions into the West, but rather of adapting the way Buddhism is taught and practised so that it meets the needs of men and women from all walks of life. Part of this effort lies in cultural exchanges, for example by way of the dialogues he has initiated between Buddhist thinkers on one side and scientists, politicians and other religious leaders on the other side, so as to explore ways in which Buddhist thinking can make a creative contribution to modern life.

The Dalai Lama was born into a peasant family in a small village in northeastern Tibet in 1935. At the age of two he was recognised by religious dignitaries as the reincarnation of his predecessor the thirteenth Dalai Lama, the previous leader of Tibet, and he was educated and trained from the age of six to take on this role once he came of age. It is a Tibetan tradition to recognise the reincarnations of great lamas and then to educate them so that they are able to carry on the work they began in previous lives. The case of the Dalai Lamas is special in that they are considered human embodiments of the *bodhisattva* of Compassion, Chenresig, who choose to take birth as human beings to serve humankind. This is why the Western media have called him a 'god king', but this is not an accurate understanding of the Buddhist principle involved. From the Buddhist point of view, the Dalai Lama is the Nirmanakaya manifestation of the Sambhogakaya *bodhisattva* Chenresig.

Graham Price

Figure 19.1 The Dalai Lama

In 1950 some 80,000 Chinese soldiers invaded Tibet, and this political crisis led to the Dalai Lama assuming full political power at the young age of 15. His efforts to bring about a peaceful diplomatic solution to the Sino-Tibetan conflict were thwarted by Beijing's ruthless policies in eastern Tibet, which sparked popular uprising and resistance, first in the east of the country and then in many other parts of Tibet. In 1959, the Tibetan National Uprising in the capital, Lhasa, was brutally crushed by the Chinese. The Dalai Lama escaped over the Himalayas

and was given political asylum in India. Some 80,000 Tibetan refugees followed him into exile. Since that time the Dalai Lama has lived in Dharamsala, northern India, the seat of the Tibetan government-in-exile. Tibet remains under Chinese control. In the 1980s the Red Army was responsible for destroying almost all the Buddhist monasteries, scriptures and artwork in Tibet, and for killing, imprisoning or torturing thousands of monks.

As the Tibetan leader in exile, the Dalai Lama has tirelessly pursued a pacifist strategy to persuade China to allow autonomy to Tibet. He has always spoken out against violent resistance, and believes that the Buddhist value of *ahimsa* has definite long-term benefits, even if the situation remains difficult in the short term. Violence, he says, only breeds resentment and mistrust for generations. In 1989, the Dalai Lama gained worldwide recognition for his efforts and was awarded the Nobel peace prize in Oslo. He accepted the prize on behalf of oppressed peoples everywhere, saying, 'The prize reaffirms our conviction that with truth, courage and determination as our weapons, Tibet will be liberated. Our struggle must remain non-violent and free of hatred.'

The Dalai Lama has actively participated in ecumenical dialogue, and has met with the Pope and leaders of the Catholic and Anglican churches and the Jewish community. He explains his reasons for religious tolerance as follows:

> I always believe that it is much better to have a variety of religions, a variety of philosophies, rather than one single religion or philosophy. This is necessary because of the different mental dispositions of each human being. Furthermore, each religion has certain unique ideas or techniques, and learning about them can only enrich one's own faith.

In the course of giving Buddhist talks and teachings in the West, the Dalai Lama has called for agreement on a universal code of ethics, independent of any particular religious denomination yet compatible with all religions, and therefore acceptable to the vast numbers of people in the modern world who follow no religion at all. He believes that certain basic ethical values are common and applicable to the whole of humanity — values such as love and compassion for others, respect, tolerance and individual responsibility — and should not be seen as religious in a narrow sense. Scientists, politicians, journalists, doctors and other professionals, whether they follow a religion or not, would benefit the whole community by applying values such as these in their work. When asked to summarise the essence of his religious belief, the Dalai Lama said once: 'My religion is simple; my religion is kindness.'

The Dalai Lama has stressed the great importance of environmental questions, and in addressing these he refers to Buddhist principles such as 'dependent

arising' (or interdependence) to explain why human activity in one part of the globe affects the situation in another. He has called on every individual to nurture a sense of universal responsibility, realising that the actions of each one of us have consequences far beyond the limits of our personal lives. We all bear some measure of responsibility for the future of mankind and of the planet.

The Dalai Lama has been interested in science and technology from a young age. As a boy, he would take his telescope, camera and car apart and put them together again to understand how they worked. He has initiated conferences with scientists to explore the connections between science and Buddhist wisdom, especially in the sciences of the mind such as neurobiology, psychology and psychiatry. One of his conclusions has been that scientific approaches to the mind are based on the assumption that mind cannot exist or be active independently of matter, and this assumption he claims, is unproven. Recently he has supported a series of laboratory experiments in North American universities, testing the effects of long-term meditation on the brain and other health indicators (see Chapter 14). Initial results show significant and long-term benefits in physical and mental well-being. He is open to using scientific methods wherever they can be helpful, even in religious areas. He believes that open-minded rational inquiry is essential for sound human understanding in any field of knowledge, and in this respect Buddhism is very close to science.

Some scholars think that the strength and influence of Buddhism in the West has only developed since Tibetan masters began living and teaching here, and that the Tibetans, including the Dalai Lama himself, have been instrumental in communicating Buddhism to the population at large without distorting or diluting it for the sake of popularity. In Europe, the Dalai Lama can attract audiences of over 10,000 people for public talks, and in the USA he has attracted 100,000 people at certain events. In this sense, it may well be that, in the future, the Dalai Lama will be seen to have played a historic role in the development of Buddhism across the world.

S. N. Goenka

S. N. Goenka is a leading master of the Theravada tradition and notable for being a lay man, not a monk, in a tradition that has always been dominated by the monasteries. He has been successful in teaching *samatha* and *vipassana* meditation to people of all faiths in both Asia and the West, and is especially known for his work in introducing meditation within prisons. Vipassana Meditation centres follow his teachings in many countries around the world, including India, the USA, Canada, Germany, the UK, Australia and Japan. He

is a prominent figure in promoting the message of peace and religious harmony, emphasising that outer peace is only possible on the basis of inner peace.

Goenka was born in Burma (Myanmar) in 1924. He joined his family business in 1940 and rapidly became a pioneering industrialist with several manufacturing corporations in the country. In 1969, he retired from business and has since devoted his life to teaching meditation. He was trained for 14 years by the renowned Buddhist teacher Sayagyi U Ba Khin (1899–1971) in the tradition of Ledi Sayadaw. Goenka started teaching in Burma and India, and in 1979 began travelling more widely, in the East and to the West. He has trained over 600 assistant teachers who carry on his work around the world. Neither he nor his assistants make any financial gain from their courses.

Goenka found that *vipassana* meditation is easily accepted by people everywhere because its benefits are universal and it can be taught in a totally non-sectarian way. Whatever a person's socioeconomic background or religious beliefs, *vipassana* provides a way of finding inner peace and reconciliation with life's difficulties. It is a method for transforming negative emotions into positive ones, and gives a direction and meaning to life. In communities divided by caste and religion, *vipassana* is able to bring everyone together.

Goenka was invited to lead 10-day *vipassana* retreats in a number of gaols in India, and in 1995 he gave the largest retreat ever in modern times, attended by 1,000 prisoners in Tihar prison, New Delhi. The results have been both moving and astounding, so much so that the Indian government has since recommended that every prison in the country should organise similar retreats for both wardens and inmates. As a result, hundreds of prisoners continue to attend *vipassana* retreats every month, and thousands of Indian police officers have followed courses too. Thousands of offenders have been enabled to come to terms with their past. Results include improved integration into society after prison and a reduction in recidivism.

The effectiveness of *vipassana* as a tool for prisoner rehabilitation has led to courses being offered in prisons in the USA. Studies there have shown that *vipassana* is effective in reducing drug and alcohol addiction among inmate. In one prison in Seattle, Washington, the percentage of inmates readmitted within 2 years in 2002 was 47% for men and 28% for women among those who meditated, compared with 75% for those who did not. Goenka and his assistants also offer *vipassana* programmes for school children, drug addicts, the disabled, homeless children and business executives.

In 1981, S. N. Goenka established the Vipassana Research Institute in India to support research into the Pali Buddhist scriptures. One of the centre's key achievements is to have completed the computerisation of the Pali Canon, which is now freely available to scholars everywhere on computer in the

Sanskrit, Pali, Burmese, Khmer, Mongolian and Thai languages. This is a major contribution to Buddhist scholarship.

Goenka emphasises the universality of the Buddha's message, saying that the Buddha never taught 'Buddhism' or any sectarian religion, but taught the Dharma, the way to liberation, which is universal and belongs to whoever wishes to follow it. This non-sectarian approach is one of the main reasons for Goenka's appeal, along with his firm conviction that Buddhist methods are of immediate and practical benefit. He says: 'May the stream of pure Dharma keep flowing in the world, for the happiness of everyone, for the benefit of all.'

Conclusion

Although these three significant figures in the story of Buddhism are each very different, it is interesting to note that they all have one characteristic in common. Each one has believed that the message of Buddhism is universal and carries a truth and a benefit that go far beyond the limitations of sectarian religion. It is this universality of the Dharma that each has succeeded in communicating, thereby changing the attitudes and lives of countless people. This they see as the point of the Buddha's message: their aim is not to convert people but to benefit them and bring them a greater measure of happiness.

Questions

1 Assess the contribution made by one person in Buddhism to the development of *either* social justice *or* reform within the religion.
2 Describe and assess the contributions which Ashoka made to the early development of Buddhism.
3 Evaluate the reasons for arguing that Ashoka's influence was fundamentally good for Buddhism.

Chapter 20

The existence of God

A significant part of the philosophy of religion in the West is concerned with arguments for and against the existence of God. Paradoxically perhaps, few Buddhist texts address this question, and it is an assumption of most Buddhist doctrine that God does not exist.

One of the philosophical treatises that does set out the Buddhist arguments on this question is the *Tattvasamgraha*, by the eighth-century Indian scholar Shantarakshita. This work is like an encyclopaedia of Buddhist thought and has been compared to Thomas Aquinas's *Summa Theologica* for its thorough and comprehensive treatment of philosophical questions. This chapter is based on that work.

What do we understand by 'God'?

It is important to know how God is defined to appreciate why Buddhists deny his existence, because the Buddhist refutation is a logical and precise one. We should also bear in mind that in the Indian context Buddhist scholars were refuting the Hindu idea of God and not the Judaeo-Christian idea of God. The following characteristics are commonly ascribed to God by theists, and are those that define the 'God' that Buddhism refutes.

- **He is the creator of the universe.** The theist argument for this is based on the idea that insentient matter cannot produce itself, therefore the cause of the universe cannot be material and must be intelligent and mental/spiritual. In ancient India no distinction was made between theist and deist conceptions of creation, that is, those where God remains involved in his creation and those where he does not.
- **He is omniscient.** This theist argument follows from the previous one: if God created the universe, then he knows everything it contains.

- **He is eternal.** The meaning given to this divine characteristic is that God has no beginning and no end and is not produced by anything else.
- **He is distinct from the soul.** Some philosophers argue that God is distinct from the soul since he is both eternal and omniscient and the soul is neither of these.
- **He is the first cause and only efficient cause.** As creator of the universe, God is the first cause, meaning that the chain of causality begins with him. All the other physical and mental factors that are involved in the creation of things — such as atoms, virtue, lack of virtue and so on — are only contributory causes. The example given is that God causes things to arise just as a potter creates a pot. God is an intelligent cause.

There are two other theistic arguments cited by Shantarakshita for the existence of God:

- The world is a place of suffering only because it is controlled by an intelligent being or cause. Suffering cannot be produced by unconscious matter. The very existence of suffering is therefore a proof of the existence of God.
- Things must be perceptible to someone, because they exist. Humans cannot perceive all things all the time; only God is able to do this. So the very fact that all things in the universe exist means that God must exist.

The Buddhist refutation

The following points present the key arguments used by Buddhist scholars to refute the existence of God as defined above.

1 Even if one accepts that there is a natural order in the universe, Buddhists claim that this argument could equally be used to *disprove* the existence of God. If things function harmoniously according to natural laws, they say, then what need is there to posit the existence of a God?

2 The metaphor of God as a cosmic builder is based on the analogy of an architect who builds a house. Buddhists argue that there are no good reasons to extend this analogy to the natural world. For example, there is no evidence to suggest that mountains and other natural features are 'built' in the same way as houses. In the case of houses, the architect does not build them alone but employs many builders to help him; so how would this analogy work with the idea of God as the universal builder? If God needed the help of other agents to produce the universe, he would not be the supreme creator.

3 It is impossible to prove the existence of an eternal being. Such a being would be unitary and would be an eternal substratum embracing all things and consciousness itself. It follows that our consciousness could not

conceive of such a being or prove his existence because he would be beyond the capacity and limitations of our minds.

4 It is a contradiction to say that an eternal being created the world. Eternal things cannot produce effects because the notions of consecutive time and concurrent time are contradictory to the notion of eternity. Causality logically implies that the cause precedes its effect, and therefore that causes and effects exist consecutively in relation to each other. The Indian idea of 'eternity' means 'out of time' or beyond time, so this contradicts the notion of an act of creation producing the universe because such an act necessarily occurs in time. If the universe has a beginning, the creation must happen at a particular time. Buddhists argue that it is irrational to say that a being who is beyond time acts within time, because these two are mutually exclusive.

5 Following on from the preceding argument, if objects exist consecutively, they must be known consecutively. In other words, something cannot be known until it exists. This contradicts the idea of God's omniscience because it would make it impossible for him to know all things at once. (In Buddhism, the omniscience ascribed to buddhas refers to the way they understand the *nature* of all things as they arise. Enlightened knowledge is not set or static, it flows with the movement of the world.)

6 Buddhists argue that if God is an unobstructed, all-powerful cause, and if nothing can conceivably obstruct his ability to create, then he would have to produce everything simultaneously. This is because there can be no reason *not* to produce something, and there can be no reason to produce a thing at one time rather than another. If a theist responds to this argument by saying that it is the auxiliary factors involved in causation that constitute the reasons for producing things at one time rather than at another, Buddhists reply that if this is the case it means that God's power to create is constrained by these other factors, which should not be the case for an all-powerful being. The conclusion is therefore that the idea of God as creator has internal contradictions: it would imply that God is dependent on auxiliary causes.

7 Some theists respond to the previous argument by saying that the reason God creates different things at different times is simply because he wishes to do so, and this is a sufficient reason. Buddhists dismiss this argument on a number of counts. First, they say that the notion of wishing is irrelevant here; a wish in itself is ineffective unless one has the power to create, and therefore the issue here is not God's wish but God's power to create. Second, they point out that there is ample evidence in the natural world for things being produced without any wish being involved. For example, a sprout appears

without the wish of a seed. Wishing is therefore not a necessary factor in the process of causation.

8 According to theists, God's omniscience is justified by his creatorship of the world, but because Buddhists reject the latter they reject the former as well.

9 Another refutation of God as creator is that there is no certainty that the creator of one thing must be identical with the creator of another thing. For example, the architect of one house is not necessarily the same person as the architect of another house. The argument that there must be one creator of the whole universe, and only one, is unproven.

10 Likewise, there is no certainty that the creator of a thing must be unitary and single rather than many. For example, there are many people involved in the building of a house, so why could this analogy not be applied to the universe? Could it not be the case that the universe was created by several gods?

Conclusion

The gist of all these Buddhist arguments is that the theist's position is riddled with self-contradiction. For Buddhists, theistic arguments are irrational in that they defy logic. Buddhists suppose that the truth of things is always compatible with reason, for if this were not the case we could never know anything at all. This is why Buddhism does not accept the existence of God in the sense of an omniscient, all-powerful, eternal creator who is self-existing.

It may be useful to add, however, that some masters have modified the Buddhist presentation on this question as a result of Buddhism's recent contacts with Christianity. One modern interpretation of the Buddhist view is to say that Buddhists do not accept the existence of God as a *person* who acts, creates, judges, rewards and punishes in a similar way to the way human beings act. This is too much of an anthropocentric view of God, an understanding that describes God in the image of man. For this reason Buddhists believe it is a mistake to think of God as a person; it is more consistent to think of God as a universal principle. The Buddhist equivalent of this in the Mahayana tradition is the Dharmakaya, the body of truth out of which all things naturally manifest, first as energy and light (Sambhogakaya) and then as matter (Nirmanakaya). And the Dharmakaya mind of enlightenment is characterised by clarity and lucidity on the one hand, and by boundless compassion on the other hand. In this sense, Buddhism does not reject the idea of an intelligent and loving principle at the heart of the world, and many Buddhists may have no objection to calling this 'God', provided that no personal embodiment is implied by this term. The Trikaya principle can be taken as one Buddhist answer to the question of how everything in the world arises (see Chapter 4).

Buddhism

1 It is a central tenet of Christianity, Judaism and Islam that God created the world. Discuss this claim in the light of Buddhist philosophy.

2 'The fact of our existence demonstrates the existence of a creator God.' How might a Theravada Buddhist respond to this statement?

Chapter 21

Buddhism in Western society

Outlining the issues

A different approach is needed when we study the way Buddhism is taking shape in the modern world. This is because it is happening here and now, and changes occur all the time, so in general it is not a subject we can read about in books. A small number of books have been published on some aspects of Buddhism in the West, but even the best studies become quickly outdated as things evolve. The most up-to-date sources of information are to be found via the internet on the websites of various groups and on some general Buddhist websites, as well as in the small number of magazines on Buddhism mostly published in North America.

One striking feature of contemporary Buddhism is that for the first time in history many different traditions and schools of Buddhism have been introduced virtually simultaneously into Western countries and are practised side by side. One way of studying how Buddhism is adapting to modern society is to study it tradition by tradition, looking, for example, at how Theravada, Japanese Zen, Japanese Pure Land, Tibetan Buddhism and Chinese Buddhism are developing in their new homelands.

Another way of approaching the study of Buddhism in contemporary society is to consider the various issues that have been raised in the process of adaptation. These are all issues that arise from the meeting of different cultures — the Buddhist cultures of Asia and the Christian or secular cultures of the modern West.

- **The matter of religious authority.** Is it acceptable that ultimate authority rests with leaders in Asia, who may be unfamiliar with Western concerns? What are the criteria for determining or justifying authority? What is the process for Westerners to be given authority?

- **The status of women.** Are the patriarchal social structures of traditional Asian society integral to Buddhism, or can Buddhist customs change in line with the new freedoms and equality of women in the West? If they can change, how are changes decided in practice?
- **The significance of monasticism.** How crucial is the monastic institution to the Buddhist religion? In an increasingly secular society, is monastic life realistic or even desirable?
- **The economic base for Buddhist institutions.** Since Buddhism is a minority faith in Western countries, there are no state or institutional mechanisms to fund monasteries, or to support those wishing to follow intensive study programmes or take several years of retreat. How can the development and practice of Buddhism be supported economically?
- **The social benefits of religion.** Is Buddhism relevant if it does not bring immediate and tangible benefits to individuals and society? How innovative and how significant are the forms of socially engaged Buddhism developed particularly in the USA and Britain?

All these questions are quite complex and there is no single Buddhist approach to any of them. Each has to be examined in relation to a specific Buddhist tradition, since each tradition holds a particular view or places particular emphasis on one point or another. In addition, there are differences not only between, say, Thai and Tibetan Buddhism, but also between individual Buddhist masters within the same tradition. It is therefore helpful to learn about each of the main Buddhist groups in the UK and in the USA to gain precise examples of the entire range of ways in which Buddhism is being adapted and interpreted. This chapter provides the information necessary for you to explore whatever interests you.

Buddhist groups in the UK

The following are some of the main Buddhist groups in the UK, categorised according to the Asian tradition they follow, with details of their websites. For comprehensive details about all Buddhist centres throughout the UK, refer to the *Buddhist Directory* published by the Buddhist Society in London.

Theravada

Chithurst Buddhist Monastery (http://www.forestsangha.org/cittavi.htm) is a monastery in Sussex founded by Ven. Ajahn Sumedho, a Western disciple of the famed master Ajahn Chah of the Thai forest tradition. The monastery follows closely the traditions as they are taught in Thailand. It hosts retreats and runs courses for lay students.

Amaravati Monastery (http://www.buddhistcommunity.org) is located in Hertfordshire, north of London. This monastery was also founded by Ven. Ajahn Sumedho in the same spirit as Chithurst. The resident community of monks and novice nuns offers meditation classes, Dharma talks, short retreats and educational support in schools.

London Buddhist Vihara (http://www.londonbuddhistvihara.co.uk) is run by Sri Lankan monks and is mainly dedicated to the needs of the expatriate community. It also runs courses on Buddhism in collaboration with London University and regularly hosts school visits.

Samatha Trust (http://www.samatha.org) is a lay-led organisation that teaches mindfulness of breathing samatha meditation in many classes around the UK. It was founded by Nai Boonman, a monk from Thailand. It runs a meditation centre in Wales.

Zen

Throssel Hole Priory (http://www.throssel.org.uk) is a Soto Zen centre in Northumberland directed by the Abbot, Ven. Master Daishin Morgan. It runs a programme of residential training and retreats and has local groups throughout the UK.

Nichiren

Soka Gakkai (http://www.sgi.org) is an association of 12 million members in 190 countries, under the direction of its Japanese president, Daiseku Ikeda, a writer and peace activist. All members are lay believers. The organisation emphasises the practical aspects of Buddhist wisdom promoting peace, culture and education. It is also politically engaged in Japan.

Tibetan Buddhism

Samye Ling Monastery (http://www.samye.org) is based in Scotland and directed by Lama Akong Rinpoche. It hosts a small community of monastics, has facilities for short and long personal retreats, and offers courses to the public.

Rigpa (http://www.rigpa.org) is based in London and is part of a network of centres in 16 countries throughout Europe, North America and Australia, under the direction of Lama Sogyal Rinpoche. It offers a structured programme of courses on the practice and study of Buddhism, organises group retreats and invites Buddhist masters of all traditions to teach.

Jamyang Centre (http://www.jamyang.co.uk) is part of the Foundation for the Preservation of the Mahayana Teachings (FPMT), a worldwide network of centres directed by Lama Zopa Rinpoche. It offers courses on the study and practice of Buddhism in its London centre and by correspondence.

New Kadampa Tradition (http://www.kadampa.org) has centres in 40 countries under the direction of Geshe Kelsang Gyatso. It arranges structured study and meditation classes, retreats and major festivals, and has an active publishing arm. Students include both monastics and lay people.

Eclectic mix of several traditions

Friends of the Western Buddhist Order (http://www.fwbo.org) was founded by Sangharakshita, an Englishman who became a Buddhist monk in India but who disrobed on returning to the UK. His concern is to ensure that Buddhism is adapted to Western culture, and he combines Theravada, Mahayana and Vajrayana practices in his own unique formula. There are no monks or nuns following the Vinaya but a new order of Members and supporting Friends. Many students live in small communities within large houses, often single-sex, and many have developed 'right livelihood' businesses according to Buddhist ethical principles. One of the most successful of these is Windhorse Trading (http://www.windhorsetrading.co.uk). There are FWBO centres in many towns and cities across the UK offering classes in meditation and yoga.

Engaged Buddhism

For some Buddhists, the idea of Engaged Buddhism is a controversial one. The stated goal of the Buddhist path is enlightenment, a mystical accomplishment that is likely to take many lifetimes to achieve. How does this fit with the need for religion to bring benefits to an individual in this life, and to help society and the world right now?

In fact, these two aspects of religion need not be opposed to each other, and most people see it as a matter of finding the correct balance between the two. In Buddhism, insight and wisdom express themselves in the world as compassionate action.

The concept of Engaged Buddhism emerged in Vietnam in the 1930s as part of the national drive for independence from colonial oppression. It was further developed by the Zen monk Thich Nhat Hanh, who helped to care for many people during the Vietnam war, and afterwards placed them on fishing boats so they could leave the country. Other Vietnamese monks burned themselves alive in public as a form of non-violent protest and were instrumental in bringing the war to an end.

Other Asian countries have developed their own forms of engagement, for example with the Sarvodaya Movement and other development groups in Sri Lanka. Engaged Buddhism is now also a significant movement in the West.

Is Engaged Buddhism a modern innovation or has it always been present within Buddhism? Stephen Batchelor argues:

> While many of these movements [in Asia] drew upon the values of ideologies that were not explicitly Buddhist (such as nationalism, democracy, liberalism, socialism), their roots lay in Buddhist traditions with long histories of social and political engagement. In this sense, Engaged Buddhism in Asia is merely the renewal of a dimension that had either lain dormant or been suppressed during the colonial period.
>
> Likewise, in the West today, as the alienated and disaffected generations of the second half of the 20th century outgrow their romantic fascination with Buddhism, it is no surprise to find a growing concern among them for social, cultural and political issues. Whether or not one calls such concerns Engaged Buddhism is irrelevant. They are simply a sign of the Dharma's mature unfolding in Western culture. For this is the way the practice of Buddhism works: insight into the selfless and interconnected nature of life expresses itself in the world as appropriate compassionate action.
>
> Stephen Batchelor, *The Awakening of the West*

In Chapter 13 we saw how part of the traditional role of a monk in Thailand and Sri Lanka was to contribute to society through education, counselling, and administrative support, so social engagement has always been a part of the Buddhist religion. Batchelor does not mention two of the most powerful ideologies that have accelerated the activity of Engaged Buddhism in the West, namely secular values attached to immediate and tangible benefits, not to the hereafter, and the Christian tradition of social action.

However, two of the leading proponents of Engaged Buddhism in the West, Thich Nhat Hanh and the Dalai Lama, both root the principle of social engagement firmly within the values of Buddhist thinking, in the idea of interdependence. If all things are interdependent, then my happiness depends in part on the actions of others and the happiness of other people depends in part on my own actions. Thich Nhat Hanh calls this the truth of 'interbeing', while the Dalai Lama expresses it as the sense of 'universal responsibility'.

While some Buddhist groups in North America and Europe have no social action programmes at all, others are well known for their Engaged Buddhism activities, through which they set out to help specific groups in need.

Angulimala (http://www.angulimala.org.uk) is a Buddhist prison chaplaincy organisation that supports prisoners following the Buddhist faith. It makes the Buddhist teachings available to any prisoners who are interested, offers meditation classes in prisons, and provides aftercare for prisoners after release. It also organises professional workshops.

East-West Detox (http://www.east-westdetox.org.uk) is a UK charity that enables drug addicts to benefit from a unique detoxification treatment run by the monks of Thamkrabok Monastery in Thailand. The treatment is based on herbal medicines, strict daily discipline, rest and meditation, following Buddhist ethical values. It is available to people of all religions and is more effective than conventional treatments: in 1997, only 35% of 300 Australian addicts treated there returned to their addictive habits within a year, compared with a 98% re-addiction rate after NHS treatment in the UK.

The Peacemaker Institute (http://www.peacemakerinstitute.org) was founded by Roshi Bernie Glassman of the Soto Zen school, who also cofounded the Zen Peacemaker Family (http://www.zpc-usa.org). It is based in New York with partner organisations throughout the USA. It organises workshops for social change, teaching skills in conflict resolution, leadership and the organisation of grassroots communities. It holds 'street retreats', where for 10 days participants (such as social workers) live rough on the streets of a USA city to experience first-hand what life is like for the homeless.

The Tiep Hien Order or **Order of Interbeing** (http://www.interbeing.org.uk) was founded by the Vietnamese Zen master Thich Nhat Hanh. This order offers a charter of guidelines for ethical, mindful and harmonious living which is followed by the various communities under his direction. A key principle of this approach is that inner peace is necessary for peace in the world. The community offers retreats and mindfulness practice.

Questions of authority

In order to illustrate how the issues of adaptation to Western culture apply to Buddhism, let us take the example of religious authority. Following the framework of analysis used in Chapter 17, the key points raised for each type of authority are highlighted below.

Scripture

Many of the scriptures are now available in print and can also be downloaded from the internet. The scriptures are published in their extant Asian languages, and many have been translated into English. However, a large number of Mahayana and Vajrayana scriptures remain untranslated into any Western language. The main difficulty is that translations have not been standardised, and a given Pali, Sanskrit, Tibetan or Chinese term may be translated in different ways by different translators, which can be confusing. The authority of the Buddhist scriptures themselves is not generally questioned, although scholarly analysis may question the authorship and dating of some texts.

Tradition

There are several difficulties in knowing how to respect the authority of tradition. In Western countries there is no existent community of elders, for example, with the result that there are no role models for ordinary people to follow and no group that can be referred to for advice and knowledge. Elders living in Asia are generally too inaccessible and may speak only their own language. This is a difficulty specific to Buddhism's early stages of development in the West and should ease if Buddhism becomes established here over generations.

The student–teacher relationship is sometimes difficult to understand, especially in Zen and Vajrayana Buddhism where submission to the master is considered necessary for spiritual transmission to take place. Some Westerners have problems with power and authority and find the notion of spiritual authority hard to accept. This can be an obstacle to following the Buddhist path.

For centuries, the teaching of scriptural interpretation safeguarded the tradition from misguided and partial views. But the situation in the West is quite different because many Buddhist scriptures are published in translation and available in bookshops, so anyone can read a scripture at home without any guidance from a Buddhist teacher. Individual and personal interpretation of scripture is therefore widespread, and the lineages that explained the meaning behind the text are often ignored. The criteria for determining whether a particular scriptural interpretation is authoritative are yet to be clearly established in the West.

Religious experience

The principle of the authority of religious experience in Buddhism is generally accepted in the West, but the main difficulty is how to know when one has a genuine spiritual experience. In the absence of a community of experienced elders, such a decision is hard to make for oneself. This is where the personal relationship between a student and a teacher is very important. Also, in societies with little or no knowledge of the spiritual path, it is quite easy to make claims about one's spiritual attainments that others cannot assess and that they may well believe through naivety. This situation allows self-made and self-proclaimed teachers to succeed where they would fail in a society with established religious institutions and peer pressure.

Reason

The authority given to reasoning in Buddhism sits well with Western intellectual approaches. The difference is that, when Buddhism is taught traditionally, reasoning is always combined with regular meditation practice and each is seen

as necessary for the other if liberation is to be attained. So, for example, mere intellectual conviction that all things are empty of substantial existence is not enough to take adherents to enlightenment; the personal experience of *shunyata* that comes through meditation is necessary too.

Generally speaking, the academic study of Buddhism in Western schools and universities does not combine reasoned understanding with religious practice, so it becomes just another philosophy, a set of interesting ideas, rather than the spiritual path it is intended to be. From the Buddhist point of view, the purpose of reason and logic is to clear away misunderstandings and confusion, and thereby strengthen wisdom; its purpose is not merely to satisfy interest or curiosity, or even to acquire knowledge for its own sake. Some Buddhists believe that a solely academic approach may lead to an impoverishment of Buddhism.

Buddhism and science

Buddhism is making an important contribution to Western culture, in the way it is redefining the nature of the relationship between religion and science. As Alan Wallace puts it in his book, *Buddhism and Science*, dialogue between scientists and Buddhist thinkers is in the process of breaking down the barriers between these two disciplines. This is having an effect on the work of certain scientists themselves, and it also has implications for philosophy of science.

There are a number of different philosophical views on how science relates to religion. Most Western thinkers believe that they are independent fields of knowledge, and each has little or nothing to say to the other. This argument can be used to affirm the split between facts and values, facts being the fruit of science and values the fruit of religion; or again, the split between the outer world and the inner life. Others, such as Richard Dawkins, argue that religion and science are but different aspects of a single body of human knowledge and that they can therefore be compared. When compared, they are found to be in conflict with each other. This type of conflict has been resolved by some thinkers on the principle that religious truths must be subjected to empirical testing according to objective scientific methods, on the assumption that scientific validation is the only acceptable way of establishing a truth of any kind.

When we try to apply these views to the relationship between science and Buddhism, the main sticking point is that Buddhism does not define itself as a religion in the sense that the word is understood in the West today. These are some of the differences we need to watch out for:

- We have already seen that psychology is an integral part of Buddhist teaching and of the Buddhist scriptures themselves, and is not considered a separate discipline.

- The Abhidharma scriptures develop Buddhism as a philosophy of spiritual liberation, without separating philosophy and religion as distinct or incompatible disciplines.
- These scriptures also address questions of what the universe, including both subjective and objective phenomena, is composed of and how it works.
- The repeatable and duplicable methods of meditation can be seen as empirical ways of establishing knowledge about both the mind and the universe.

If we categorise Buddhism as 'religion', or 'philosophy', or even 'science of the mind', we must therefore be careful to redefine our terms so that we do not interpret Buddhism through unconscious Western assumptions and biases. In particular, the Buddhist approach is generally less dualistic. It avoids a split between 'inner' and 'outer', 'subjective' and 'objective', and instead emphasises the connection between the subject who knows and that which is known. All knowledge in Buddhism is seen to depend upon, and be relative to, the particular mind that investigates. This is very different from science which, until very recently, has never been concerned with the state of mind of the subject but simply with the object of knowledge.

If we are prepared to learn about Buddhism on its own terms, therefore, and abandon our culture-bound ideas of these various fields of knowledge, we might see Buddhism as a form of 'natural philosophy', the term used for early European science, investigating the deepest questions (as in religion) by means of rigorous logical analysis (as in philosophy) and empirical investigation (as in science). Alan Wallace, who is both a Buddhist scholar and a physicist, states:

> In terms of the interface between Buddhism and science, we must…entertain the possibility of learning about the world from Buddhism, as opposed to studying this tradition merely as a means to learn about Buddhism.
>
> Alan Wallace, *Buddhism and Science*

Since 1987 the Dalai Lama, the Buddhist leader of Tibet and a remarkable scholar in his own right, has engaged every other year in formal conferences with scientists from around the world, sharing views and discussing differences. The proceedings of these conferences, which are organised by the Mind and Life Institute (http://www.mindandlife.org), are published in a series of books, each of which focuses on a particular theme. The subjects range from the mind sciences, to ethics, the new physics, cosmology and quantum mechanics.

In addition, the Dalai Lama has encouraged attempts to validate some of the truths, principles and practices of Buddhism by scientific means. Chapter 15 of this book, for example, mentions the recent laboratory experiments carried out on Tibetan masters in the USA, which provide evidence of the neurological and

chemical effects of prolonged meditation, and their associated impacts on thoughts and emotions.

Care must be taken not to conflate Buddhism and science and to say, for example, that quantum physics is simply a modern way of expressing the age-old truth of interdependence. Clearly, the goals and assumptions of science and religion are distinct, and this must be taken into account. Nevertheless, dialogue has been fruitful in reviewing intellectual assumptions on both sides, and especially the view that mind is a physical phenomenon.

Some statistics

Buddhism is a religion that is growing slowly in Europe and North America. Growth rates vary considerably from one country to another — in France, it is now the fastest growing religion. The census of 2001 gives the most recent official figures for Buddhism in the UK, but it should be remembered that some Buddhists might not declare themselves as such on a census form, while others might declare themselves to be Buddhists when they have just read books on the subject and meditate occasionally. The census data do not therefore reveal a totally accurate picture of how Buddhism is being practised on the ground, but the figures based on the census, in Box 21.1, give some indication of the general picture of Buddhism in the UK.

Box 21.1

UK Census 2001 (round figures)

Total population   58.8 million

Religion

Christian	42 million	**Religion and ethnicity**			
Buddhist	152,000		**Buddhism**	**Hinduism**	**Islam**
Hindu	559,000	**White**	56,000	7,000	180,000
Jewish	267,000	**Asian**	14,000	533,000	1,140,000
Muslim	1.6 million	**Mixed**	4,650	5,700	64,000
Sikh	336,000	**Black**	1,500	3,000	106,000
Other religions	179,000	**Chinese**	34,300	150	700
No religion	9.1 million	**Other**	33,200	29,250	56,450
Religion not stated	4.3 million				

Age profiles

Christian   71% of total population, but 19% are 65 or over
Muslim   Very high proportion of young people: 33.8% are under 16, 18.2% are 16–24
Buddhist   12% are under 16; 52% are 25–49; less than 2% over 65
Jewish   High proportion of older people: 22% are 65 or over

The census figures show that of the 152,000 people who declared themselves to be Buddhist, just under 40% were white 'converts', while around 24% were ethnic Chinese and a further 24% were from 'other' ethnic groups. These may include various nationalities of Asians who did not identify with the categories listed on the census form. This means that there are about 60,000 ethnically European people in Britain who have converted to Buddhism.

Research by Robert Bluck of the Open University has shown that there are now around 1,000 Buddhist groups in Britain. The largest are groups of the Friends of the Western Buddhist Order, Sokka Gakkai International and New Kadampa Tradition, which together may account for some 15,000 members, but the national total includes numerous local groups each with only a handful of members. Bluck therefore concludes that the majority of Buddhists in Britain have no formal contact with a Buddhist group, and practise on their own or with friends, possibly visiting a Buddhist centre very occasionally.

Survey of Buddhism in France

A detailed survey of Buddhists in France, published in *Le Bouddhisme en France* by Frederic Lenoir in 1999, gives an interesting picture of why some Westerners are beginning to practise Buddhism as a religion. The broad trends probably apply to most European countries, with some national variance.

Official statistics show that there are 600,000 Buddhists in total, of whom 50,000 are Chinese, 400,000 refugees from southeast Asia, and 150,000 native French. Box 21.2 on page 234 shows the results of some of the survey questions.

Conclusion

The practice of Buddhism as a religion has been growing steadily in Europe and the USA over the last few decades. The number of followers is modest as a percentage of overall populations, but the percentage of Buddhists in these countries who are white 'converts' is exceptionally high when compared with figures for Hinduism and Islam. Although our understanding of current religious trends is incomplete, it would seem that the reasons for conversion to Buddhism are quite different from those behind conversion to Islam or Hinduism, where social factors are often dominant. In the case of Buddhism, the main attraction to Westerners appears to be intellectual and emotional: sympathy for the Buddhist values of compassion, non-violence and tolerance; interest in meditation; the personal inspiration of Buddhist teachers; and the psychological benefits that Buddhist practice can bring.

Buddhism is at an early stage of development in the West. For example, the establishment of a monastic sangha of monks and nuns has hardly begun, and

Box 21.2

Survey of native converts in France

How did you come across Buddhism?

28%	through books
25%	through a friend or relative
7%	through martial arts
7%	through travelling to Asia
16%	through meeting a Buddhist teacher
17%	other

Which Buddhist tradition do you feel closest to?

60%	Tibetan
30%	Zen
8%	Buddhism generally
0.4%	Theravada
1.6%	other

How often do you visit a Buddhist centre?

45%	once a year
22%	once a week
17%	once a month
6%	daily
4%	never
6%	other

Were you brought up in a particular religion?

89.6%	Catholic
6.7%	Protestant
1.5%	Jewish
0.8%	Christian Orthodox
0.3%	Muslim
1.1%	other

Do you still feel close to your childhood religion?

46%	quite close
22.6%	no
22.4%	yes, very
5.3%	absolutely not
3.6%	don't know

Why are you drawn to Buddhism?

12%	compassion and respect for life
11%	direct contact and inspiration of a master
10.7%	meditation and silent contemplation
8%	practical help and personal experience
7.7%	freedom to follow one's own path
7%	clear explanations, psychological help
6.4%	no God and no dogma
5.6%	tolerance
5.5%	helps work on my body and emotions
5.1%	law of karma
4%	explanation of suffering and evil
3.6%	helps to eliminate suffering
13.4%	various

Do you believe in reincarnation?

63%	yes
31%	don't know
6%	no

What does Buddhism give you that you feel you don't get from Christianity?

38.8%	psychological and spiritual support
32%	values and explanations that I can believe in
26.6%	freedom from dogma, rigid morals, feelings of guilt
2.7%	other

---

some Westerners even wonder whether the monastic way of life is desirable in modern society. Many questions remain unresolved in terms of how Buddhism will adapt to modern Western cultures: the process raises issues such as how authority functions, how authenticity is safeguarded, how social and economic relations need to evolve. Different Buddhist groups are finding their own answers to these questions, and in the absence of an over-arching Buddhist hierarchy there is no generic Buddhist response to them at present.

The cultural influence of Buddhism in the West is already considerable, and quite disproportionate to the relatively small numbers of Buddhist followers.

Buddhists are active and innovative in many areas, ranging from interfaith dialogue to the environment movement and to conflict resolution; and from training in compassionate management to the rehabilitation of prisoners and drug addicts. Buddhists of all traditions are aware how important it is to demonstrate the tangible benefits of a spiritual way of life, and even to prove them scientifically. At the same time, it is believed that a spiritual approach to life is our only way out of the conflicts and tragedies of our modern world. Speaking of the value of compassion and love, the Dalai Lama has said: 'Compassion is not a luxury; it is a matter of survival'.

Questions

1 How successful has Theravada Buddhism been in adapting to society in the UK?

2 How do you account for European interest in Buddhism as a religion?

3 Explain how the Friends of the Western Buddhist Order have adapted Buddhism to Western societies, and assess the reasons for their success.

4 How difficult would it be to live as a practising Buddhist in Britain today?

Glossary

Note: All words are in Pali except where marked. Jap = Japanese, Skt = Sanskrit, Tib = Tibetan.

Abhidhamma (**Abhidharma, Skt**)	Scriptures containing philosophical and psychological analysis
Amitabha (Skt); Amida (Jap)	The buddha of infinite light and life, devotion to whom ensures rebirth in his pure land after death; he is the main buddha revered by the Pure Land School
Anatta	The doctrine that there is no permanent, inherent essence to anything that exists
Anicca	Impermanence, change
Arhat (**Skt**)	Literally 'worthy one'; one who has attained nirvana (nibbana), the highest level in Theravada
Aryans	People who invaded India from central Asia in 1500 BCE
Asuras	'Demi-gods'; jealous beings who dwell in one of the six realms of samsara
Atman (**Skt**)	The impersonal essence of a person according to Hinduism
Bardo (**Tib**)	Literally 'interval'; specifically, the intermediary period between the end of one life and the beginning of the next in Tibetan Buddhism
Bhikkhu	Monk
Bhikkhuni	Nun
Bodhichitta (**Skt**)	Literally 'awakened mind' or 'mind of enlightenment'; the mind that strives to realise enlightenment for the sake of all beings in Mahayana Buddhism
Bodhidharma	Considered the first patriarch of Ch'an (Zen) Buddhism, who brought Ch'an from India to China (*c.* 470–543)
Bodhisattva (**Skt**)	In Mahayana a person motivated by *bodhichitta* who follows the path in order to liberate both themselves and all others; advanced *bodhisattvas* may deliberately choose to be reborn in one of the six realms to help suffering beings; some are considered to be present in Sambhogakaya form and are objects of prayer and devotion

Brahma (Skt)	The supreme personal God of Hinduism
Brahman	The supreme impersonal principle that governs the universe in Hinduism
Brahmin (Skt)	Priest in the Vedic religion and also in Hinduism
Brahminical	Social or religious order where brahmins are dominant
Canon	Collection of scriptures
Chittamatra	School of Indian Mahayana philosophy which taught the doctrine of *tathagatagarbha*
Dharmakaya (Skt)	The body of truth, the enlightened mind
Dogen	Considered to have introduced the Soto school of Zen into Japan (1200–53)
Dukkha	The first of the Four Noble Truths: suffering, pain, frustration, insecurity, anxiety and angst
Eisai	Considered to be the founder of the Rinzai school of Zen in Japan (1141–1215)
Karma (Skt); (kamma)	Literally 'action'; this also refers to the universal law of cause and effect that governs the moral results of intentional actions, including rebirth
Kathina	Festival at the end of the rains retreat in Theravada
Koan **(Jap)**	A seemingly paradoxical riddle or statement used as a training method in Zen Buddhism to force the mind to abandon logic and conceptual thought
Lama (Tib)	Spiritual teacher or master in Tibetan Buddhism
Madhyamaka	School of Indian Mahayana philosophy which taught the doctrine that all things are empty of inherent existence (*shunyata*)
Mahayana	Literally 'Great Vehicle'; one of the three major traditions of Buddhism teaching *bodhichitta*, *shunyata* and the *Bodhisattva* Path
Mantra (Skt)	Phrases composed of sacred syllables representing the speech and mind of a particular buddha or *bodhisattva*; in Vajrayana they are repeated as meditation aids and for prayer
Nagarjuna	Founder of the Madhyamaka school of Mahayana philosophy in the second/third century CE
Nembutsu **(Jap)**	The Pure Land practice of reciting the name of Amida Buddha 'Namu Amida Butsu'
Nirmanakaya (Skt)	The body of manifestation, the physical dimension of reality

Nirvana (Skt); (*nibbana*)	Literally 'extinguishing, blowing out'; the goal of Theravada Buddhism, which is liberation from the cycle of rebirth and suffering
Pali	Sacred language of Theravada Buddhism
Pretas	'Hungry ghosts', beings with excessive greed who suffer in one of the six realms of samsara
Samanera	Novice monk
Samatha (*shamatha*, Skt)	Calm abiding meditation
Sambhogakaya (Skt)	The body of enjoyment, the dimension of energy and light in Mahayana and Vajrayanam
Samsara (Skt)	The cyclic existence of birth, death and rebirth characterised by suffering
Sangha (Skt)	The third of the Three Jewels; this generally refers to the monastic community, but nowadays also to the lay Buddhist community
Sanskrit	Sacred language of India, especially of Mahayana and Vajrayana Buddhism, and of Hinduism
Satori **(Jap)**	Sudden glimpse of spiritual insight or enlightenment in Zen Buddhism
Shunyata **(Skt)**	Literally 'emptiness'; the doctrine that all things are without essence and arise in dependence upon other causes and conditions; it is the characteristic doctrine of Madhyamaka philosophy
Stupa (Skt)	Religious monument that may house the relics of buddhas or saints
Sukhavati **(Skt)**	'Land of bliss', the pure land or heaven of Buddha Amitabha (Amida Buddha)
Suttas (sutras, Skt)	Discourses of the Buddha on meditation, the Four Noble Truths and so on
Tathagatagarbha **(Skt)**	'Buddha nature', the potential of enlightenment that exists in everyone according to Mahayana
Theravada	Literally 'Way of the Elders', the only surviving school of Nikaya (Hinayana) Buddhism
Tipitaka (Tripitaka, Skt)	The Three Baskets or categories of the Buddhist scriptures: Vinaya, Sutta and Abhidhamma
Upanishads	Hindu scriptures composed from seventh century BCE onwards
Upasaka	Lay man

Vajrayana	Literally the 'Diamond Vehicle'; one of the three major traditions of Buddhism, also known as Tantric Buddhism
Vassa	Rains retreat in Theravada
Vedas	Scriptures of the Vedic religion
Vedic religion	Religion believed to have been introduced into India by the Aryans from around 1500 BCE
Vihara	Monastery (Theravada)
Vinaya	Scriptures on monastic discipline
Vipassana (*vipasyana*, Skt)	Insight meditation
Wesak	Festival celebrating the birth, enlightenment and passing away of the Buddha (Theravada)
Yana	Literally 'vehicle'; this refers to one of the three major traditions or vehicles of Buddhism: Hinayana (Nikaya Buddhism), Mahayana and Vajrayana
Zazen (Jap)	Sitting meditation in Zen Buddhism

Resources

Books

Scriptures

Carter, J. R. and Palihawadana, M. (transl.) (1987) *Dhammapada*, Oxford University Press.

Conze, E. (transl.) (1959) *Buddhist Scriptures*, Penguin Classics.

Easwaran, E. (transl.) (1985) *Dhammapada*, Nilgiri Press.

Mascaro, J. (transl.) (1973) *Dhammapada*, Penguin Classics.

Watson, B. (transl.) (1993) *The Lotus Sutra*, Columbia University Press.

Other books

Bechert, H. and Gombrich, R. (eds) (1984) *The World of Buddhism*, Thames and Hudson.

Carrithers, M. (1996) *Buddha: A Very Short Introduction*, Oxford University Press.

Chah, A. (2001) *Being Dharma*, Shambhala.

Conze, E. (1993) *A Short History of Buddhism*, Oneworld.

Coward, H. (2000) *Scripture in the World Religions*, Oneworld.

Cush, D. (1993) *Buddhism*, Hodder and Stoughton.

Dalai Lama (2000) *The Meaning of Life*, Wisdom.

Dalai Lama (1991) *Mind Science: an East–West Dialogue*, Wisdom.

Embree, A. T. (ed.) (1988) *Sources of Indian Tradition*, Columbia University Press.

Freeman, P. (2004) *A Student's Guide to A2 Religious Studies*, Rhinegold Publishing.

Gethin, R. (1998) *The Foundations of Buddhism*, Opus.

Gombrich, R. (1988) *Theravada Buddhism*, Routledge.

Hanh, T. N. (1988) *The Heart of Understanding*, Parallax Press.

Harvey, P. (1990) *An Introduction to Buddhism*, Cambridge University Press.

Harvey, P. (2000) *An Introduction to Buddhist Ethics*, Cambridge University Press.

Keown, D. (1996) *Buddhism: A Very Short Introduction*, Oxford University Press.

Keown, D. (2000) *Contemporary Buddhist Ethics*, Curzon.

Klostermaier, K. (2000) *A Short Introduction to Hinduism*, Oneworld.

Rahula, W. (1959) *What the Buddha Taught*, Oneworld.

Reat, N. R. (1994) *Buddhism: A History*, Asian Humanities Press.

Rinpoche, S. (1992) *The Tibetan Book of Living and Dying*, Rider.

Saddhatissa, H. (1997) *Buddhist Ethics*, Wisdom.

Sangharakshita, Ven. (1992) *Buddhism and the West*, Windhorse.

Strong, J. S. (2001) *The Buddha: a Short Biography*, Oneworld.

Thomas, E. J. (1993) *The Life of the Buddha as Legend and History*, Motilal Banarsidass.

Unno, T. (1998) *River of Fire, River of Water: an Introduction to the Pure Land Tradition of Shin Buddhism*, Doubleday.

Williams, P. (2000) *Buddhist Thought*, Routledge.

Websites

Access to Insight (http://www.accesstoinsight.org) is a reliable website on Theravada Buddhism and the Pali Canon.

BuddhaNet (http://www.buddhanet.net) has links to many different groups, magazines and scriptures. It covers especially Theravada and Chinese Buddhism. There are audio tracks of Theravada chanting.

BBC (http://www.bbc.co.uk/religion) has a useful section on Buddhism which includes 13-minute audio talks on each of the Four Noble Truths.

Dharma Net International (http://www.dharmanet.org) offers articles and links to many Buddhist centres.

Tricyle (http://www.tricycle.com) offers articles and news from one of the biggest magazines on Buddhism in America. It has a Buddhist Basics section with free introductory articles.

Wisdom Books (http://www.wisdom-books.com) specialises in distributing books, videos, posters etc. on Buddhism. This site gives its online catalogue.

Films and documentaries

Films

Kundun: directed by Martin Scorsese, on the life of the Dalai Lama of Tibet; approximately 2 hours; 1997.

Little Buddha: directed by Bernardo Bertolucci; approximately 3 hours; 1993.

Documentaries

Doing Time, Doing Vipassana: video documentary on S. N. Goenka and meditation in Indian prisons; Karuna Films; 50 mins; available from Insight Books, The Sun, Garway Hill, Herefordshire, HR2 8EZ.

Kill or Cure: Constant Cravings: BBC2 documentary on treatment of drug addiction at Thramkrabok Monastery, Thailand; 60 minutes; first screened 2003.

Legendary Trails: pilgrimage route in Nepal and India related to the Buddha's lifestory; BBC Everyman special; 50 minutes; first screened 28 November 1993.

The Life of the Buddha: BBC; 60 minutes; first screened 23 March 2003.

Zen on the Street: documentary on Zen master Bernie Glassman's work in New York on the streets, in hospices and in an AIDS clinic; 77 minutes; 1999; available from Wisdom Books.

Index

Buddhism